The Art of Attack

The Art of Attack

Attacker Mindset for Security Professionals

Maxie Reynolds

WILEY

Library of Congress Control Number: 2021941139

ISBN: 978-1-119-80546-5
ISBN: 978-1-119-80628-8 (ebk)
ISBN: 978-1-119-80547-2 (ebk)

Cover image: © Getty Images/Gearstd
Cover design: Wiley/Michael E. Trent

SKY10027856_070221

About the Author

Maxie Reynolds is widely considered one of this generation's most successful social engineers. She started her career in oil and gas as an underwater robotics pilot working in Norway, Venezuela, Australia, Italy, Russia, Nigeria, and the United States. She then transited into cybersecurity at PricewaterhouseCoopers in Australia, working in ethical hacking and social engineering. She later studied digital forensics with SANS and has performed digital forensics for law enforcement and corporate America, and as an expert witness.

Maxie was born and grew up in Scotland, dabbled as a stuntwoman, and achieved some success as a model in both the UK and the United States. She has a degree in computer science, a degree in underwater robotics, and is educated in quantum computing. She is also a published author, and in her spare time she works with the Innocent Lives Foundation and National Child Protection Taskforce.

Maxie has published articles on complex human behavior and its effect on a social engineer's ability to influence and has given speeches on the mindset and science behind the art of social engineering. She teaches various courses on social engineering and the attacker mindset. This book, *The Art of Attack: Attacker Mindset for Security Professionals*, is the first book of its kind to be published. It looks at the cognitive skills and requirements of the mindset, how to engage it, and why.

Acknowledgments

Attackers don't acknowledge people. They target them.

Contents

Introduction

There is nothing either good or bad but thinking makes it so.
—William Shakespeare

I was recently told by someone I consider to be a subject matter expert that introductions in books, although seldom read by typical readers, are meant to respect the reader. Introductions are not intended to insinuate to readers that they will only understand the book's subject matter once they've read it cover to cover. Instead, the introduction should tell its audience how the core message of the book will be broken down. I think this is true, so this introduction acts only as a way to summarize what's to come, not to aggrandize it.

The core subject of this book is the attacker mindset, the gathering, processing, and applying of information for an objective. That's the key takeaway of this book. If you stop reading now, you will have received its central message. However, what I'm hoping will keep you reading, rather than repurposing the book as a doorstop, is that the whole book is about *how* to do this as an attacker—*how* to process and apply information for the benefit of the mission.

The Art of Attack looks at all aspects of the attacker mindset (AMs), focusing on the cornerstone pieces. In breaking these pieces down to their fundamental components, the book empowers you to build them back up into something recognizable as your own brand of attacker mindset. I will describe the principles of this mindset and how to interweave them with the process most attacks follow, namely: reconnaissance, initial approach, privilege escalation, redundant access, and escape. Through this attacker lens, this book explores tools you can implement as attackers and the psychological principles, too. I will also call out all the times you should take snacks with you on a job, which doesn't seem important now, but wait until you've been trapped in a bathroom stall for six hours.

To help you remember the material packed into this book, I'll provide stories (both successes and fails), which should make transferring AMs from theory into practice much easier. As a practitioner of social engineering, I will mainly concentrate on examples of the attacker mindset in my stories from the field. However, as a trained pen tester there will also be crossover.

The tagline I've used to put attacker mindset into shorthand over the years is: *there really is nothing good or bad, but your attacker mindset makes it so*—this line is effectively how this book came into being: Countless hours of trying to teach people the art of the attacker mindset allowed a reduction of it to that statement. The attacker mindset allows us to *hack* information, which may on the surface be neutral to the untrained pedestrian, but to you or I as attackers, could prove lethal when leveraged correctly. There's no information that you will come across that's simply *good* or *bad;* information is processed through the lens of the attack and its objective.

I wrote this book solely to teach this mentality, but each of you will build your own version of it that reflects your strengths and weaknesses. This book should teach you *how* to think, not *what* to think. It contains chapters on open source intelligence (OSINT) and social engineering, too. However, other books and courses exist that break down how to perform OSINT and how to become a social engineer (SE). My aim is to show you how those fit into the AMs's executive functions.

Who Is This Book For?

The attacker mindset should be taught to those who need it most—those who we, as a society, want to protect from malicious attackers. Companies should use physical testing as well as network testing to evaluate their security postures regularly, which will help build their populations' intuition and security. The attacker mindset should be used in boardrooms and other government and corporate settings as a way to scrutinize and analyze blind spots and vulnerabilities. Members of the cyber and information security communities should be consulted as think tanks and task forces. So, my aim is for this book to speak to those decision makers as well.

However, because I will look at the attacker mindset through the lens of a security professional, this book is first and foremost intended for those who wish to partake in a modern battle of stress testing and ethics: security professionals. Ethics and morals will come into play quite a bit. Knowing how to portray the bad actors is not the same as actually becoming them. The line that separates us from them is the line of ethics.

There's also a case to be made that says ordinary individuals can benefit from learning about AMs. Awareness of how this mindset might present itself can prove pivotal in assessing whether an attack is being mounted against you and what to do if it is. Because of this, my aim for *The Art of Attack* is for it to be useful for the general public, too.

Finally, every chapter in this book, every paragraph, every sentence, has the capacity to offend or irk someone. Those with a detailed military background will need all of their patience to forgive what cannot be known about warfare recon without having been in the thick of it; those who guard the realm of the ethical hacker will need to find a way to subside their rage given this book speaks as directly to malicious attackers as it does ethical. Alas, I cannot control who reads this and what they do with the information within it. For those very sensitive or pedantic, putting the word *ethical* before the word *attacker* will not make what I say in this book invisible to any malicious actors reading it. To subside this rage, all I can offer is this: as a society increasingly in need of effective security measures, focusing on the need to better understand attacks and attackers is prudent. Understanding how and why an attacker performs is one thing—and it's important. But being able to think like them, looking at ourselves through their eyes, we become more powerful, more dominant, and far safer.

My final sentiments are a cloned copy of Tai T'ung, who, in the 13th century said of his book, *History of Chinese Writing*: "Were I to wait perfection, my book would never be finished." Of course, I am not writing a history of the attacker mindset. I am setting out to show the full breadth of it and its modern-day uses and functions.

What This Book Covers

- The idea behind this book is to document and teach the attacker mindset, without taking individualism and obliterating it.
- Different strengths will have to be played to by all of us who use this book to build an attacker mindset and execute attacks. Nonetheless, I'll pick apart the attacker mindset so that we can find the commonalties and still leave room for each of us to apply our own personal brand to it.
- The greatest and sharpest attackers are trained to see opportunities in the moment, and there's no way for this book to list the infinite opportunities an (ethical or otherwise) attacker might come across out in the field. But what it will teach is this: how to form the attacker mindset and how to apply it.
- In the name of ethics, the final part of this book will explore the "tells" of an attack and what businesses, organizations, and institutions can and should do pre- and post-attack to protect themselves.

- Finally, the end goal of the attack, after you've sprinted 18 flights of stairs, hidden under desks, been wedged in between two 20-foot containers, sweated the foundation off your thumb tattoos (all fun stories for later), and handed in the report, is to leave each company, boardroom, and client stronger for having employed you. It's almost all that separates us from the bad guys.

Here we go. Enjoy.

Part I

The Attacker Mindset

Chapter 1
What Is
the Attacker Mindset?

War is 90 percent information.

—*Napoleon Bonaparte*

It is 5 a.m., and I still have an hour before I meet my team. I've been up for the last hour going over plans because this is how I always start my attacks: with a niggling amount of nervous energy, I pace the floor of my hotel room, playing a game of mental chess in my mind. I go over my initial approach, consider my possible moves if I do get past security, and then again if I don't, I start to wonder *How will I pivot?* The game of mental chess carries on. This is the most efficient and successful way I have found to hone my mental agility.

From this thought I dive into a myriad of others, imagining new ways I might get into the building, new ways to escalate my privileges and deepen my foothold after my initial breach, whether that starts in the basement or the lobby. *If someone happens to ask me why I am in the basement, could I say I got in the wrong elevator from the parking garage and ask for help. . .?*

I visualize the layout of the building internally—another luxury afforded by solid open source intelligence (OSINT) findings—and use faceless silhouettes to represent staff I might pass along the way. Sometimes I imagine them asking me questions; sometimes I imagine myself just nodding at them in silent acknowledgment. After all, the largest component of executing an artful attack lies in the attacker's ability to adapt to the people and surroundings in which they find themselves, even when those things are brand-new.

I continue to walk myself through it all a few times, picturing different obstacles: *Would it be better just to tailgate, or should I walk in front of the building declaring myself a visitor?* I imagine the payoffs of each and weigh them. *Working the visitor system should give me almost unfettered access for the day, but it's a high-risk move,* I tell myself, *whereas tailgating in through a less visible entrance leaves me at the mercy of sloppy, albeit well-intentioned, employees holding any one of hundreds of fire and security doors open for me. . . .* Taking a moment, I come to a conclusion: *No, stick with the A-plan: go to security and get access,* I tell myself.

The whole time I'm performing this mental pre-attack ritual, I am reminding myself of the same things over and over: get in, get the flags, never let them know you're a threat, and stay within scope. In my mind I am always making my way to the 38th floor, and I am always mentally preempting the challenges I'll face as I try to walk into the CFO's office and place a USB drive into their computer port. That's my job. And, although I like to warm up by running as many possibilities through my mind as I can come up with, I have yet to predict obstacles and pivots correctly even once in my career. That is irrelevant, though—the mental warm-up is what I need—it induces the power of thinking on my feet and knowing I've learned from prior failures and successes.

I soon start to focus on making sure I've disguised myself as a threat. I've based my pretext off the OSINT I've found so far. For this bank job, I am a lawyer here to help wrap up the mergers and acquisitions deal that was all over the news only weeks ago, albeit without much context. It took a lot of searches and piecing together information to choose the nuance of this pretext; I am not just any lawyer, but a lawyer who is now needed to help the deal over the final few hurdles, equipped with an abundance of paperwork—my prop and my seeming legitimacy. And, unless the security guards happen to be a team of lawyers, I won't be found out by the typical questions people ask a lawyer: *What are you here for? What firm do you work for? How long have you been practicing, what school did you go to? Do you know how I can get out of a parking ticket?* I call these my *pretext layers*, and depending on the job, I might need to go many layers deep, to the point I need to know much more than you might expect, from common jargon to how a piece of machinery works.

The start point of the operation is as hermetic as it's ever going to be. I have my props, which in this case are an ID card from my "firm" and a portfolio filled with "legal documents," categorized by tabs that have the words "Signed by [CFO's name]" and today's date. I also have a fake guest pass card that one of my teammates was able to print for me based on a picture of a legitimate one we'd found on Yelp. Blessed be Yelp. I have lock picks; I have my radio-frequency identification (RFID) duplicator and fobs just in case the opportunity arises to clone a working security card I can't slip into my pocket; and I have the most important thing I'll carry all day: my letter of approval. It is a piece of paper with my point of contact's name and number and a short statement asking anyone who detains me to contact him before the police. I also have my fake ID, although I am sans a snack, which is unlike me. The snack is not important. Yet.

With another huge thanks to mighty OSINT, I've already prepared my outfit for the day, too. I've had it picked out for about a week now, and it will be a big part of the operation. I've chosen it with meticulous care to be professional and versatile. This is not a job where I can wear a costume. I won't be going head-to-toe in scrubs or coveralls, like in some of my other jobs. I put on my wardrobe for the day with a sense of gravity and focus that I generally don't use for throwing on my usual working-from-home attire (sweats on the bottom, work-acceptable T-shirt on top). It is the middle of summer in New York, yet I have on a long-sleeved blue shirt under a white silk shirt, but for a good reason. There is a chance I'll need to ditch the top layer so that the security team can't quickly identify me by the color of my clothes, should someone start to become suspicious. I have a hairband tied around my wrist, too, to throw my hair up in case I need to hide its length and color. I've put foundation on the rather unfortunate tattoo I have on my right thumb. I'll be returning to this office soon enough, and I don't want anything about me to be too recognizable. These seemingly inconsequential things matter.

Finally, dressed and mentally prepared, I leave the room to meet my team. They won't be joining me, but they will be on standby in case of trouble, which is a company policy and one I've been thankful for on more than one occasion. After a pep talk, making sure we can stay in constant communication, I make my way to the bank's offices and try to break in, knowing that if it all goes well, I'll be out in time to do it a second time under the cover of darkness. I'll need my team for that and a few more games of mental chess.

Using the Mindset

The *attacker mindset* (AMs) is a set of cognitive skills applied to four laws. It is evident and relevant across all professions, trades, and businesses, although it often goes under the guise of *expertise*. Many people exhibit AMs qualities within their domain, as we will look at shortly. *The Art of Attack,* however, is about gaining and using this mindset for malicious activity over any domain—but in a way that ultimately results in the betterment of an organization's security.

The laws say that you must know your end goal, be able to constantly collect information that you can weaponize and leverage to achieve that goal, develop a pretext that you never let slip, and have every action you take be for the advancement of the objective. As you will see, the cognitive skills needed to uphold these laws in an attack are broad, but they all have a single common thread: they relate to information, and most importantly, information as you perceive it. There is no attack without information, and learning to tie it back to your objective is the essence of AMs.

A woman spills coffee on herself, and it burns her. We hear, "Someone had butterfingers," and comprehend hot liquids scald.

A lawyer hears "The coffee was too hot" and the winds of a lawsuit. This particular woman's lawyer took facts and bent them and shaped them to fit the objective set out by the law. This is what the attacker mindset looks like at work. Your attacker mindset will differ from that of a lawyer's, but the central principles remain: the building of an attack is based on information as you perceive it; the execution is based on the information as you apply it. AMs is nothing more or less than a way of taking information in and applying it to an objective. The mark of a good attacker is the ability to repurpose information in ways not intended by the source. This is made possible by using the first and second laws of the attacker mindset: the first law states that you start with the end in mind, and the second law states that you gather, weaponize, and leverage information as a means to that end.

As an example, if you hear of a company holding a conference, you may be able to phish them by gathering information on who their vendors are and impersonating those vendors by way of vish (a call in which an attacker attempts to gain information or perform an attack), phish (an email in whch an attacker aims to gain information or gain access to a user's machine/network), or even in person to gain sensitive details or access. If they are holding the event virtually, a well-crafted phish will have a high probability of being undetected. You might start by finding out which platform they are holding the event on and phishing them, pretending to be that platform. You might be able to phish their attendees or their speakers, appearing as if you are in fact reaching out from the hosting company itself, gaining access to potentially thousands of people's sensitive data. Most people's reaction to that possibility is that this sort of attack would be illegal. This is actually up for debate, depending on where in the world you live. Some governments can authorize this sort of *test* if you have a bank account in that country, as an example. Typically, though, it will be a company that hires you, and you will not be able to test their attendees.

Let's look at another example of how this mindset can take seemingly innocuous information—in this case given by the source—and use it to create a vulnerability. Say you are able to circumvent a company's technical defenses upon searching current or historical job postings. In this example, a company was looking for a candidate who had "an overview or understanding of SAP product and service portfolio (SAP Cloud Platform Integration, SAP PI/PO, API Management)." They were also looking for that person to have "sound knowledge of JavaScript and Groovy Script. [Be] able to configure Sound NetWeaver. Should be comfortable with Java Programming. Nice to have worked in UI developments using SAP Web IDE \#."

There's a lot of information in this that could prove vital in various attacks against this target, including network, web app, phishing, and vishing attacks.

A *network attack* is an attempt to gain unauthorized access to the target's network, with the objective of stealing data or performing other malicious activity. Thanks to this job posting, I know that the target uses systems applications and products (SAP) systems, which are tempting to perform an attack on because they store and manage the lifeblood of any organization: critical information and business processes. SAP systems can be based on different platforms: ABAP (Advanced Business Application Programming), Java, or HANA. We can assume this is based on Java, given the job description. The main SAP platform is SAP NetWeaver, and ExploitDB (www.exploit-db.com)—a popular website repository—shows that vulnerabilities exist for version 7.4, one of which showed that SQL injections are possible. This type of attack allows attackers to inject their own evil SQL commands, creating requests and paving the way for access to critical data in a database of users' passwords, account information, and anything else stored in the database.

A simple vish could be made with this knowledge to multiple departments in the organization to gain more information based on these findings or to weaponize this information immediately to attempt to gain forgotten credentials. You may be able to gain entry to a secure building upon learning of an upcoming event they are holding and vishing to find out which type of ID is required to enter. If it's their work badge, you may be able to find a clear enough picture online to re-create one. You may be able to circumvent a whole building's security team by finding out what time the guards change shifts.

The possibilities are truly endless when you have information, and you can weaponize it and leverage it correctly. All of this neatly brings us to the cognitive skills an attacker must exhibit: an attacker must have curiosity in abundance; persistence to drive that curiosity into action so as to be moving forward all the time; the ability to process information into workable categories; mental agility enough that allows repurposing of information when a situation calls for it and the agility to adapt the information in ways not always intended by the source; and finally, this mindset requires self-awareness. Self-awareness is invisible. No one can "see" that you are self-aware, but almost everyone can feel if you are or not. You must leave people *feeling* however you need them to in order to fulfill your objective. I will cover this in a later chapter on target psychology.

The Attacker *and* the Mindset

It's silly to argue about the "true" meaning of a word—a word means whatever people believe it to mean—but for me, "hacking" information through AMs means using information in ways unanticipated by the original source. Just as a hacker uses *something* in a way it was not intended to be used, an attacker uses information in a way it was not intended. This gives AMs a sense of neutrality on the surface, but delving a little deeper into it, it encompasses the art of the mindset seamlessly: information exists, and we are free to process it and apply it however we want. A great attacker will always apply information for the good of the attack; they will always bend and twist the information in a way that furthers the mission or gains the objective.

In the most traditional sense, an attacker is an individual, or a group of individuals, who seeks to destroy, expose, alter, disable, and steal information or to gain unauthorized access to or make unauthorized use of an asset or person. Attackers are often portrayed as ruthless individuals with almost otherworldly skills and the means to win against their victims. They will try to find the path of least resistance for the biggest gain. To an extent this is true, but as we have already covered in part, an attacker's main ammo is the leveraging and weaponization of information—without this, they are powerless. The world runs on data now, so information is abundantly available. Malicious attackers will use information to gain information from their targets; ethical attackers will do the same but will teach the targets *how* their own information can be used against them, how to recognize when that is happening, and how to prevent it.

There are two main states of attacker mindset: there's before the vulnerable information has been carved out and there's after. One commonality exists between them: every step you take as an attacker must go in the direction of the objective. The nature of AMs means it boils down to forming information around the objective, inferring in cases, leveraging information where possible, and concealing other information where needed. These are the core competencies that make up AMs, and we are about to start untangling them. But it is prudent to note that you do not need the skills to understand the laws of AMs, and you do not need the laws to use the skills. It's the application of the skills against the laws that makes the mindset:

- The first law of AMs states that you start with the end in mind, knowing your objective. This will allow you to use laws 2, 3, and 4 most effectively.
- Law 2 states that you gather, weaponize, and leverage information for the good of the objective. This is how you serve law 1.
- Law 3 says that you never break pretext. You must remain disguised as a threat at all times.
- Law 4 tells you that everything you do is for the benefit of the objective. The objective is the central point from which all moves an attacker makes hinge. You cannot diverge from the objective set out because of law 1.

It is the interwoven use of five cognitive skills that form the backbone of the attacker mindset:

1. You cannot become a good ethical attacker without a healthy dose of curiosity.

2. Your curiosity will not pay off without persistence.
3. You will have nothing to persist in if you cannot take in information and leverage the most mundane of it correctly.
4. You will need to have mental agility enough to actively adapt information in the moment.
5. If you have all of these skills, you will still only succeed if you have a high level of self-awareness, because you must always know what you bring and how to leverage it. Self-awareness will allow you a higher level of influence over someone else. These five things play a role in every job you will get as an ethical attacker looking to succeed.

AMs Is a Needed Set of Skills

Defenses against attackers generally center on building technological protections to combat ever-lurking adversaries. Businesses typically try to fortify their assets by closing off the most obscure entry points, which is commendable. But it becomes irrelevant if they leave the front door wide open rather than employing an active defense. Attackers are often relentless and dogged types (and need to be in order to succeed). Protecting against this can be difficult, because the threat is somewhat faceless and motionless until one day it's not—how can we truly protect ourselves against such a faceless, shapeless entity, you may wonder? Something that doesn't seem like it's a threat at all until one day it appears, and it is tangible, dangerous, and consequential. Looking the threat in the face leaves most companies wondering how they could have missed imagining the scenario in which they find themselves, and the truth is there are infinite attack scenarios. Imagining and barricading against them all is futile. Learning to think like an attacker, seeing how information about you can be used against you, will not stop it from happening, but it will make halting attacks in their tracks that much easier. It's the closest thing to a security panacea I will see in my working lifetime, of that I have no doubt.

People, typically not in the cybersecurity or information security industries, wonder if it's safe or even ethical to teach people how to think like an attacker, whether that be teaching a penetration tester how to break into networks or a social engineer how to elicit information and use it against a target. My response is always this: the solution to successfully fending off attacks and staying ahead of them is to be able to think like those who would seek to attack us. I am not teaching people to be malevolent or corrupt; I am teaching them to how to be ethical—testing people, companies, and security for our greater good. When a company is attacked, regardless if they left themselves open to it or not, it affects the people who work there; it affects the people who used the services. This should not be overlooked or taken lightly. Because of the stakes, we must have only trusted individuals within our workplaces, or the information security/cybersecurity sectors test our businesses.

Also, as I have said in the introduction and countless times before, whether it be when asked by people curious about my profession or in interview and training settings, putting the word *ethical*, or some variation of it, before the word *attacker* will not make the words that follow invisible to malicious actors. I also cannot control who buys this book. But I believe that learning to think like a malicious attacker can and will help us, as security professionals, get ahead, stay ahead, and beat them. We take their power when we can think like them, but with a purer intent.

As a society, we test everything: we test our cars to see how they'll fare on impact, we test buildings for structural safety, we even test markets before launching products. We train our emergency personnel, too, and rightly so. We wouldn't simply place a person in front of a burning building with a hose expecting them to put it out; we test our firefighters, give them experience and build their skills. The same goes for many other professions. As businesses, we can and should test everything. "Everything" includes human-based defenses. Testing people against ostensibly malicious attacks is tactical, daunting, and dynamic, but it works as a way of upping security, and it's the next great defense in security for businesses, and for us all. One of the most effective ways to uncover flaws and weaknesses in a business's security posture is to carry out planned attacks, exposing gaps in their defenses before a malicious attacker can take advantage.

Finally, while testing people is of course not teaching them the attacker mindset, it is teaching them how an attack might rear its ugly head and that alone gives them defenses against it. So, as security professionals, it's also our duty to form attack methods that, once executed, have no long-lasting adverse effects on the population tested—a major contrast when compared to those breeched by a malicious attacker. After all, some of the most devastating attacks haven't been the most technical—they've simply been human versus human. The catch is that only one human knows about the attack as it unfolds. By offering insight into the principles of AMs, we should be able to move the needle on security in the right direction without adversely affecting the population.

A Quick Note on Scope

The word *scope* will be used frequently throughout this book and chapter. It refers to a document that is an agreement on the work you're going to perform for a client. It outlines what you can and cannot do. It is your get out-of-jail-free card if you are caught (if you stuck to the terms of it) and possibly your never-go-to-actual-jail card if you are caught (if you stuck to the terms of it).

The scope will permit you to do a whole host of things, like enter a building from any given area or use real employee names in a phish. It might let you break into a building during the day but not at night (within normal working hours), or it might allow you to impersonate employees, both in person and over the phone. It is decided by the client.

Here's the bottom line of scope: you don't have to do everything scope permits. You cannot do a single thing it prohibits. Ensure you understand scope before you embark on the work. Make sure it uses clear language, and make sure you clarify anything you are unsure of.

Collectively, as a team, we've broken into hundreds of servers and physically compromised many of the world's most tightly guarded corporate and government facilities, including banks, corporate headquarters, and defense sites. However, I am always struck by how James Bond–like people think the job is. Each job is a long process that looks at legalities, operational conflicts that have to be worked around, and deliverables.

The first phase of the process is aligning with the target, picking a period in which to attack and defining the scope. To discuss that in great detail is beyond the range of this book, although an important point about scope should be made: scope limits *what* you do, not *how* you think. Breaking that down a little further, the scope matters to you because it tells you what you are and are not allowed to do—if you are not allowed to impersonate an internal employee, then you might pivot to impersonating a contractor. You may not be allowed to spoof numbers or name drop, so your AMs will have to forge ahead, giving you deceptive and creative ideas to offset those limitations. For instance, if you can't spoof numbers, you might get a burner number that's a few digits off from the one the target will expect. If you can't name drop, you might use names that sound close to the one. If scope limits you from using tools, like card cloners, then you might have to use a look-alike card and feign a technical error when it won't permit you access. Basically, scope adds complexities to your job, but it doesn't limit the power of your AMs; it simply exercises it in different ways.

There are good and bad outcomes that arise from having a scope in place. Primarily it is a protection for you as an attacker, which is why stepping outside the lines of them can be so damaging and devastating, both to your company and to your career. They are protection for the target, too. Most often you will hear new people in the field saying a real attacker would never stick to scope, so why should they? This is more complex than you'd first think. The first part of the statement is true; an attacker does not have a scope to stick to. However, if the client is asking you to go after the same asset that a real and malicious attacker would, the outcome is the same. Your clients should train their staff on how to spot attacks even when they are using spoofed numbers and impersonation, but if you are able to successfully breach them with these limitations in place, you further hit home to them how vulnerable they are. Scope is an attacker's blessing in disguise.

There are, however, grounds to challenge scope. If the client is too extreme in either direction, without good cause, you should—professionally—be able to point out to them how it precludes valuable testing. For instance, if you are vishing a bank and the client doesn't want you to use any semblance of an existing department as your pretext, you might point out that such limitations are heavily skewed in a way that will impact the findings and go against their security posture and future mitigations. It's too far removed from a realistic attack scenario.

However, if you are breaking into a government facility and the client doesn't want you to take any device in that's able to film or photograph, that shouldn't be too much of a concern for you as long as a mechanism is in place for you to prove your successes (and failures). Some clients will want a representative to accompany you; others will want you to check in at different points throughout the building. In the case of most pen tests, you will usually screenshot your progress. However, some clients will prohibit this and use their own logs as an example.

We will not cover report writing, although it is a large part of a job for most clients. What I will say about reports is that they should not be approached with fear or loathing. Equally, they should not be treated as precious. They are a way for you to give a coherent and exhaustive rundown of what you did from start to end and to give recommendations based on all of that. Giving the client all the vulnerabilities you saw but didn't take is important, too. I care more for a simple and easy report to both write and to read. There's still an element of AMs law involved in writing them: you must know the objective of the report (to show them where they are vulnerable and how to close those vulnerabilities); you must be able to take the information you gathered and describe it effectively, leveraging it for the report; you will have to stay professional the entire report—it is not a document for you to write your moves out like a screenplay; and you must always keep the objective of the report in mind so that it doesn't drift in the direction of fiction or in the direction of data only, without fixes.

Summary

- Attacker mindset can be used from your computer, but it really can't be taught there. It's a set of skills and laws working in combination.
- AMs is a set of cognitive skills applied to four laws. Used together, they produce an advantage for the attacker and a disadvantage of the target.
- Teaching the attacker mindset to those who don't seek to harm us, but to protect us, will greatly impact our successes in information security going forward.
- The following chapters present a complete system for building this mentality and untangling the complex web of thinking and resulting actions that make an attacker mindset so formidable.
- Reports are, for most people, the least fun part of the job but the most important part for the client.

Key Message

War is 90 percent information; the rest is how you apply it to the objective. An attacker takes in information to achieve an objective, but instead of profiting in the end, an ethical attacker seeks to strengthen defenses they circumvented or defeated. AMs' largest commodity is information; it is the use of this information that defines the attacker and the attack.

To carry out the acts of an attacker requires curiosity and persistence, which are interdependent as one often drives the other. Information processing is another important skill. A subset of information processing is mental agility—you cannot use information agilely if you cannot first parse it. Self-awareness is the ability to use yourself in a way that is beneficial for the objective.

Chapter 2
Offensive vs. Defensive Attacker Mindset

Before we dive into the components of the mindset, it is worthwhile to categorize it into its offensive and defensive sides. In this chapter, we will briefly look at what offensive and defensive security is and how they differ from each other. Then we will look at the offensive and defensive side of the mindset and what each side brings to its security counterpart in terms of skill and functionality.

Many millions of dollars in public and private investment have been spent on new technologies, usually for defensive measures rather than offensive. Offensive security is a proactive and an oppositional approach to protecting computer systems, networks, and individuals from attacks. The offensive part of the attacker mindset is also oppositional and dogged.

Defensive security, however, uses a reactive approach that focuses on prevention and detection of attacks. The defensive mode of your AMs will allow you to be reactive, helping you see ways in which you might be caught and hopefully circumventing those defenses with the help of your offensive prowess. Afterward, your defensive AMs will allow you to see ways to prevent attacks, making you extremely valuable to any client.

In terms of technology, currently there is an enormous defensive preference in security. Unfortunately, this means that the time between a defensive weapon's creation in comparison to that of its offensive counter is often huge. Another problem with this defensive preference is that even with the best defensive security protocols and technologies in place, as a social engineer or red teamer, there is a chance I'll be able to slip right past them, which is often a lot easier than getting past a technological defensive protection and can be just as damaging, maybe more so. Additionally, technology is becoming further and further intertwined throughout the broad population's professional and personal lives, which makes the overall goal of security more complex. Because of this, both sides of technology are needed and both sides of the mindset are needed.

Both offensive and defensive securities have their purpose, and each is important from a business standpoint. Offensive cybersecurity strategies shrink the chance of attacks by promoting a permanent state of readiness and actively analyzing the environment; they can and should be critical in keeping people like me out, which is a big win when undergoing testing, and the malicious digital pentesters, too.

Defensive security relies on a comprehensive understanding of an environment and being able to analyze it in order to detect latent flaws. The barrier to perpetual, effective defensive security is the inability to always accurately predict the future.

A like-for-like scenario might be that of an earthquake. In the United States, we construct buildings meant to withstand earthquakes within a range of magnitude, but we can't always accurately predict all the other chaos, mayhem, and destruction it might bring with it. So, after a hurricane strikes, the clean-up begins and measures like riverbank management are put in place so that the situation is not repeated in the future. However, the next earthquake that strikes might do unforeseen damage to other critical infrastructure. So, that is then hardened, and the loop continues. As an example, Hurricane Sandy, when it hit New York in 2012, shone a light on the inherent flaws of keeping generators in basements. When flooded, generators are relegated from use. The aftermath of Hurricane

Sandy also saw the city build more emergency shelters, repair public housing to make it more storm-resistant, and construct flood protection in the form of greenery around Manhattan. City officials estimate that the storm cost $19 billion in damages and lost economic activity.

Defensive cybersecurity deals with the prevention of attacks and the strengthening of the defenses that keep them at bay. These defensive measures often follow a successful offensive attack—hence the constant lag and uneven playing field. If a metaphorical hurricane hits a business, they have to quickly address the points of failure, put in place short-term mitigations, and find ways to make their environment more resilient and less vulnerable to malicious damage. That reality means it's imperative for the business to start preparing immediately to protect its employees, infrastructure, and revenue from those future catastrophes.

Offensive security mainly refers to penetration testing, for which a broad definition has been given already, and physical testing, which is a main focus of this book. Threat hunting, which traditionally is the proactive seeking and destroying of cybersecurity threats before they compromise an organization, may also be considered as a form of offensive security. For the purposes of this book, threat hunting is a core component of AMs and, in particular, the offensive part of the mindset; instead of seeking and destroying threats to the company, an ethical attacker (EA) will seek out information or gaps and turn them into threats. It's an alternative way of thinking about threat hunting, and it only applies through the lens of this book and context. The defensive side intersects here because it seeks out defenses to first circumvent them and then, after the attack, to patch and bolster them. Offensive security doesn't just build protections and resistance. It sees pervasive penetrations for what they are—an active form of asymmetric warfare that threatens security at the highest levels. Offensive security thus aims not just to defend against threats, but to neutralize them.

With all that said, it seems fair to say that there are advantages to both sides of security, and that having neither side would result in mayhem for everyone. Technology has a lot to offer to us all now and in the future, but our greatest challenge will always be keeping it all secure. Even the most cutting-edge techniques and methodologies of today will have to evolve in the future, and so part of every business's (and individual's) security strategy needs to be devoted to this task of staying ahead of the curve. Here is where I come to the point: taking all of this into consideration, there is a solid case for an EA to have strong offensive and defensive skills from a mental standpoint. The remainder of this chapter will look at the mental portion of these categories and how they manifest, as well as their function as part of a mindset.

The overview I will start with is this: both are needed, and one cannot exclude the other. The defensive attacker mindset (DAMs) minimizes how long a mitigating control or interference can obstruct you from achieving your objective by identifying defenses. The offensive attacker mindset (OAMs) promotes a permanent state of readiness, allowing constant analyzation of your environment and the ability to detect vulnerabilities and impose costs on those defenses.

The Offensive Attacker Mindset

The offensive attacker mindset (OAMs) allows you as an EA to direct an event in the direction of the objective. More specifically, it allows you insights normally invisible to others (namely defense). It is always scanning for vulnerabilities and creating them from information. OAMs is oppositional and unyielding, and it uses information and environments only to further your position. It does not care about anything outside of its focus, which is always the objective. Typically, your objective as a pentester is access to an asset, information, or place within a building(s) or on a network.

This mindset uncovers a catalog of valuables and vulnerabilities, and not only those you've identified for your own, relatively narrow objective—it also helps you identify what else the target deems important in the moment. It will reveal vulnerabilities that you might not be able to use due to your scope of work or that you've missed because they do not suit your objective but may still be a critical or severe vulnerability. For example, if your objective is to get into the building and to the network operations center (NOC) without using any other entrances or exits other than the front door, you should still note if there are opportunities to do so, whether it be the loading dock or parking structure.

In another example, you may believe due to your scope and objective that the NOC is the thing the company wants to protect most. However, upon entering an environment, you may figure out that actually they are preparing for a market-disrupting move that executives are meeting for, talking about, and writing about. This is valuable information—it doesn't change your scope or objective, but it is worth noting in your report or directly to your point of contact (POC).

OAMs is also what keeps you in a sort of *hunt mode* as the attack unfolds, identifying any opportunities that present themselves and exploiting them with seeming ease and poise—all without letting the target know that you have any ulterior motive or missing a beat as you deviate from your original plan. It leads you to learn new things about your target and apply those lessons for the good of the objective. For example, you might not learn until you get on-site that they have upgraded their visitor system to a digital kiosk that can be circumvented with the standard out-of-the-box key code.

There is also a sense of competitiveness with OAMs. It doesn't want to be beaten. Ever. It doesn't want to be merciful or helpful. It wants only to win. Your competitive drive is always influenced greatly by your determination to set and achieve goals. It should keep you striving for progress with a quiet but unrelenting focus. It's the peak of your curiosity and persistence combined. It is your competitive desire combined with critical thought that helps you match and surpass defenses meant to stop you. Your OAMs is powerful—a force to be reckoned with, neatly hidden behind a pretext or stealthy moves.

OAMs also guides the achievement of our objective through certain advantageous vectors. It does so by revealing facilitation in places you might not have considered looking otherwise, like vendors, suppliers, insurance providers, and building maintenance contractors. It helps you look at the world in an adversarial and alternative way. It sees through a lens that only identifies *helpful* or *unhelpful* data and information. OAMs wants to proceed and succeed. It's the machine that weaponizes information.

Comfort and Risk

My position is this: comfort with risk is one of the most essential offensive skills. Comfort with risk does not equal discomfort with caution, however. Too much discomfort with caution will not serve you in this field.

If you are going out on a mission (say to an armed facility), the risk is in going; you should remain cautious at every step, but, again, too much overt caution in the moment will have you stand out. . .a *surefire* way to get shot (no pun intended). For the rest of the operations and engagements you go on, you will need to be comfortable with risk; too much caution in the moment will equate to too little confidence, and this may result in you seeming unnatural, which is the antitheses of your role most often. There are of course times where you will be nervous; my advice is that, in such moments, use those nerves as part of your pretext. Let your nervous energy come out as you tell security that you are running late for a critical meeting.

This position on caution remains valid no matter the vector you are using—being too cautious on a vishing call where the target expects authenticity will likely lower your probability of success. Being cautious with a phish is a thing—it will show up in the length of the email you send. You will likely try to answer every question you can possibly come up with from the target's perspective in the body of your phish—a big no-no. Phishes are to be succinct and not say quite enough, piquing the target's curiosity or piquing some other mood or reaction so that they click on the phish's link. Too much caution on a network pen test will likely prevent you from seeing gaps and exploiting them. You need to be able to take calculated risks.

It's notable that there's a difference between being comfortable with risk and failing to analyze a situation, but OAMs has you strike a balance between the two. The balance can be found in seeking a solution as a problem comes into view. The slight caution that OAMs affords you is what aids the swift identification of a problem. Implementing the solution is a function of comfort with risk. Being comfortable with risk doesn't mean you avoid a problem or deny it exists altogether—it just means that you can be comfortable finding another avenue that isn't your first choice or that puts you at greater risk.

The way to reach something that resembles equilibrium between caution and risk-taking is to apply it with another component of AMs—visualizing outcomes. By further playing that game of mental chess, you should be able to think through the risk factors of the operation. Every move you make comes with a risk, and some risks are the unintended consequences of simply executing an attack. If you try to think about every single measure of risk involved, step-by-step, you will walk straight into failure. But keeping your end goal in mind and thinking through how your next move may impact how you achieve that goal is a good start. It will keep you balanced and on track. Keep a holistic assessment of the risk running in your mind.

To sum up, when executing the attack, you should not be overly or overtly cautious. There has to be a sense of comfort with risk when executing. There is, however, lots of room for caution preceding the execution, which, as you'll see, your DAMs will take care of. The biggest issue of discomfort with risk when executing an attack is that it can reveal you as an intruder. OAMs allows you to maintain a relaxed approach and to act without showing hesitation and avoid the dangers of overthinking.

Planning Pressure and Mental Agility

One of your greatest advantages as an EA is that you know you are attacking, whereas the target is typically oblivious. Often this advantage translates to the illusion of control—the tendency for all of us to overestimate our ability to dominate and manage events. Strictly speaking, you do not have control over the outcome of any operation; it's down to randomness or "luck." You can do things, however, to steer the outcome in your favor. The initial reveal here is that an abundance of caution will hamper this ability to steer, whereas a relaxed, but risk-aware, approach will function and perform far more highly. This may seem difficult given that, as an attacker, you need to maintain extremely strong offensive mental agility.

You should be focused, intense, aiming to win, and primed to take advantage of any opportunity for success that real-life attacks provide, also known as mental agility. Note that, even if you plan an attack within an inch of its life, you will still not be able to accurately account for the actions and reactions of your targets. Without mental agility, an attacker may be good, but they will never be great.

Planning in and of itself will not lead you to feel pressure, but insisting you stick to the plan will. It is also likely lead you to failure. You must be able to interact and react to the environment. No one wakes up and says to themselves, "Well, today is the day I will not react to my environment."

Sometimes we get so set on winning that we get tunnel vision on the one route we want to take, not the one that's opening up in front of us. You must be able to adapt. When nothing is going as planned, you have to be able to pivot. When everything is going as planned, you should still recognize the opportunity to pivot, especially if it leads to a shortcut.

I've had to pivot more times than I've had hot dinners, and thankfully, not all have led to success. One of my first jobs saw me turn up at a small office as an IT consultant, which wasn't all that far from the truth. I was promptly introduced to the facilities manager, who was exceptionally nice to me. She gave me a cup of tea, and I told her about my love of British biscuits because I saw some in the kitchen, and I am not above hinting. Mere minutes later I had enough to eat and to take home. News of an IT consultant's arrival soon traveled, and not too long after I had staff coming up to me inquiring about some issues they were having on their computers— enter the pivot!

I, of course, agreed to take a look so that I could open a command prompt—allows you to run programs, manipulate Windows settings, and access files by typing in commands, the perfect low-key privilege escalation I'd been looking for. After a few minutes poking around pretending I knew what I was doing, I opened Terminal and took a discreet photo and thought I'd be on my merry way—except someone asked me a very simple question that any IT professional would know, and I crumbled like a two-day-old British biscuit. They saw me crumble, and minutes later the whole operation was on its knees because the manager of the office insisted on calling my cover company, which didn't exist. All because I couldn't recall what RAM stands for. (I can now at all times.) I still managed to pivot. When there was no answer on the other end of the line, mainly because it was ringing the burner phone in my pocket, I soon began to act indignant. I left papers to sign and told them where they could send them and got on my way.

This is the other advantage of OAMs: when you're under pressure, an offensive edge makes continuing the operation less challenging. Being able to pivot suddenly to continue trying to achieve the objective is a specialist skill. Mine let me down only when I got so flustered by an unexpected question that I couldn't recall the words random access memory. But it picked back up when I felt the heat rise and the possibility of arrest become a real threat.

Using OAMs to combat the pressures of planning and pivoting is, admittedly, easy to comprehend in theory but hard to practice. Learning this mental skill on the job is among the trickiest of things to do, but it's possible. There is definite value in seeking out stories from people who succeeded in pivoting and from those who have not.

Ultimately, using OAMs under pressure provides the ability to develop effective contingency plans, which is a critical mental skill for frequent decision-making, not only while in an active attack scenario but leading to that time as well. As an aside to this, for some people it will take time to learn this particular offensive strategy—working under pressure is on a spectrum, not a case of "you can" or "you can't," so we can all do it to varying degrees. Finding ways to build up this skill is tantamount to success as an ethical attacker, because it's a constant when you're out in the field. It may be adding a little more stress to your current role; it may be building up physical challenges. The point is that you have to build up your tolerance from stress and become increasingly immune to its effect on your critical thinking. For some people, it will seem to come naturally. Many of the individuals I've come across that have found picking up this skill easy have had seemingly tough initial conditions or have had experiences that have made using skills like this one second nature. It is definitely something you can learn if you aren't quite a whiz under pressure yet. Breathing is your greatest tool, as nuts as that sounds. But checking in on your breathing in moments of stress isn't some hippie-dippie technique. It works. It helps you process what you are feeling, which is most likely what's prohibiting you from thinking clearly. Lean into it and let it pass. You will become better and better, faster and faster at it.

Emergency Conditioning

Another component of OAMs is the ability to visualize, create, and construct scenarios based on information, which should serve to keep things straight in your mind. There's a game of mental chess to be played before each attack, as I've mentioned frequently. However, you cannot assume that you will conjure up the exact scenarios you will walk into, because there's no conceivable way to picture every act, action, and reaction that may occur. This ability to visualize is not shorthand for "manifestation." It's simply a good offensive warm-up strategy that can get the offensive juices flowing, so to speak. It's a skill you can build up now that will help your future self—and it makes thinking critically in the moment easier.

The brain is the strongest force in the body. It can overcome many adverse things, especially if you practice mental preparation. This practice can allow you to far exceed your physical and even mental limitations, but you have to train your brain for it. This sort of training relies on two things that you will need to do and use:

first, be prepared to use the fourth law of AMs; make every move count in the direction of the objective.

Second, you must also be able to employ *situational awareness*, which is essentially knowing what is going on around you. That's a broad definition, but there are items that you should look at. Above all else, start with entry control and access. There are two ways you must pay attention to these things: you must know how you are entering and how you can exit. This is true of network pen tests when exfiltrating information and covering your tracks, to vishing tests where starting and ending the call naturally enough so as to not invoke a negative feeling from the target is often essential. You never want to raise suspicions. You must also try to gauge how porous the establishment is overall. Both may include looking at doors, gates, fences, walls, windows, skylights, even sewage pipes. Look for how easily vendors gain access, where they park, and so forth. You should look for wall and ceiling cameras and even body cameras. You should try to be aware of motion sensors and other barriers. In a sense, attacker mindset and attacking is part of the built environment; the design of any structure always implies a way to exploit it.

Just as architecture and crime intersect, so, too, does efficient crime intersect with cities and even neighborhoods. You should also consider both of these. For example, if you were to think like an attacker breaking into a bank in Los Angeles, you might consider how far you are from one of the Freeways, the main links connecting downtown and the suburbs, which spread throughout the region in a vast network of concrete ribbons. You would study where exactly you were headed after the heist and not time the operation for rush hour. As an ethical attacker you might not *need* to think of these things as you have tangible confirmation that you are there to test security, typically in the form of a letter from someone high up within the organization, but because a real attacker does not, they will think about the broader logistics. You might also consider that Los Angeles, a sprawling county composed of a series of widely dispersed settlements, is heavily policed from the air—more so than any other US city, and that getting away without law enforcement being informed is of the utmost importance to your get-away being a success. But Manhattan, NY, on the other hand, is not anything like this. Its long, skyscraper-lined streets make policing from the air more cumbersome. It would also be notable to an attacker that Manhattan is surrounded by water, making alternative methods of escape plausible. Not to mention the elaborate, comprehensive subway system—another area hard to police effectively. However, the streets of New York lend themselves to police cars chasing suspects pretty well, and the plethora of alleyways that result in dead ends can make escape hard should the authorities or security be alerted of your operation.

In a network pen test, gathering as much information as possible for the compromised environments and the domain network means having situational awareness. Pre-entry, reconnaissance on infrastructure can tell you quite a lot about the target's network, too. Tools like NsLookup (`www.nslookup.io`)—a command-line tool for querying the Domain Name System (DNS) to obtain a domain name or IP address, or other DNS records—and theHarvester (`https://github.com/laramies/theHarvester`)—used to gather information of emails, subdomains, hosts, employee names, open ports, and banners—can give you a lot of information to start building your attack and increasing your awareness of the target's environment.

Including situational awareness in assessing whether your next step is for the good of the objective or not is non-negotiable. You cannot blindly attempt to obtain the objective; you must use the information you know and the information around you, reevaluating the further you get into the target's territory. Of course, this is true for actual events, but if you are practicing emergency conditioning in your mind you will have to imagine variations of what is included when assessing your surroundings. Which leads me to this: when practicing emergency conditioning, the purpose is to not get fixated on any one move or outcome.

The best analogy I have for it is this: if you have to picture yourself crossing a busy road, envision getting hit by a vehicle. . .a fun task. You have no way to know the color, make, model, year, or speed of the car, you won't know if it has a dashboard camera attached, and you won't know the direction it will hit you from, but you can imagine being hit by it at all speeds, what you'd do depending on the speed, where you get hit, and so forth. And then you can try to imagine dodging that car from different angles depending on its angle of approach. You can imagine it all a hundred ways or more, and you should always imagine surviving.

By imagining it, you will think of the sounds a car driving at a high speed makes, the difference in volume as it skids around a corner, and so forth. By doing this over and over, slightly differently every time, you might be better prepared when the time to cross the road actually comes. You would likely be quicker to dodge a car, even if in our imaginings it was yellow, and in actuality, it was a truck. I know, that was very uplifting.

This type of mental exercise is akin to *emergency conditioning*, which is just a training technique used to make unknown situations seem familiar. You are basically tricking your brain into being familiar with an experience so that when it, or something similar, actually unfolds in the real world, it doesn't seem as intimidating or daunting and your reaction rate will go up.

Notably, there is an upside to experiencing moderate levels of stress—even if you are just imagining the stress. Stress is often viewed as an absolute negative. It occurs when someone feels an imbalance between a challenge and the resources they have to deal with it. But it turns out that there are different kinds of stress and that, in smaller quantities, it can be very helpful. Eustress (beneficial stress) is a common form of stress. It's the sort of stress you feel before performing, and as EAs our job is to perform, in the sense of both execution and acting.

The factors that lead to eustress result in short-lived changes in hormone levels in the body. Normally, this type of stress does not last long and will not have long-term negative health effects. These smaller levels of stress can enhance our motivation. Small doses of stress can also force people to problem solve, ultimately building the skill and their own confidence in it. However, the relationship between the brain's health and stress is a very selective one, and there's no universal preferred amount of stress, because each of our brains is different. Most importantly, this effect is only seen when stress is intermittent. When stress continues for a prolonged period of time, there is a buildup of cortisol in the brain that can have long-term effects. Thus, chronic stress can lead to many health troubles. When chronic stress is experienced, our bodies produce more cortisol than it can release, and high levels of cortisol can wear down the brain's capacity to function properly. Several studies indicate that chronic stress impairs brain function by disrupting synapse regulation—resulting in the loss of sociability and the avoidance of interactions with others—by killing brain cells and even reducing the size of the brain. The prefrontal cortex, the area of the brain responsible for memory and learning, undergoes a shrinking effect when high levels of cortisol are present due to chronic stress. It can also increase the size of the amygdala, which can make the brain even more receptive to stress. A vicious cycle that has no upside.

The following graphic shows where optimal performance lies in conjunction with optimal stress and what can occur as a result. However, as noted previously, there's no universal preferred amount of stress. You will have to figure how much stress has the *Goldilocks* effect for you.

Optimal Performance

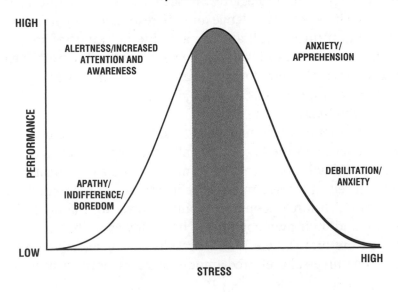

Finally, confidence in OAMs' skills allows you as an attacker to stay on the offensive in live attacks, to be in a state of readiness. The bottom line of OAMs comes down to being able to analyze an organization, identify the security gaps and exploit them effectively, knowing the risks and acting anyway. You are the storm that forces change in critical infrastructure and environment.

Defensive Attacker Mindset

Defensive skills help attackers succeed consistently and in all conditions. Defensive skills include the capacity to adapt and respond to surges in security or target resistance. The key words that describe defensive mental skills are balance, resilience, and caution.

When your defensive skills are strong, you become a consistent performer, finding success in the smaller components as well as the overall attacks far more often. Whereas with OAMs the ability to *apply* change is a coveted skill, with DAMs the kernel of success is the ability to *adapt* to change. With DAMs, adapting with resiliency is critical.

Consistency and Regulation

There's another link between OAMs and DAMs we need to explore: offensive mental skills are necessary *for* excellence, but as attackers we need defensive skills to *maintain* excellence. OAMs' penchant for stealth and competition—and the drive that comes with it—will be complemented by your defensive skills, allowing you as an attacker to be resilient and consistent in any conditions. This shows up when you pivot in a bid to win—your OAMs pushes this while your DAMs regulates it, making you consider the risks, even if fleetingly, and thus ensuring endurance. It also allows much of your agility to be executed carefully, because OAMs is primarily concerned with winning and will use persistence as a force, sometimes to the engagement's detriment. DAMs will take that power and cool it, keeping you stable.

Another way in which DAMs strikes a healthy balance with OAMs is in organization. Whereas OAMs demands that you pivot and apply new information for the good of the objective, DAMs allows for a standard to be adhered to. You must always apply information in an organized, efficient, and useful manner. You cannot blindly try things without surveying the environment for defenses that would thwart your plan.

Anxiety Control

One of the most important facets of DAMs is its capacity to help control anxiety. This becomes more critical, more vital, and even more indispensable as the critical stage of the attack approaches—this is recognizable as the point at which the significance of the operation typically increases. If you fail at that point, the operation is over. There is no room for error and no second chance.

At this point, there is less room for flexibility with options and opportunity typically becoming scarcer, too. I like to think of this as a funnel effect; the further you get into an attack and the closer you get to reaching your objective, the fewer options and less freedom you have. There may be only a few moves that would allow you to achieve your desired outcome. Anxiety-inducing stuff.

Here's an example: When approaching a building, you may have the choice of 10 entry and exit points to try. Once inside, you may have three or four routes to the security operations center (SOC), for example. Getting into the SOC may come down to two potential moves: up through the tiled roof and down the other side *or* through the door should you able to get it open. There's the bonus "option" of randomicity, which may show up as someone walking out of the SOC's security doors, allowing you to walk effortlessly in, but you typically wouldn't count on this. As the funnel effect unfolds, it's easy for anxiety to build.

When the body perceives a stress, it goes into "fight or flight" mode. Our attention gets highly focused and a slew of other bodily changes take place. This innate response is what allows parents to flip cars off their children and injured soldiers to continue fighting. Alas, there is a limit to how beneficial stress is. Too much stress causes performance to suffer. You may also take time to identify the root cause of your nervousness.

Clammy hands. Dry mouth. Shortness of breath. Shaky. Tense body parts. Sound familiar? Nerves. They get too many of us too often. As I've already confessed, I break out in a weird, patchy rash when I am really nervous. The old-age method of picturing your team or target in their underwear is by far the worst idea you'll have on the job, and thankfully you might not need to. Employing your DAMs means you should be able to quash, or at the very least quiet, those nerves before they've taken root. Identifying the root cause of your nerves will help you conceptualize them, which means that you can apply reason to them. This is important for multiple reasons, not the least of which is stamping out that anxiety and enjoying critical thought processes again. The first step is to interrupt that feedback loop.

Anxiety often begins in the amygdalae, which is where your brain processes memory and interprets emotions. It's now understood that you can reduce anxiety signals from your amygdalae if you assign names or labels to the emotions that you're experiencing at the time.

Another effective way to bring back critical thought processes is a breathing technique practiced by the Navy SEALs called *tactical breathing*. It focuses on slowing your rate of breathing down by pushing the breath through the nostrils, counting to four for each inhale and exhale. This technique might seem simple, but it has a huge impact.

Now, I'd like to note that your DAMs will have to work in concert with your OAMs at many times. For instance, if the root reason for nerves is fear of loss of control, you will have to employ functions from the OAMs "comfort with risk" structure. Sometimes all your DAMs can do is help you identify the origins, which is still a huge help that shouldn't be overlooked. In other cases, DAMs is enough; if the root cause of your nerves is that you feel you don't have enough information, you've underprepared. DAMs will help you ensure this never happens—if you employ it by ensuring you prepare and consider the defenses you will go up against.

Remember, the defensive side of the AMs is what helps a great attacker win consistently and in all conditions. Defensive skills include the capacity to adapt and respond. Through DAMs you know there are many uncontrolled variables, and it's easy to get overwhelmed. Simply knowing this is enough to begin turning the tide. DAMs can give you a high level of understanding and allows you to control anxiety, because defensively you know neither stress nor anxiety will aid your performance and that OAMs has you covered on the opposing side.

Instill in yourself the point of any defensive strategy—to fend off and block what doesn't serve you or that wants to harm you. Prepare and remember your goal, adapt to the situation, and respond with confidence in knowing the attack will never overtake you. You are performing it. DAMs is a regulator; it keeps you calm and allows for a modest amount of caution. Whereby OAMs allows you growth in stressful moments, DAMs regulates the stress you feel so that you actually use it as a driving force, recognizing it as a reason to adapt to, and then apply, your own changes.

Recovery, Distraction, and Maintenance

The skill of quickly recovering from setbacks is a defensive mental skill that pays dividends in lengthy engagements. This, coupled with the ability to focus despite distractions, is a potent combination completely in your favor as an attacker. This is critical at times where distractions increase in proportion to the size and importance of the job. It also helps prevent false positive opportunity identification. Not every incident or event is an opportunity for you as an attacker—sometimes it's just good enough to be able to observe them, with no need to act.

Finally, mental maintenance skills, or the ability to maintain simple, effective thoughts under pressure, is often the difference between having a great plan and executing a great plan. DAMs should amount to consistent performance and continued success on jobs.

OAMs and DAMs Come Together

There is overlap between the two sides no matter how you slice it. Having them categorized within our minds isn't important. Looking at the skills and building them up together is the real goal.

Offensive mental skills allow attackers to achieve what most ordinary people would find hard to believe, never mind actually perform. Defensive mental skills give attackers consistency and resiliency. The combination of both will result in a powerful attacker, able to test the most hardened of defenses and also able to provide solution-based feedback for clients left feeling shattered, most often because they could not have conceived of such an attack mere hours before it was performed. The performance of an attacker missing either of these skills will be diminished.

Summary

- OAMs: offensive attacker mindset
- DAMs: defensive attacker mindset
- The offensive attacker mindset allows you to direct an event in the direction of the objective and be comfortable with the risk of doing so.
- A defensive attacker mindset will help an attacker win consistently and in all conditions.
- DAMs also teaches you that getting to the root cause of an anxious feeling will help take it from a feeling to a thought that can be broken down and dealt with and, hopefully, eradicated.
- Whereas your OAMs wants you to pivot at every possible opportunity that presents itself, your DAMs holds you back when necessary, knowing that not every incident or event is an opportunity and that observation without action can be just as powerful.

- Whenever the two are in conflict, OAMs will push you to do what it takes to win; DAMs will pull you to use caution, urging you to not take big risks.
- If there's no life-threatening danger, and you are closing in on the end of an attack, you should go for the win. If the risk you need to take in that moment threatens the rest of the engagement, fall back and reassess.

Key Message

Being able to think straight and maintain effective thoughts under pressure is key when working in a hectic or fluid situation. Preparation and staying aligned with your goal and adapting to the situation are critical. Your mental agility is a great asset, as is believing the attack will never overtake you. You are performing it. You have as much control as you will ever have. The rest is chance. Find comfort in that.

Chapter 3
The Attacker
Mindset Framework

The Attacker Mindset Framework (AMsF) is the method and systematic approach for achieving an objective. It's the life cycle model for an attack. The remainder of this book is a support for this framework. By using the AMsF, you become familiar with building strengths like mental agility, objectivity, and critical thinking. Through the use of exercises and stories, you start to think like an attacker.

The AMsF is formed by functionally overlapping elements. The base elements covered here are development, execution, and ethics, which are further broken down into their own primary components. These three groupings are what make up the attacker mentality. With these at play and executed well, you can probably compromise most businesses worldwide with seemingly devastating results. Obviously, if you are a malicious attacker, you will likely forgo the ethics portion and gain similar results but with more risk. As professional, ethical attackers, we cannot afford to execute without ethics.

The good thing about any framework is that it gives you the freedom to apply it differently in any circumstance and for any objective. This framework also allows for individual differences in effort and execution (see Figure 3.1).

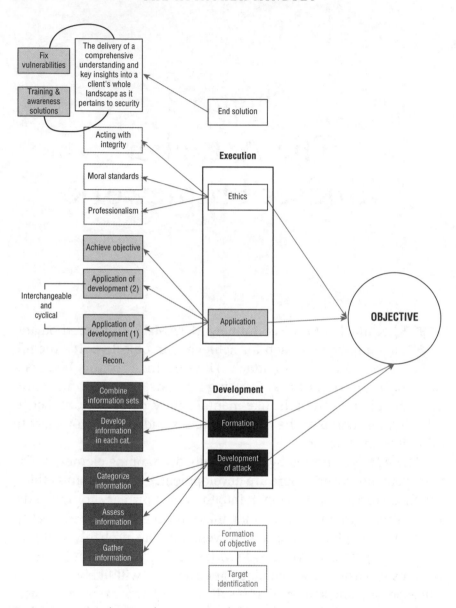

Figure 3.1   Attacker Mindset Framework (AMsF)

Development

The development phase of the attack cycle leans heavily on the first four cognitive skills needed to practice this mindset: curiosity, persistence, information gathering, and mental agility.

There is no attack without information. Likewise, without processing and using the information well and for the good of the objective, the attack will falter. Looking back to the very first example given in Chapter 1, "What Is the Attacker Mindset?," where a woman spilled hot coffee on herself and I thought, *I bet she was going over a bump! instead of Oh, she should sue!*–information is critical to the mindset and the direction you take as an attacker, and so is how you process it. Had I known that McDonald's was heating coffee perpetually at 180–190° F, and that coffee at that temperature, if spilled, causes third-degree burns in 3 to 7 seconds, I'd have known how to get approximately $3 million in putative damages from McDonald's. I didn't have that information. And more important, I didn't think to look for it. I was not at all curious about the coffee or any information to do with it. I was only focused on the woman. Worse still, I went with what I thought I knew, which is that it's not anyone else's fault if you single-handedly spill coffee on yourself (speed bump or no speed bump). This thought process in and of itself highlights two interesting points. The first is that this is a sort of bias that we all fall victim to and must fight hard not to. It takes a lot not to operate from bias because it is most often invisible to the operator in every way.

The particular bias I was suffering from is known as *anchoring bias*; I relied too much on one key piece of information and the first piece I received. I also fell victim to the illusion of validity, which meant I overestimated the accuracy of my own perception and judgment. These examples are two of a huge number of cognitive biases that hamper critical thinking and, as a result, the validity of our decisions and stances on things. This neatly plays into the second thing of note, which is that it is always best to get a good picture of both sides of the story—for instance, finding out the temperature of the coffee.

There's another, darker side to be considered with regard to information weaponization for the good of the objective. To explore it, we must look at the world of spies. Ana Montes was a prolific and damaging Cuban spy. But to those she was deceiving, she was thought of as a star. She had been selected, repeatedly, for promotions and showered with honors, accolades, and even a medal from the CIA. One of Montes's former supervisors even described her as the best employee he had ever had.

She was a Cuban analyst, what is known as a GS-14. But she was also on the clock for Fidel Castro for her nearly 20-year career. For the entire time, she passed along secrets about her colleagues, she spied on the American spies working against Cuba, and she leaked classified US military information frequently. Moreover, she manages to blindside her brother Tito, an FBI special agent; her former boyfriend, Roger Corneretto, an intelligence officer for the Pentagon specializing in Cuba; and her sister Lucy, a 28-year veteran of the FBI who has won awards for helping to unmask Cuban spies. Montes never removed any documents from work, nor did she send them digitally. Instead, she kept the details in her head and simply typed them up at home. She would then relocate the information onto encrypted disks, meet with her handler, and turn them over.

But what did she do from an attacker mindset point of view? Well, she stuck to all four laws and used all the skills. Montes most certainly had an end in mind; it was believed to be a shared end between her and her employers and her country to a degree; she weaponized information and applied it to the objective time and time again. She weaponized information she got from being on the inside and applied it to her own objective. She altered other information so that it could not be properly weaponized by those who believed her to be working along with them.

All of that is a given, and it was not easily detectable by her peers because they all thought, and Montes seemed to be, working from the same scope for the same objective. Her real power came from the fact she never broke character. If she had, for even a second, she would've been in jail a lot sooner. Her duplicitous game meant everyone thought she was working for the same goal they were, and because she continuously bent the information to her own objective without breaking character, she was able to deliberately distort the US government's views on Cuba. Her pretext was not for the good of everyone else's goal. It was only to disguise her as a threat from it.

Eventually, though, Montes did break character and took actions that could not be aligned with the mission she was supposed to be working on. In other words, she acted in a way that was not congruent with the American objective. She deviated from the normal course of action and acted in a way that benefited her own objective.

In 2001, an analyst at the National Security Agency (NSA) approached Scott Carmichael, a counterintelligence officer, with sensitive information: the NSA had intercepted and made sense of a coded Cuban communication. It revealed a prominent Washington figure who was secretly working for Cuba. They called this person Agent S and noted that this double agent had interests in the 'Support for Analysts File Environment' (SAFE) system and had traveled to Guantanamo Bay in July 1996. (SAFE was the computer system of the Defense Intelligence Agency [DIA]). Carmichael cross-referenced any DIA employees who had traveled to Guantanamo Bay in July 1996, and a familiar name came up: Ana Montes.

Consequently, Montes is in jail at the highest-security women's prison in the nation. She's shared a *home* with a woman who strangled a pregnant woman to get her baby, a nurse who killed four patients with massive injections of adrenaline, and a former Charles Manson groupie who tried to assassinate President Gerald Ford. Montes took actions that were outside the scope of what was best for her seeming objective, and it was an immediate red flag. Law 4—everything you do as an attacker must be for the good of the objective—will always out a traitor or someone detrimental to the mission because at certain points they will have to choose their true objective over the one they are pretending to act on behalf of.

Stepping out of the world of spies and infiltrators, I come back to information. Information is the lifeblood of any operation, and so knowing how to collect and process it is integral to achieving and using the mindset. In this beginning phase of the attack, you gather information, assess that information, and categorize it into one of three classes: useful from a pretext standpoint, useful for the actual attack insofar as helping to achieve the objective, or not useful at all (to be disregarded). Learning new ways to process, follow, and apply information becomes easier with practice. This is development, and it's the first major piece of the AMsF.

The development of an attack can be split into two subcategories. The first is assessing information, and the second is creating vulnerabilities from it. Achieving this involves processing the information and mental agility.

The ability to assess a business's vulnerabilities through your AMs lens means parsing seemingly innocuous information to help form an attack. Examples of this apparently mundane information are things like job postings for the company that specify particular systems and software used; pictures of office space and lists of upcoming events that employees will attend, or even those that they have attended in the past; and even social media postings allowing insight into the culture of the place. One of the best places to look for information on a company is on sites that *allow* employees to critique their place of employment. Of course, not all information is *seemingly innocuous*, but if you happen across information that is crippling (aside from reporting it to your point of contact pretty pronto), you have to be able to use it in a way that's not tactless or revealing about your motives. Examples of this would be finding that the domain controller is on the demilitarized zone (DMZ) or that an employee has accidentally posted a picture with the company credit card displayed. In both cases, you would have to operate with discipline and control. In both cases, you would quickly have to inform your point of contact.

The development stage also involves creating vulnerabilities from information for the same outcome. Usually, development means starting to build a pretext, which is typically the first step in an attack's formation. In the next section, brilliantly titled "Phase 1," I will look at an example of a case in which a pretext is developed from apparently harmless information.

As a helpful aside so that you aren't blindsided later, I further categorize useful information into two classifications: *advantageous* and *elite*. Advantageous information is made up of items that can help us but that can change at any time. An example is a company's leadership, software used, or a vendor. Advantageous data is typically stable, but it's not elite. Elite information doesn't change over the course of its lifetime, unless the company is sold or acquired. Other examples include the company's Employer Identification Number (EIN); its core services, profits, and losses each year; and other historical information.

When we're attacking a person, an example of elite information would be health data, such as blood type and mental conditions. We live in an age of genetic sequencing, whereby the best of current-day science tells us that all humans are 99% alike and that only 1% of DNA accounts for our differences. In other words, your DNA is responsible for your psychological traits and personality; it can reveal your mental illnesses and abilities. Behavioral problems show great genetic influence, too. This puts elite data in a category entirely of its own. With the rise of personal genomics, a person's mental strengths and weaknesses can be predicted from birth. That's valuable information, and it is available to us now as attackers.

Advantageous information would be a person's address and their email. Typically passwords change over time, too.

This level of categorization is not needed, but you might find it helpful to label things this way, depending on how detail oriented you are and if categorizing things this way is beneficial to your client.

Phase 1

The first phase of development concentrates its efforts on sifting through broad and voluminous information without any direction. The searches you perform and the information you gather will obviously pertain to the target, but it won't all be in the same category. As an example, you might collect information on the public appearance of the company, the services they provide, the hierarchy, and other even simpler information, like the address of their headquarters or if they sponsor employee events. Gathering all this information and sorting it into categories will allow you to hone your avenue of attack and gather more information to design and craft a pretext in the second phase of development.

Because I'm never in the mood to be sued, I'll start with targeting the Lehman Brothers, a company I've chosen because they have long since gone out of business. I search Google using the Time Tool, a search function that can collect search results for your query before a certain date, during a date range, or after a date when set. I set it to display information between January 1, 2000 and December 31, 2007. I find two items that allow me to begin developing a pretext as if I was building an attack, circa 2002. Notably, this is a *very* straightforward example, and it showcases the simplest of attack development to get us started.

Finding No. 1 (see Figure 3.2) supplies me with the target's physical address. Eventually, after searching that address, I am taken to Finding No. 2, which gives me information on the building. The same page leads me to a PDF document that includes the architect, engineers, and suppliers of the building (Figure 3.3).

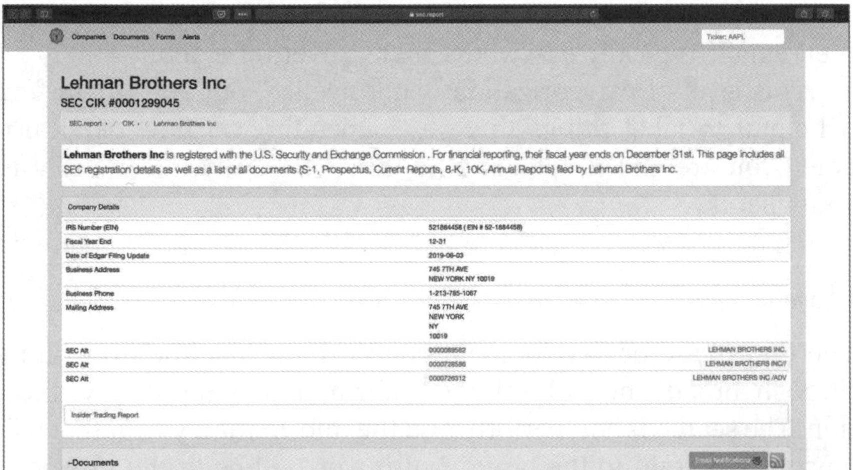

Figure 3.2　Finding No. 1: Lehman Brothers's corporate address
SOURCE: https://sec.report

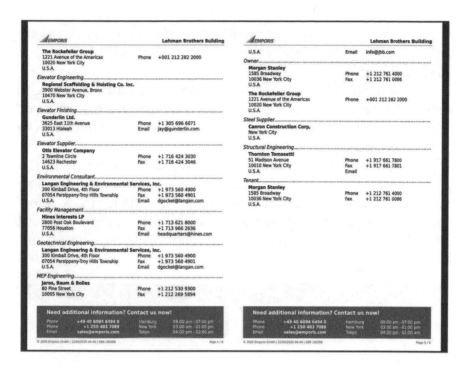

Figure 3.3   Finding No. 3: Lehman Brothers's building engineers and suppliers
SOURCE: www.emporis.com

From here I have a few choices. I hesitate in choosing which line to follow first. If I could impersonate the elevator supplier or engineering company representative, I'd probably have free access to the whole building. But pretending to represent the facility management company would also gain me a lot of freedoms and cover. Because of this, I start by searching for the facility management company, which turns out to be Hines Interests LP. But ultimately, I choose Otis Elevator—they are well known, and the use of an Otis Elevator UTF fire service key would likely gain me access to any floor I want.

Admittedly this is pretty easy stuff, so I'll provide one more example. This example shows another avenue to a pretext and hints at the volume of information available without even using a Google dork. By using and mixing operators, a *Google dork* can

help a user locate sensitive, buried information that is not well protected. Using these operators, or *dorks,* a user's searches become
advanced searches.

Pivoting slightly from the first search, instead of choosing to
search the address of the business, I choose the SEC ALT number,
which is the Securities and Exchange Commission number, given
as 0000089562.

This search takes me to a page similar to the first search. The
page, shown in Figure 3.4, lets me download a document (see Figure 3.5), called a Consolidated Statement of Financial Condition;
collect the signature and telephone number of the chief financial
officer (CFO); and also ascertain their auditors to have been Ernst
& Young (EY).

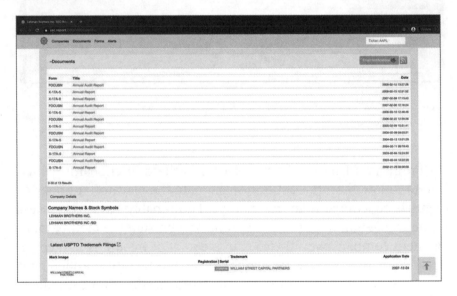

Figure 3.4   Find No. 1: SEC ALT number
SOURCE: https://sec.report

With these findings, I consider posing as a consultant from EY
and spoofing the number of the CFO to bypass reception.

From here, we can move to the second phase of development,
which is also split into two.

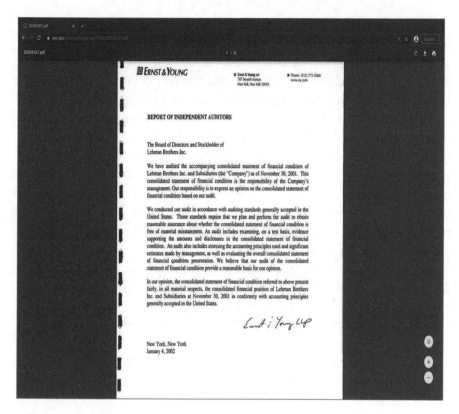

Figure 3.5 Find No. 2: Ernst & Young LLP
SOURCE: https://sec.report

Phase 2

Before delving into the second phase, let's discuss the two subsections of Phase 2. First, building the two subsections does sometimes happen simultaneously due to the nature of information—when searching for one thing, we invariably stumble onto other information that's not helpful at that exact moment but that might be of use later. Within the framework, gathering this information is referred to as "developing the information in each category" and "combining the information sets." Ultimately, this means that there's gathering information to support your pretext and there's gathering information to further your attack.

Sticking with the Lehman Brothers example, if I were to build up OSINT to pose as an Otis employee, I'd need a similar uniform and an ID badge; I'd need to know about offices and depots they have; and I'd have to see if I could find any information online about how often they service their elevators. I would also consider calling as an Otis employee to the building/maintenance company to schedule an appointment to inspect the elevators or to try to ascertain when they were last scheduled. I would also want to show up with seemingly legitimate paperwork to support my pretext. This is all OSINT heavy.

For the other subsection, recon development, I would look for information that could bolster my objective. If my objective was to get to their security operations center (SOC), I would look for information on what kind of security doors were in the building, search for building blueprints, and meticulously go through social media accounts to see if there's ever been a photo posted from within the SOC. I'd comb through LinkedIn, searching for the people who work in it.

For both phases, it is fair to say that the real test of knowledge gained isn't in its truth but in its utility.

Application

The development of an attack is the ability to assess any business's vulnerabilities through our AMs lens by parsing seemingly innocuous information or leaked information to form an attack. The application is the leveraging of that information to perform our attack.

Let's look at application from a high level. There are many ways to attack:

Physical Attacks   An attack on a physical resource, such as a facility, building, or other physical asset.
Human Attack   An attack that involves social engineering and the manipulation of people to achieve the objective, also at a physical resource/facility, but usually one with human capital, includes vishing (voice phishing).

Cyberattacks   Cyberattacks can range from installing spyware or malware onto a computer or network to attempting to destroy the infrastructure.

Phishing falls between the latter two categories, with both a human and a technological component.

Theoretical Attacks   Often used for strategy and decision making, a theoretical attack offers companies and organizations fresh perspectives for a hypothetical future. It is typically performed by two opposing teams, generally external to the organization, that test the weight of the intelligence given to them, both arriving at different outcomes based on the same information. This information can be pivotal for decision makers who can then choose a path more easily, especially when the stakes are high.

The second phase of development sees you gather information to realistically mount an attack. Earlier in that section, I said that as an Otis employee, I'd need a similar uniform, an ID badge, and knowledge of typical maintenance schedules they keep with regard to their elevators—maybe because they are required by law or regulation. This type of information feeds the application and execution of the attack. With this information and the other items I've found on them as a company, I could comfortably mount an attack. The comfort, however, isn't just in how much I can seem like an Otis employee. It is also about how I conduct myself in the face of factors that will remain unknown until I walk in the door on the day.

The application of information is powerful, but there's information that will only be available to you on the day, such as the person you're dealing with, their mood, the proclivity for security, and their job role as well as your own effect on them. To steer the odds in your favor, you should employ the following:

Confidence in Your Character   This doesn't mean to say you must act confident. If you are posing as a lost foreigner (hey, it's worked for me before), then you shouldn't really be *too* confident, but you should have confidence in your "character" or pretext choice.

Commitment to Your Character   You cannot enter as the lost foreigner or an Otis employee or any other and disengage from that character unless planned. This plan, for me, includes if I get caught. I will keep in character for as long as I can until I am sure they will not let me go (obviously I would try again) or if they threaten to call the authorities. If one or both of these occur, I explain the situation and ask for my point of contact to be reached. There is, however, a line. On my first job for my current company, Social-Engineer LLC, I went in as a satellite specialist there to renew a license. I also got someone to let me on the roof to check the equipment. This was overkill. I was in the building, I was getting all the flags required by scope, but I wanted to see how far my character could get me—it was close to a pointless exercise, and the equipment on the roof wasn't in my flag list. However, I offered the information to the client because I wanted to (a) be transparent and (b) show all the weaknesses I found. I said earlier it was *close* to a pointless exercise. It's useful for the client to know how far you can get. Since it was considered within scope, and the roof hadn't been struck off, I committed to my character too much and essentially did the job of the person I was impersonating.

Commitment to character might end when commitment to another begins. If you enter a building as an outside specialist but get deeper into the environment and need to assume another identity to get further, you absolutely can. You just can't be both at the same time, and you should leave as the character you walked in as so as to not raise flags.

The third law states that you never break pretext. This law actually means that you are never yourself. You are always in character. You are always disguised as a threat for the sake of the fourth law: the objective is the central point from which all other moves an attacker makes hinge from.

Narrative Effect   As humans, we love stories. In reality, we don't always see the truth. We rely on a biased set of cognitive processes to get to a conclusion or belief. This natural tendency to view our thoughts as facts to fit with our existing beliefs is known as motivated reasoning—and we all do it.

Though we may see ourselves as rational beings, we are very reactionary. Most of our decisions aren't rational. This is why the application of pretext is important and not only the application of information we have to use against the client. As human beings we're wired to interpret information as confirming our beliefs and to reject information if it runs counter to those beliefs. So if I show up in an Otis uniform and the building has no elevator, that's going to send up a few red flags.

According to Sara Gorman, a public health specialist, and her father Jack, a psychiatrist, "[R]esearch suggests that processing information that supports your beliefs leads to a dopamine rush," and as we know, dopamine is addictive. On the flip side, information that is inconsistent with one's beliefs produces a negative response. This leads people to see what they want to see so they can believe what they want to believe—so *preload* them.

Preloading

Preloading is influencing your target before the event takes place. In other words, the attack starts before you've walked in the door— how you walk, how you carry yourself, what you are wearing, and your demeanor, posture, facial expression, everything down to your gait, are all factors in your success—it's all part of the attack. Get people to believe what you want them to, what fits the narrative you're selling, and you will find yourself with an easier target. It's a great way to begin the application phase.

"Right Time, Right Place" Preload

Preloading can work by simply being in the right place at the right time. Imagine you are a target for a moment; you are at a work event and someone approaches you, seemingly interested in you and your job. It doesn't seem too threatening—after all, it's just someone interested in learning about your job and at a place that seems appropriate to do so. Before long you're talking about how you deploy patches or how you store customer information; they are captivated and so curious about it all—finally, a perfect stranger cares about databases as much as you do. Much of this is accomplished through preloading. They were where they were supposed to be and were interested in something that doesn't seem too far-fetched, given the circumstances, location, and backdrop. The attacker presented themselves in the right place at the right time.

If, as an attacker, you can preload by merely being in the right environment, half of your job is done for you.

Preloading is one of the best tools at your disposal in the application phase. It does much of the heavy lifting, and combined with your commitment to character, you become powerful as you apply information to gain information—all to achieve your objective.

Ethics

As the good guys, all of what we're learning here is underpinned by something a malicious attacker will never have or use: ethics and morals. Keeping the moral line between us and them and choosing to be bound by ethics is the staple of the mindset I am trying to teach. You can't—and don't—always show it in the moment, since it's the antithesis of our job when in attack mode, but our moral compass wins in the end, when you help rebuild the pieces. In doing this, you make companies, employees, and the public safer.

There is another point of consideration when delving into ethics that I often find myself talking about in speeches I give to agencies and companies alike: believing you're doing the right thing can still make you *feel* as if you are not. And vice versa—feeling you are doing the right thing doesn't necessarily mean you're *actually* doing the right thing. Ethics is a field that isn't always black and white.

Intellectual Ethics

To intellectually believe you are doing the right thing will require analysis of the situation on your part. To intellectually believe you're being ethical, you will need truth, knowledge, and understanding. These three things are what distinguish intellectual ethics from the presumption of ethics at play or merely *feeling* you are operating ethically. The line of ethics is movable; it's decided by the spectrum your target sits on. If you hunt terrorists, you don't have to apply ethics against your target or environment, as professional social engineers often do. You must apply ethics against the greater good. The Innocent Lives Foundation tracks and traces pedophiles. Ethics are not applied against the targets in these cases, either. They are applied against the greater good.

As an attacker, sometimes your job is to deceive people for the greater good, even if they are good people, and ultimately, you will lie for a living. That can chip away at even the most stoic among us. But, intellectually at least, there are different kinds of lying. First and foremost, there's anti- and prosocial lying. If you truthfully understand that, after assessing all the information available to you, you're conducting your actions on behalf of something bigger than yourself in that moment, something that will in the end produce a safer environment for its population, then you can intellectually believe that you are operating ethically.

Prosocial lying requires empathy and compassion because you need to be able to posit that what you say or do may cause harm in the hypothetical future—which is a responsibility that shouldn't be shrugged off easily. But in having a sense that what you do matters, that it is for a cause, not a seemingly malicious act for the sake of it, you should remain intellectually safe.

Reactionary Ethics

I refer to the "feelings" of being ethical as *reactionary ethics* because they are most often a reflex to a situation relative to you and your beliefs. There are two things that can help you navigate reactionary feelings hinging from a job: the scope and the objective.

If the scope permits your actions, then any negative feelings you have are resolved in the context of your response. The objective is also another indicator of whether the feeling of operating ethically or not is sound. As an aside, choice is something that's included in ethics, and you should always feel you have the choice whether or not to execute. I personally base that decision on the weight of the greater good.

You have a morally ambiguous job as an attacker. It is centered around dishonesty, duplicity, and confidence. As I most often describe the job of attacker, we are the intersection of corporate spy and con artist, at least as social engineers. Network pentesters aren't a stone's throw away from that description, either. Their job is to surveille and exploit. So, where do morals come into play and what's the metric?

The primary moral virtue of an attacker is integrity. Integrity comes from serving and protecting your clients. To accomplish this goal, you must be able to explain your technical and ethical limitations with regard to each contract. Additionally, the only line between an ethical attacker and a malicious one is *intent*. Your intent is never in question as an ethical attacker—you should never be wondering if you do or do not agree with protecting the client. If you are wondering that, you've probably flipped, and if that were me, I would recuse myself from the project. For example, I know I would never take a job for the Ku Klux Klan. A ridiculous statement, but nonetheless it shows that you won't always agree with your clients' ethos, and when that occurs, you are not the right person for the job. Say no.

However, your morals cannot stand in the way of you and influencing a target for the sake of the mission. As an example, you cannot be so in love with your client's business that you hold back from trying to beat it. In this case and in these moments, your morals must be applied to the greater good. As attackers, we have to solemnly believe that everything we do is for something bigger than ourselves and winning in that moment.

There's one other nuance to morals that's worth covering: the greater good of a mission, rather than the acts of it, are items to be concentrated on when executing. This guideline is most applicable to those who have a harder job than mine: hunting terrorists, human traffickers, and other such factions. Morals and ethics aren't applied to the targets of these operations and investigations. Our moral psychology as humans dictates that we apply morals to those who are hurt, not those who are responsible for the hurt.

Ultimately, you may have to look at what you are doing through the lens of the consequences that will ensue and see if you can reconcile the two from a moralistic standpoint. Notably, guilt and morals or sadness and morals or any other emotion and morals aren't mutually exclusive, but knowing your intent matters. It gives a sense of meaning to otherwise difficult work.

Moreover, the field of ethics (or moral philosophy) involves systematizing, defending, and recommending concepts of right and wrong behavior. It is widely accepted that ethical theories can be divided into three general subject areas: metaethics, normative ethics, and applied ethics. We will skip the first and look at normative ethics. For us, as social engineers, we look to the Social Engineering Framework, written by Christopher Hadnagy:

> Set out in this framework is The Social Engineering Code of Ethics which accomplishes three important goals: it promotes professionalism in the industry, establishes ethics and policies that dictate how to be a professional SE, and provides guidance on how to conduct a social engineering business. More than this it defines moral standards that regulate right and wrong conduct. It involves articulating the good habits that we should acquire, the duties that we should follow, and the consequences of our behavior on others. The following 10 bulleted points comprise the Social Engineering Code of Ethics:
>
> - Respect the public by accepting responsibility and ownership over your actions, and their effects on the welfare of those in, around, and involved with the engagement.
> - Before undertaking any social engineering engagement, ensure you are fully aware of the scope and effects on others and their well-being.

- Avoid engaging in, or being a party to, unethical, unlawful, or illegal acts that negatively affect your professional reputation, the information security discipline, the practice of social engineering, others' well-being, or the parties and individuals in, around, and involved with the engagement.
- Reject any engagement, or aspect of an engagement, that may make a target feel vulnerable or discriminated against. This includes, but is not limited to, sexual harassment, offensive comments (verbal, written, or otherwise) related to gender, sexual orientation, race, religion, or disability; stalking or following, deliberate intimidation, or harassing materials. Additionally, lewd or offensive behavior or language, which may be sexually explicit or offensive in nature, materials or conduct, language, behavior, or content that contains profanity, obscene gestures, or gendered, religious, ethnic, or racial, slurs are all to be avoided. Employing any of these tactics reduces the target's ability to learn and improve from the engagement.
- Do not negatively manipulate, threaten, or make others uncomfortable in any way, unless specified by a client due to unique needs and testing environment.
- Minimize risks to the confidentiality, integrity, or availability of information of your employer, clients, and individuals involved in engagements. After performing a social engineering engagement, ensure the security of obtained information is a priority. Never disclose information to outside parties as private and confidential information must remain private and confidential. Do not misuse any information or privileges you are afforded as part of your responsibilities.
- When training future social engineers, consider that training will leave a lasting impact on your students and the methodology with which you train will echo through all students' future engagements. Provide students with the knowledge and tools to create positive learning environments and productive scenarios for their future engagements and clients.
- Ensure the social engineering practices of yourself and your students include conscientious, thoughtful, and considerate ways to escalate engagements to eventually emulate real-world attack vectors. Recognize our clients are seeking ways to improve their

security posture and work with them to increase the difficulty of realistic attack vectors.

- Respect that social engineering engagements involve human vulnerability and avoid publicizing vulnerabilities, whether through a blog, social media, or other medium, that result in harmful effects, emotions, or feelings for your client and the individuals and parties in, around, and involved with the engagement.
- Do not misrepresent your abilities or your work to the community, your employer, or your peers. Ensure you have the experience and knowledge promised to your clients and stakeholders.

Refer to the framework at `www.social-engineer.org/` `framework/general-discussion` for further insights.

Social Engineering and Security

Switching gears a little, let's look at social engineering in conjunction with AMs because they are closely related. Much of what makes up AMs is facilitated in the real world by using social engineering. Although many social engineering attacks are diverse and dynamic in nature, common patterns emerge when we break down attacks. For instance, social engineering most often uses OSINT followed by rapport building and elicitation of help and assistance themes, which we will delve into later. Some attacks use fear as a theme, and others use greed. Nonetheless, after performing OSINT, social engineers typically rely on their social skills to advance an attack, which is both deceivingly underwhelming and terrifying all at once, that a social engineer may be able to elicit information from a person to create and then exploit a vulnerability should not be ignored. It's the weaponizing of a person who, if effective, can circumvent the most modern and hardened defenses.

There are many forms of social engineering; the main vectors are phishing (email), vishing (voice call), SMShing (text message), and in person (this includes impersonation). As attackers, we need to be able to execute attacks down any and all of these vectors. Network pentesters have to apply the attacker mindset to identify, exploit, and resolve security vulnerabilities and weaknesses affecting a target's digital assets and computer networks, too. Then, in some cases, they must use social engineering to further their attack or hold.

However, this book does not strictly cover social engineering. This book is (obviously) about AMs, and AMs and social engineering are not one and the same; rather, they are relatives. Given that, there's no doubt that social engineering has become a serious occurrence in information security. I often describe it as the intersection of social skill and business stress testing, but what it boils down to is human versus human. As has already been pointed out, social engineers employ certain tactics, like fear, authority, scarcity, and rapport—building techniques, to strengthen their attacks. All of these can prove powerful for an attacker to leverage against their target, but we cannot afford to focus on them here. This is because you can be a social engineer but possess no real form of the attacker mindset; it is neither acting skills nor influential acumen alone that makes an attacker's mindset, although both can be helpful. It's truly the discovery and application of information that forms this mentality.

As I will cover in this book, curiosity and persistence are the driving forces of the discovery of information, but this discovery requires a methodology—a systematic approach to OSINT is therefore paramount. Understanding that data is abundantly available is something I consider to be a strong and optimistic outlook; being aware that you will have to parse large amounts of data efficiently and effectively, and filtering it to the items that are critical for the success of the mission, is a skill that requires self-discipline and an unwavering dedication to the objective at hand. You should always keep in the back of your mind that sometimes you have to apply information to gain information.

The application of information is made easier if the primary step of collecting it is performed properly. Seeing weakness through the lens of the information you are collecting and applying it is the logical extension of the discovery phase.

Social Engineering vs. AMs

Again, it's beyond all doubt that social engineering is a serious discipline with serious consequences. Neglecting to comprehend the nature and power of it over security will only ever serve to decrease the security posture of our organizations. KnowB4.com estimates that 98 percent of cyberattacks rely on social engineering (https:// blog.knowbe4.com/social-engineering-is-a-core-element-of-nearly-every-cyber-attack). As a social engineer, my job is to influence others to obtain my objective. But I could do that without any presence of AMs at all. For example, I don't need any real semblance of AMs to make a call, follow a script, and hope that the target unwittingly helps me achieve my objective, but I could still be classified as a social engineer. You can see this lack of AMs in other related industries, such as "script kiddies" in programming and ethical hacking—not having an underlying skill doesn't preclude you from achieving an objective at times.

At the same time, forming an objective and knowing how to collect information and how to apply it to a target to reach my objective—but not being able to make the call, write the phish, or approach a target—would make me a terrible social engineer. I'd be hitting all the AMs targets by about 80 percent, but my execution would suffer. So, social engineering and AMs are closely related but not always mutually exclusive—they do overlap. In fact, they can and should be used in a way that makes them functionally reliant on each other because they are most powerful when used together, not separately.

Not all professional social engineers seem to exhibit the qualities of an attacker; rather, they are readily able to follow scripts and hope for the desired outcome. This way of working directly affects those businesses and people we are trying to secure because often a play-by-play of the attack is offered with limited insight into how to solve for future attacks. I fundamentally believe that the best of all social engineers should have a sharp and effective attacker mindset. Blending social engineering with an AMs will place you in an elite category whereby you can identify, exploit, and explain security gaps. This blend is a massive benefit to your clients, who depend on you to give them more than a step-by-step account of the actions you took to circumvent their defenses. To best protect them, you should be able to give them a comprehensive understanding of their whole landscape as you perceive it, not only how you bypassed some of their defenses arbitrarily.

No business should be without an attacker mindset specialist—not if they want to accurately see themselves as the targets malicious attackers do, yet protect themselves and their customers as ferociously and as comprehensively as they possibly can.

Summary

- Social engineering is a dominant discipline in which influence is used as a method of evading security measures at a human level.
- AMs and social engineering are not one and the same, but they are closely related. By understanding the detailed characteristics of social engineering, you can build an effective AMs more easily.
- All social engineers should be able to think like an attacker because, as previously mentioned, social engineering is involved in 98 percent of cyberattacks.
- Social engineering is a way to use your attacker mindset, not a way to form it.
- How you gather information makes the mindset as well as the direction you take as an attacker.

Key Message

Social engineering is a formidable practice in which persuasion is used as a technique to circumvent security measures and gain information or access to it. You can be a social engineer but possess no real form of attacker mindset; it is the discovery and application of information that forms this mentality. AMs and social engineering are most powerful when used together, not separately.

Our belief in ideals and ethics are what make up a society. If you believe in those and you are defending them, you are working for the greater good. With AMs working for the community, not against it, and with your intentions set toward good, you'll have fewer hard days at work.

Part II

The Laws and Skills

Chapter 4
The Laws

Let all your efforts be directed to something, let [your mind] keep that end in view.

—Seneca

There are four laws of the attacker mindset. They are all heavily interlaced and interdependent. In this chapter, we will look at them and explore how to use them effectively.

Law 1: Start with the End in Mind

Assuming you already have a contract and a contact in place, there's really only one correct place to start an attack—at the end. To start with the end in mind is the first law of AMs. But doing so is material to how the rest of the skills are used, too. You cannot blindly point to information about anyone on anything and then build and execute an attack. You need to know a couple of points to start: who you are attacking and to what end. The "who" is generally solved for you— the client typically approaches you or you will sell your services to them. Either the "what end" is defined by the client—who will know what they wish to protect but want to know how easily it can be accessed or destroyed—or the client will not define their assets as such, asking you to simply penetrate their defenses as deeply as you can.

Given that, there's an almost infinite list of objectives to be achieved for an impossibly large list of businesses the world over, so I won't try to list them all. But most often for a security professional, the items most likely on the list of objectives will be (a) gaining information or (b) gaining access to an asset. So, with those goals in mind, we have our immediate ends in sight.

This phase of the attack is the only one in which your AMs has absolutely no barriers or boundaries. At this point, you aren't particularly concerned with ethics—you're only looking for information or vulnerabilities to use against your target. The attack will later be adjusted for ethics and the after processes will be a direct result of them, but at least for now, your AMs can create, craft, and plan unincumbered, stopping only to consider scope.

End to Start Questions

Just as in chess, where the central objective is to checkmate the opponent's king by placing it under an inescapable threat of capture, your central objective is to capture your target's information or asset one move at a time. To do this, there is a short list of important things to be considered. Starting at the last to be considered physically, but the first to be considered in planning, we have the following:

- How to leave with the information or asset intact?
- How to secure the information or asset (to ensure you maintain custody of it)?
- Security surrounding information or asset?
- Location(s) of information or asset?
- Weak point in security and means needed to circumvent it?
- Larger area around information or asset and means to traverse area around it (the building it's housed in or the network security active to safeguard it)?

- Pretext for approach and entry?
- Economy of force (applying personnel in the most effective way possible)?

I've had a job where my end goal was to move money from the bank to "my" account. My top question, "How to leave with the information or asset intact?" is pretty easy to answer on this one—it will be intact when it hits my account. But the second question on my list, "How to secure the information or asset?" becomes a bit of a headache, because to ensure safety of this transaction, I'd ideally like to be there to see it happen, to see it *being sent.* Having not actually robbed a bank before, I can't say for certain, but I feel sure it's not like in the movies where an 8-bit green bar fights to make its way across the screen, with the evildoer sweating and staring at it until it flashes "100%." But whatever it looks like, I'd want to see it and know the attack was complete and a success. That was not possible on this job because I performed the attack via a series of vishing calls.

Putting the phone down after being assured too many dollars to disclose were indeed in the ether, on the way to my account, made that particular night a long one. Thankfully, although not for the security of the bank, the ungodly sum did show up in the account it was supposed to. Thanks to its appearance, I got to write a very detailed report. I also got to keep the original account's balance of zero dollars and zero cents afterward.

The two fundamentals to look at when forming an attack are your objectives and what your cover story will be. Working backward from the question at the top of that list, though, is a strong linear sequence that helps answer both. It will help you decide the equipment you require, as well as the number of people you need to execute the job. It also helps optimize other things, such as the time of day you should attack and the number of people needed to achieve the objective (economy of force) and how will they be used? Some might be at the physical location, whereas others are not physically there but instead *in* the network.

I had considered all of these things as I entered a very prestigious building in New York to, essentially, begin robbing it.

Robbing a Bank

Robbing a bank is no easy feat, even if you are a pro. Where we last left off on this story in chapter one, I'd met with my team; I'd drunk copious amounts of hot chocolate because, apparently, I hated myself around that time and was trying to abstain from coffee. The team and I had gone over the plan until it felt like the words were meaningless and melding together, looked over the floor plans that we'd come into possession of through some very nifty OSINT, and looked over some of the interior pictures people had put on Facebook when they'd "checked in" for meetings, and so on. We were keeping to our plan of sending me in first, with all of us returning that same night. We were ready.

After doing some final checks on our communication methods (primary and backup), I was soon walking from our temporary office in the city to the target's main building. I knew the security surrounding the information and asset I was aiming to get to was mainly in the form of humans, which can often be a pesky hurdle. There was also going to be security in the form of technology. I knew from pictures I'd found online that there were motorized turnstiles, also pesky because they generally beep obnoxiously when you jump over them. But, as I told myself then and believe now, humans are often distrustful of technology, which is one way to neutralize both.

As I made my way toward the revolving doors, the mental games of chess I'd had been running in my mind up until that point ceased. I was only going over the details of my pretext now: Lawyer. Merger. Documents. Appointment. Late to meeting I knew had already started. Rinse and repeat.

I walked inside looking to the reception desk, stretched out somewhat menacingly over the sterile-seeming foyer. I almost stopped dead in my tracks. It took every bit of self-discipline not to look around in search of what I had always imagined I'd find upon entering the prestigious lobby of a well-known, reputable bank. There was no guard. There was ostensibly no security personnel present.

My initial feeling was one of relief—this meant that there was no one to stop me. Mere milliseconds later my brain was throwing me a curveball in the form of paranoia. If security wasn't at the desk, were they watching me from the sky? Stopping myself from a 360° spin to check *for* any security in my general vicinity, I immediately curved to the right as if it had been my intention all the time and headed for the turnstiles. I reached into my pocket as if this was not the first time in my life I was pulling this card from it and scanned it on the machine's reader. As if I expected it to open, I pushed my briefcase into the glass doors of the turnstile that, for the people who actually had access, would've normally *whooshed* to the sides by now.

Nothing happened. Obviously.

I tried the card again, pretending I expected the typical results. Still, though, no one appeared.

"Hello?" I shouted over the barrier, hoping someone would hear me and turn up. Moments later a security guard appeared from the side of the turnstile I wanted to be on. As he approached, I remember wishing that I'd hit the building at a busier time because congestion would've been imposed a greater sense of urgency on him to fix the problem—it would've said for me, "Let me in so that all of these other fine folks not aiming to rob you can get to work." But that isn't how jobs work. You have to take what you are given and be agile enough to respond to the circumstances as they unfold.

"Having issues?" he asked calmly.

"I am. This turnstile won't let me through, and I'm late," I said gently, almost like I was defeated, rather than in a rush. My play on humans' distrust of technology was in full swing.

"I am sure we can fix that," he said, maintaining eye contact. "Try this one!" he said, gesturing to the turnstile one over.

Aw crap, I thought to myself, *Why didn't I think of that!* I had obviously pictured him just letting me through the side gate; I had not envisioned him making me try all the turnstiles so we could both be certain my keycard was a dud. *Well,* I thought as I walked to the next turnstile, *just stick to law 3: adhere to the pretext.*

Bringing It All together

You'll remember we started this chapter with eight questions:

- How to leave with the information or asset intact?
- How to secure the information or asset (to ensure you maintain custody of it)?
- Security surrounding information or asset?
- Location(s) of information or asset?
- Weak point in security and means needed to circumvent it?
- Larger area around information or asset and means to traverse area around it (the building it's housed in or the network security active to safeguard it)?
- Pretext for approach and entry?
- Economy of force?

Up until the point I just described, standing in a Manhattan bank's lobby, I knew all of the answers to these questions. Certainly, I'd known some in more detail than others. For example, I knew the answer to the first question (leaving with the information or asset intact). The answer was to walk out with my phone on me because it would be housing photos of this attack, as the client had requested, and I knew I could further secure the asset by sending those photos to my company's secure portal periodically as I moved around the building. This also took care of the next question you should ask and answer when committing to a job: securing the information or asset (to ensure you maintain custody of it).

As for "Location(s) of information or asset?" I was aware that the CFO's office was on the same floor as three of the bank's largest meeting rooms. This knowledge helped lead me to impersonate a lawyer, given I also had found information pertaining to an imminent merger that had hit some speed bumps.

The security surrounding the CFO's office was minimal after the ground security.

I knew the weak point in the security was the information I was able to find out online—no one should be able to duplicate a guest badge that they've found online to get past a business's defenses.

Pretext for approach and entry was informed by all the previous answers on the list combined with OSINT that had led to the
discovery that the business was in the middle of a large merger and
acquisition (M&A). I knew that, as long as I wasn't discovered right
away, one pretext would be sufficient to get the job done. It was
designed to get me from the front door to the target's office and
complete that portion of the mission.

Economy of force was the easiest question to answer in this case
because it was decided by scope. I was slated to go in during the day,
but we were also engaged to do night break-ins too. We were instructed
to try all entrances and exits on our night trip and achieving that,
especially in a skyscraper in New York City, would take a team.

The Start of the End

In case you weren't convinced, there is evidence that points toward
the end as a starting point being the right place. In philosophy it is
often accepted that all things are created twice—first in the mind,
and then in the real world. Physical creations follow mental ones,
from the computer I'm typing on to the book you are reading. This
book started off in my head, and now it exists outside of it. The same
thing is true of my computer and the desk it sits on, along with
almost everything else in the room. Attacks should be no different;
beginning with the end in mind is to visualize your specific project
the way that you want it to end up *before* you begin pursuing it. This
results in greater precision than pinballing your way there. Again,
this is not a form of "manifestation"—it's a form of agile planning.
The main reasons this "begin with the end in mind" philosophy is so
important come down to clarity, efficiency, and your objective, each
of which we will briefly look at in the following subsections.

Clarity

Remarkable clarity comes from knowing exactly where you want to end
up. As you've witnessed multiple times throughout this book already,
there's nothing more clarifying than an objective. When you have it,
you are able to plan accordingly with only that in your crosshairs.

There's another, often underrated benefit of this strategy: when you begin with the end in mind, you'll also gain clarity as to what *not* to pursue. If your goal is to get onto a network without detection and maintain persistence, you would avoid using any noisy tools. If you were aiming to get into a facility that did not allow cameras or phones but where your objective was to photograph the inside and walk through the front door (it has happened), you would not walk in with your devices on you. In this case, I attempted to hide devices around the perimeter and upon getting in, I waited until I could tailgate out a back door, collect the device, and come back in. I did eventually get arrested on this job, because I was viewed on camera with my phone in my hand taking photos. Was it my best moment? No. Am I still proud of trying? Also no. I had to go to a chiropractor for about three months after that arrest. They do not pin you to the ground softly. The better idea here would've been a piece of jewelry with a small camera inside. In hindsight, that's definitely a better idea.

Starting with the end in mind provides a straight shot to clarity holistically and that's valuable.

Efficiency

When you begin with the end in mind you gain clarity, which will naturally help you become more efficient. You'll be able to plan and strategize for the best route to your goals. Let's say your job is to break into a bank and get to the vaults. That's your goal. Great, you can now plan the most efficient way to achieve it. Instead of chasing erroneous objectives, you'll focus on just the steps you need to take to get to the vaults. I would, in a case like this, set myself up for success weeks in advance—months if the scope and project timeline allowed for it by vishing the facility first.

Efficiency comes from always pushing in the direction of the objective. This will always generate efficient results.

The Objective

Finally, when you begin with the end in mind, you gain purpose. Some clients come with a loose set of goals. Most typically, you will hear the words, "Just whatever you can get." These are generally preceded or immediately followed by a beautiful sentence that goes something like, "But there's no way you will get in anyway." I tend to listen to neither.

If I am told to get "whatever" I can, I will research the most damaging thing I can get. This is not to humiliate the client; it is to illustrate how dangerous their mindset is. They should be able to identify what is most precious to them.

If they tell me I won't get in, I always feel a sense of relief for my attacker life—their security is likely lacking because of exactly this mentality and "security ego," as I like to call it. Security ego is the best thing to happen to an attacker, ethical or not. It's also the worst thing to happen to both a business and me afterward as those report and awareness programs tend to be *very* long.

The key here, though, is focusing on what you really want to achieve in any given engagement and working toward that only. You don't have to get caught up in every security flaw and attack it, but you should note it for your client. As has been previously discussed, your job is not to give a play-by-play of *your* attack. It's to tell your client what happened, while also painting a picture of their whole security landscape as you saw it.

How to Begin with the End in Mind

So far, we've covered the "what" and "why" in regard to beginning with the end in mind. Now, let's tackle the "how." There are five steps.

When you begin with the end in mind, you set yourself up for success. There's no better way to identify what you actually need, why it's important to get it, and how to get it. To implement this philosophy into your AMs, you can follow these five steps and build on each for your own projects:

1. **Narrow objective:** What is it you need to achieve for this engagement and client? The attack objective should be the one you place here, not the overarching one, which is to strengthen security as a security partner.

2. **How long to get there:** How should you budget your time? Most engagements have solid start and end dates. This is both good and bad for the client. It's good because they will know that, most likely, any attacks they see during the window of time they have authorized are being executed by you; it is bad because a true, malicious attacker will not perform all of their operations under a neat timeframe. Some take months or years to execute an end-to-end attack. However, the long and short of it is that a business is unlikely to pay you to be its everlasting threat, so you will be given a timeframe and you should budget your time accordingly. You may not need three weeks of OSINT. You might perform perfunctory OSINT only to get yourself familiar with the environment and to gain you a pretext that does what all good pretexts should: conceals you as a threat and makes you seem as though you should be there at that time.

3. **Design:** Designing an attack is a complicated task in some ways. I aim to keep mine to their simplest form, but that can still become intricate. Planning to attack a bank or prison isn't an easy task, but it should be trimmed consistently to be the simplest it can be—take the simplest route, adding complexity only where necessary.

4. **Fully commit:** Fully committing takes two things: one is comfort with risk—you cannot plan for every eventuality or every reaction or every unknown thing; you can plan, craft, and design so that the odds are in your favor, though. The second is that you must commit to your pretext and the utilization of it. If you do not feel your pretext properly asserts you as a person that, in all the ways you can conceive, should be there or that conceals you as a threat, then you might consider adjusting or forming a new pretext. Alternatively, you might need to switch pretexts as the attack unfolds, but doing so should be inconspicuous.

5. **Implement:** This is *go* time. You should have been able to form an objective and budget your time effectively for each step in achieving it. Now it's time to execute.

Law 2: Gather, Weaponize, and Leverage Information

The true art of the attack doesn't come from being able to act like an attacker—it comes from being able to think like one. For instance, when a company puts out seemingly innocuous information, it's the attacker's mindset—their thoughts, outlook, and approach—that molds it into exploitable intelligence to be used against them. The ordinary reader or listener will simply process the information as intended by the source, and an ordinary person will take the information and search for more of the same if curious; a good attacker will use it as a starting point, exploring a surplus of information through the lens of their objective, disregarding all that cannot be used in a future attack and building on all that can. An attacker only gathers information to build, forward, and execute an attack. Information is the star of the show.

Picking this apart, there is one other thing that is crucial to successfully adopting and maintaining this mindset: the *tieback*. Similar to the *callback* in comedy, the tieback is the act of binding information to the needs of the objective. If the information you are sifting through is not beneficial for pretexting or using information against a target; it should be disregarded. There's not a set list of things that *do* and *don't* matter—the objective dictates these kinds of things. Intuitively parsing information as it comes to you is a deft skill that cannot be overlooked in the name of both efficiency and AMs sharpness.

Let's look at a simple example to start. If I am gathering information on a single target, with the objective to compile a seemingly legitimate phish, nearly any information becomes valuable and potentially weaponizable. Knowing the make and model of their car is valuable if I want to make them think they have a ticket and send them a link to view all the related information, but I'd have to consider whether a personal message like that would go to their work email account. The name of their child's school is valuable if I want to register for a one-on-one session to discuss the progress their child is making. None of this is valuable if I need to phish them using a professional pretext, as dictated by scope. Their home address is valuable if I want to phish them from HR, citing a mistake in their details. Sometimes you may need to know little else about a person other than the country they live in. For instance, if I know a target lives in the UK, an SMSish from Royal Mail is a solid bet for a click. In the United States, the US Postal Service is a likely candidate to get a click. For a phish, I mainly just need their email address to be factual. I can use almost any other information I come across to build into a phish, taking personal and professional information and tying it back to the objective.

Simply knowing where someone works is a great start to making a tieback—you can check online forums to search for records about the hardware or software the company uses and call when IT is citing issues with it.

For physical jobs, you will need to know the location, and you might want to know the shifts of guards to make getting in and out that much easier—that tieback of that information to the objective is easy. You might also want to look at the entries, exits, underground access points, aerial views, and surveillance spots—you should be able to tie all that back to the objective and work out how to use all that information. The rest will be specific to the location, including terrain, surroundings, staff numbers, likelihood of visitors, and likelihood of unfamiliar people going unnoticed or unchallenged. Most information you come across that exists in part outside of the organization, such as vendor or contractor information, is typically easier to weaponize and leverage.

I once broke into a large warehouse with the help of a very gifted pentester and social engineer who has asked never to be named. Our job was to get inside and access any computer terminal, taking photos as evidence. For this, we needed to know employee shift times and attempted to gain information on the types of locks they used and the type of computers through recon.

No matter the type of job, the same principle applies: you need to gather information, weaponize it, and leverage it.

The weaponization of information in the moment is also a vital skill that cannot be overvalued with regard to an ethical attacker's performance. There's a certain amount of opportunistic ability and situational agility that an EA must be able to apply when executing an attack. It is what I refer to as an attacker's *opportunistic aptitude*. It's the ability of the EA to see and act on opportunity in the moment, never letting their target(s) know it's haphazard. A level of opportunistic aptitude can be taught, but building it up into a deft skill will fall to the EA themselves. This ability to pivot while maintaining character *and* to focus on the objective falls under the umbrella of mental agility, specifically, "persuasive performance." Agile, persuasive performance provided by an EA is the effective exploitation of human weakness through covert adversarial behavior. Bit of a mouthful, but broken down, it means that the attacker mindset, when executed properly, is versatile and adaptable and doesn't falter from the objective.

The critical finding here is that a plethora of information may exist for any one client you get. Your job is to be able to parse that information by applying it to the objective, both prior to the attack and when executing it. To parse information effectively and efficiently, I tend to think of it as a puzzle of sorts: if I can't get the information to fit to the central piece (the objective), I disregard it and move on.

In summation, the weaponization of information that is commonplace to everyone else is the true mark of a security expert with a strong, effective AMs—in both the act of attacking and the planning of it. The information you gather will go into three buckets: (a) useful for recon and building familiarity, (b) useful for pretext, and (c) not useful at all. But I am now getting ahead of myself. We will cover more about information processing in a later chapter, in Chapter 6, "Information Processing: Observation and Thinking Techniques."

Law 3: Never Break Pretext

Now we move to pretexts. A persuasive performance is crucial in defeating an unwitting target. To be effective under your pretext, two things must be true. The first is that you must be able to play the part of your pretext accordingly—for instance, it would likely be detrimental to most operations for me to show up as a repair technician. I don't know enough about repairs of any kind to pull that off, nor do I easily fit the part of a repair technician. I could go as an inspector from a repair company, though—there to take notes and inspect some items.

With a pretext, you must be able to see clearly what other people think of you and lean into it when beneficial. This self-awareness will allow you to know your shortcomings, and it will allow you to play the parts that suit you. Attacker behavior is not politically correct, and neither are the biases you must play into.

The second thing is that pretexts must be built off of information. You cannot pull a pretext out of thin air and hope for the best. Just knowing that most companies have vendors doesn't give you the vendor pretext card. It certainly doesn't permit it without detailed searches of your target company's specific vendors.

Sure, there are times you will have to go in blind because the information doesn't exist. These are rare and extreme cases. However, inferences can still be made, and you will likely need to employ hardier recon tactics—likely military-level recon. Military-level recon takes into consideration the effects of forces like weather on the target terrain, and determines at what point the enemy can observe them. It also takes into account the target's known recon capabilities, typically things like infrared, thermal, light enhancement, and enlarging capabilities.

Military-level recon also takes into consideration route investigation: an attempt to obtain detailed information of a specified route and all terrain from which the target could influence movement along the route. Most often this is beyond the range of a job, with only the very immediate surroundings of the target environment being investigated. Some jobs, perhaps for government engagements, will require this level of recon.

Military "reconnaissance-in-force" is a deliberate combat operation designed to discover or test the enemy's strength, dispositions, and reactions or to obtain other information.

Whether your job dictates that you direct effort to military-level recon or red-team/social-engineer–level recon, the common thread still remains: information is key. A scrap is not ideal, but it will do. And if you use laws 1 and 2 against that scrap of information, you will end up with more than you started out with.

A pretext is one of the most powerful and unique laws of the four. It exists to serve the others, but the others cannot function without it. Delving back into the world of spies, a good spy could know their desired goal, gather and weaponize information, and attempt to apply that information for the good of the objective. They would immediately be in Guantanamo if they wandered into their target's environment and laid the truth out. Pretexting is important.

Take Adolf Tolkachev. He was a chief engineer at the Soviet Radar Design Bureau, which focused on the development and prototyping of advanced aero-navigational systems. Tolkachev had the highest-level access to Soviet state secrets. He approached a CIA agent in 1977 at a gas station in Moscow and slipped him a note stating that he wanted to become an American spy. The CIA was naturally suspicious of a KGB trap, so they said no to Tolkachev—on multiple occasions. Finally, his attempts met with success and the CIA gave him the codename "Sphere."

Tolkachev was stable and believable in his role—he fit it perfectly. He remained an engineer, and so the KGB never suspected him of being a spy. Tolkachev used his own devices and procedures to get information to the CIA since he realized many of the procedures provided were simply ineffectual. For example, he modified a civilian camera and used it instead of the camera provided to him for his endeavors. He knew it would not fit his pretext and would actually be a point of potential failure. Through his pretexts, Tolkachev revealed top secret research documents on weapons to be created years into the future, including details such as air-to-air missiles, surface-to-air missiles, and fighter aircraft information. As a source for the CIA, he reported detailed data on new Soviet weapon systems that would not have been available for years, if ever. Tolkachev provided complete documentation before the systems were even fully operational.

Tolkachev never broke character and would have likely never been caught. He used all the laws together and had skills beyond reckoning. He never gave anyone pause for thought. Despite being very careful, he was captured by KGB in 1985 after CIA officer Edward Lee Howard, who defected from the United States to the Soviet Union, outed him.

As ethical attackers, we cannot quite operate like spies. There must be demarcations set that you cannot use your sexuality, looks, or compelling or coercive promises and lies to gain entry—actual network pentesting being the exception to the rule. In all other cases, a pretext whereby you talk with another human must be ethically aboveboard; otherwise, you become unable to teach someone what they should've done in a situation where they failed. As an example, I would likely let someone into a building if they threatened to kill my family. There is no teachable moment there, and we must operate well above that to prove vulnerabilities in an organization's security. It's also ethically wrong and absurd to flirt your way into a building. By nonparticipation in these sorts of actions, you are not ignoring they might work and leaving the client open to that risk. Your job is to get past security defenses and then implement or suggest processes that keep all others out that may try—however they may try. Your pretext doesn't have to be nasty. You prove a better, stronger, more valid point by using more vanilla pretexts, showing that if something as weak as a "new employee" without their card can get through their defenses, anyone can.

Law 4: Every Move Made Benefits the Objective

This is a very straightforward law. You do not deviate from your given course. You cannot switch directions, physically or figuratively for your own personal gain, for your own personal curiosity, or for any other reason. Like a spy, you can apply the first two laws to your mission, but if 3 and 4 are not also applied to the mission, you face an internal conflict and mission failure.

Everything you do has to be for the good of the mission. It might be for the short-term good, like switching pretexts or exiting a building or even a network before it is optimal. This could be so that you appear to be operating like your supposed peers—leaving at the end of the day if you cannot hide in plain sight or *actually* hide. You might need to switch pretexts depending on where you are in the mission; a network pentester has to disguise their traffic when exfiltrating data, which is likely done differently compared to how they first gained access to the network. In the same way, a physical pentester has to hide their real self the deeper they get into an environment and the longer they are there. They might gain access as a cleaner at night but transform into a nightshift worker when entering the server room. Like Tolkachev, you might modify or even forgo equipment altogether if it will prove to be a distraction from your pretext and so to the good of the objective.

No matter if the gain is for long or short term, you must not do anything just for the sake of doing it. You must at least believe that each step you take will move you in the right direction—the direction of achieving the objective.

Summary

- Working from the end of an attack backward as a way of planning, designing, and executing an attack is paramount to success and one of the best cognitive skills an attacker can have.
- If you are already inclined to act and think this way, it might appear as though there's no other way to perform an attack. However, it is not uncommon for people to only think linearly, asking how to get into something rather than first thinking about where they are going when they enter.
- There are two fundamentals to look at when forming an attack: your objective and what your cover story will be. Let all your efforts be directed to that objective, and let your mind keep that end in view at all times.

There are four rules of the mindset. They must all work together in order to obtain success.

Key Message

An attack should be kept to its simplest form. Starting from the end of the attack and backing into it is the most efficient, clarifying process and strategy you can use.

Chapter 5

Curiosity, Persistence, and Agility

Read not to contradict and confute; nor to believe and take for granted; nor to find talk and discourse; but to weigh and consider.

—Francis Bacon

What's the one thing persistence needs to exist?

It's a goal.

Persistence needs a pursuit. It could be argued that it also needs curiosity as its momentum, although I can concede there are exceptions to that rule—not all persistence is fueled by curiosity. Some forms of persistence rely on dogged beliefs and unwavering prejudice or narrow-mindedness. For instance, malicious attackers do not use curiosity as a tool. Instead, they team their persistence up with malevolent intent and pedal their beliefs that way. These two things—curiosity and persistence—don't always go hand in hand, but the combination is vital for the mindset we are seeking.

Curiosity itself is a driving force of progress within an attack scenario, but it will not pay off without persistence. There's also another point that can't go unmentioned here: you will have nothing to persist in if you cannot take in information and leverage even the most ordinary information properly. If you jump on the wrong pieces of information and try to use them persistently to your advantage, the operation will misfire early on. This is where another cognitive skill intersects: mental agility. There are two times it is pertinent. One is when you've leveraged good information against a target or environment but still end up with a less-than-adequate result and need to pivot quickly. The other is when you've leveraged the wrong information and need to pivot quickly. I will lay out an example of each, which should help you conceptualize.

There are times when you will have gathered solid data. You will know everything about your target in order to get you in the door and on the way to achieving your objective, but something out of your control will thwart you, and you will have to pivot. Imagine lining up the perfect vishing call for a target. You have her name, number, department and position, job details and responsibilities, the times she works, and her clearance level. All you have to do is call her office and convince her to give you portal access. You finally dial the number, spoofing your number to appear as if internal to the very organization you're trying to penetrate. The ringing stops and someone picks up. But it's not your target. For one thing, the voice sounds as if it's the wrong gender. Then they introduce themselves and sure enough, the person you are talking to is not the person you were hoping for. However, they are within scope.

If it were me, imagining a proxy for my target answered, I would springboard into my new attack on the same call. I would explain the predicament through the veil of my pretext and push on, wrapping my new target into the same web and aiming for the same outcome. "Oh, I wonder if you can help—I still need my portal access reset. When I talked to her a few days ago, she said it takes a while, but I need in today!"

There's a chance this approach will work, and the odds will be far more in my favor if I am agile enough to twist the information to suit the new set of circumstances I've found myself in this hypothetical situation.

Of course, there are also times where you inadvertently leverage the wrong information. Imagine entering a target's workplace with the information they are enjoying time off. Let's say you were posing as maintenance, there to fix something in the target's office that they'd scheduled you for. Imagine your surprise if it turned out they were in their office at that very moment, and the receptionist was calling them to verify you were indeed supposed to be there.

GULP.

Well, you would have to be agile enough to produce an issue of your own. You might enlist the help of a teammate by calling them in front of the receptionist and/or target to say you'd ran into an issue. You'd have to explain it like someone confused about why you'd been sent out at the wrong time. You might even go as far as to get "new information" from your office, perhaps stating you had been scheduled by someone else at the company and had confused the situation. I'd apologize and I'd likely act quietly mortified.

I'd push this as far as I could and likely have a teammate spoof a call from a legitimate source within the company that fits the role of maintenance scheduler. Without an ounce of fear or unease, I'd ask if they still wanted me to perform the work or if they wanted to book me at a later time. If they opted for a later time, I would make sure it was within the timeframe the scope allowed and I'd go back again, trying to game the system.

Mental agility is possible with real-time interactions, like the ones laid out here. However, you cannot save an operation if you use bad information where communication is asynchronous, such as a phish. If you send a spear phish as the target's spouse's divorce lawyer only to find out they were divorced 30 years ago, you will likely not come back from that. You will have to start from scratch, keeping in mind that the target is probably a little more on edge given your previous play.

Mental agility is as much about making fresh connections between different things as it is teasing out problems and thinking on your feet to solve them in the most efficient way possible. It's taking in information and applying it to your current circumstances. There is one more thing that can't go unnoted about mental agility—it's bred by calmness. If you're too anxious, there's a good chance you will miss the opportunity to pivot well. If you are too uptight, there's a good chance you'll want to do what's been done before. AMs is less about traditional thinking and more about forward thinking.

As an ethical attacker, you will also require two more things for perfect potency: common sense and morals, both of which we will briefly cover in this chapter, too. But before we discuss that, let's look at how your curiosity can pay off in the first place.

Spoiler alert: It's through OSINT.

Curiosity

Curiosity is a basic element of our cognition, yet its biological function, mechanisms, and neural underpinning remain poorly understood. It is nonetheless a motivator for learning, influential in decision-making, and crucial for a functioning and prevailing attacker mindset. Moreover, for the ethical or malicious attacker, curiosity serves as a driving force in the pursuit of information and knowledge. Cultivating it is fundamental, and the best way of baiting it is to ask questions.

Curiosity, however, can be viewed on a spectrum. You may have more or less than someone else, but the amount you have doesn't preclude or facilitate your ability as an ethical attacker (EA) for obvious reasons. The most evident is that curiosity doesn't guarantee you'll find your way to useful or valuable information or that you'll know when to stop searching for information.

Lastly, there will always be someone less curious than you, and there will also always be someone more curious than you. To help foster your own curiosity, let's perform two exercises. The first will be to foster an agile curiosity, and the second will be to build an understanding of it through the AMs lens.

The Exercise: Part 1

To cultivate curiosity, you will also have to start building on your persistence and agility. To eventually use all of them together, you must look to information. Find a news article on any company of your choosing. Identify the key bits of information and start down the mental agility course I am about to lay out. The first step is to ask yourself how you could use this information to form an objective and possibly even the beginnings of a pretext. The rub is that you can use only one article, so pick wisely.

I will start with Apple because they are my favorite company on Earth, and I want them to be secure. I would be distraught if they were attacked and they didn't have time to turn back their keyboard from butterfly to scissor-switch before the next MacBook Air comes out.

For this, exercise, I typed **Apple** into Google and selected the News tab. I was offered many articles to choose from. I went to an NBC article by David Ingram, with the title "Facebook and Apple are in a fight. Your browsing history is in the middle." Here's an excerpt from the article:

> Apple and Facebook are going to need each other in the long run, because billions of people want their social media apps to work well on their phones and tablets. But first, the two California tech giants need to settle a brawl that's playing out in newspaper ads, industry meetings and potentially federal court.
>
> In the next few weeks, Apple is planning to roll out a new feature on its devices that will alert people when an app such as Facebook is trying to "track your activity across other companies' apps and websites." People will have options such as "Ask App not to Track" or "Allow."
>
> "Users should know when their data is being collected and shared across other apps and websites—and they should have the choice to allow that or not," Apple said in a statement. "App

Tracking Transparency in iOS 14 does not require Facebook to change its approach to tracking users and creating targeted advertising, it simply requires they give users a choice."

There are two points I care about here:

1. That the article makes the leap that the two might end up in court over this
2. That Apple is stating nothing has to change in the creation of targeted advertising, except for people to opt in or out of it

The article then goes on to say:

"Apple's move isn't about privacy, it's about profit," Facebook said in a statement. It argues that Apple stands to gain if more of the internet becomes subscription-based, because Apple collects commissions from its app store.

Apple has said the new tracking notifications will start to appear in early 2021. Privacy groups such as the Electronic Frontier Foundation support them.

If I *had* to build a pretext out of this article, I would likely use the Electronic Frontier Foundation (EFF), founded by none other than Steve Wozniak, John Perry Barlow, Mitchell Kapor, and John Gilmore. I would build the attack around growing concern that Apple might be hedging its bets on a subscription-based Internet and information model, citing that the EFF would be willing to continue support as long as Apple could categorically state that it did not intend to profit from pseudo-privacy. An attack like this would best be served via vish (voice phishing call) and pish (email meant to gain access or at the very least certain details, such as that the account is active).

It could be something as simple as sending a request for comment on an article the EFF is releasing on its stance with regard to Facebook and privacy. There is no correct sequence, I could send the phish and chase a reply the next day by vish, or I could call first, portending the phish.

I might also attempt something more complex and wily such as a notice about information that has been leaked by to the EFF concerning a vulnerability in Apple's AppTrackingTransparency framework, which is a consent interface that notifies an Apple iOS user when an app requests access to your microphone, camera, or location. A call to warn them followed by the link in an email, potentially while I am still on the call, might suffice. However, in cases such as this, curiosity might kill the cat, and I might only have to send one phish and wait for the click.

The Exercise: Part 2

Stay with the same target as before or pick a new one and write down 10 or more questions you'd like to know the answers to. The true skill of an EA at this stage is to form more questions based on the first round of answers. An experienced attacker will continue this cycle until they feel they have complete knowledge on which to mount their attack. Most of the time, it's not enough to know about the company or individual you're attacking—you must have in-depth knowledge to complement both your pretext and the facilitation of objective achievement.

There are 11 rudimentary questions I'd start with for any target I had no existing knowledge of. For this exercise, I will use Nespresso, because (a) I know little about them other than their main product is coffee, and (b) I would also hate for them to be attacked and not have enough time to put a caffeinated mocha capsule into production. So I'll give them a head start by outlining how an attack might be built up against them. Here are the questions I'd start off with when considering an in-person social engineering attack:

1. What do they do?
2. Where are they headquartered?
3. How many offices do they have in the country?
4. Have they been in the news recently?
5. Who is their leadership?
6. Who are their vendors?
7. What could be considered their biggest competitive advantage?

8. Are they regulated by any government agency or authority?
9. How many employees do they have?
10. How large is their social media footprint, and who is associated?
11. According to the news, have they been successfully attacked before?

The answers to these would, for me, spawn the following questions:

1. Are there internal images online of their real estate?
2. Are there any images showing their employee ID badges?
3. Are there internal documents online?
4. For what do they use their vendors?
5. How much contact information can I get for people highest up—emails, phone numbers, assistant information?

Those questions will typically be followed by more questions, and they would start to narrow in on the pretext, which I would have started to identify with the answer to question 6 for this particular search. This process is cyclical in nature and will yield new questions with new answers that, in massive plot twist, will end up with more questions. . . The one other thing that I'd like to note here is that the further you get into this process, the more you will have to rely on Google dorks and efficient disregarding of information not critical for your needs.

If you are doing a night break-in, you will have to build a different pretext and look at different questions. For instance, if I were to be breaking into Nespresso headquarters at night, I would likely not show up as a vendor. My first 11 questions would differ slightly, too, with more concern placed on their security, security vendors, building layout, and shift patterns. Without listing them here, I'd likely turn up as a vendor spraying for pests overnight.

Also, the questions you first ask when building an attack rely heavily on the type of attack you expect to perform or are contracted to perform. If the client wants you to vish them, your questions will be greatly directed by the flags, which are pieces of information or assets, the client wants you to obtain as well as target numbers and other contact information. If your attack includes all vectors—vishing, phishing, and in-person—you will start to build a more intricate attack where all the vectors functionally overlap, allowing progress with every email, call, and step taken.

One other significant consideration will help you know when to stop an intensive search for information: it's when you have a solid pretext—when all the questions related to your pretext are answered—and when you have enough insight into the business's environment that it feels almost familiar to you. With this in mind, always remember that a pretext is to conceal your identity as a threat based on your objective.

A pretext is a narrative in which you are the details. Additionally, your pretext may have the air of a threat to it without it being a conscious decision, which is something people struggle with time to time—a lawyer could be perceived as a threat, for example. A lawyer showing up in a rush for an appointment apparently no one knows about won't always portend brilliant and joyful things to come for the people within an organization. But that's not the job; the job of a pretext isn't to leave people feeling any particular way. Its job is only to protect *you* as a threat. So sometimes you will have to let your pretext lean on society's biases and do the heavy lifting for you. Your presence doesn't have to induce feelings of happiness from everyone you meet within the organization. It simply has to divert attention away from your true intentions as an attacker.

My last point on pretexts is only to stress that you must never actively try to scare or bully someone while in character. You will not leave any room for a teachable moment if you opt for that sort of performance. You can show up as a firefighter without telling everyone you meet they are about to burn to death.

Finally, I would be remiss if I didn't state that the questions I've listed aren't magic. They may not be the right questions for your target, but I have more often than not found them to be a good start.

Ultimately, the questions they build up to answer are "What is your objective?" and "Where is this target weakest?" Also, the first stage of this cycle takes everyone a notably different amount of time to get through. I can generally achieve this over 4 to 5 hours of rigorous searching. Some people will be much faster and some, possibly, a little slower.

Persistence

Our curiosity will not pay off without persistence. We aren't talking about heroic persistence, laughing in the face of danger and defying all odds. We are leaning toward a persistence recognizable as not giving up on finding and using information against your target. Curiosity and persistence in the pursuit of knowledge mean that you are forever aiming for the Goldilocks effect—consuming information that's not too long, detailed, and complex, yet not too short, simple, and watered down. This takes some time to get perfect, and I still slip now and then. (Remember in Chapter 3, "The Attacker Mindset Framework," I described how I went in as a satellite specialist there to renew a license and literally started to inspect the equipment on the roof. There was also a time I walked into a building pretending to be a Swedish convoy only to realize that I was in the presence of people who actually spoke Swedish (I do not). So, I was quickly escorted out.) Striking the balance of using the information you have suitably is not easy. There are times, however, where persistence is critical to a mission's progress. I found this out via a restroom cubicle in New York.

Last we left off on this story, I was pinballing in and out of turnstiles, pretending to be baffled each time my fake card didn't work in front of a security guard who was not at all moved by my pleas of running late for a very important meeting. Each time I tried a new reader and it failed to read my card and grant me access, mainly because my card was a complete dud, I looked at the security card with a bemused look on my face.

"He is going to hit the roof!" I said trying my card on the last turnstile reader. "I am now so late, I'm pretty much just early for next week's meeting," I added in jovial defeat. "What should I do?" I asked as he looked me up and down. I love asking people questions like this, because it speaks right to their responsibilities, and it places an onus on them that is hard to fight. It also leaves them uneasy with the new pressure of having to decide something quite quickly with little information. Not this person, though.

"What exactly are you here for?" the guard said, staring back at me with a certain indifference to his tone.

"I am delivering the paperwork for the . . ." I lowered my voice, and leaned closer to him (with the glass gates separating us). ". . . the *thing* that's not going too well," I finished, still looking at him directly. He cocked his head slightly to the side, as if he wasn't sure what I was telling him. "The merger," I said briskly, still acting like I was sharing a secret with him.

"Oh, *that*," he said quietly as if he, too, wanted to keep it a secret. Naturally, this made no sense seeing as it was across multiple media outlets. There was absolutely no poverty of information regarding this merger, but I was about to give him information that only he would know. Making people feel trusted will generally help them trust you.

"Yeah, look!" I said, unclipping my briefcase. "There's so much to be negotiated and signed that even just this will take us days to go through, but it will all get signed by Friday!" Before he could ask me more, I made the most genius move I've ever made and went with chaos as a companion. I *accidentally* dropped all of the paper onto the floor. On his side of course. "Oh my gosh!" I yelled in alarm. "This is *not* good!" I continued yelling. "Can you help me?" I said, petitioning for access from the other side.

Completely ignoring me, he said only, "Other way, please" as he now tried to ward off a group of three people walking toward the gates from stepping on the paperwork.

"No one can see those!" I said, straining my voice. "They are very confidential!"

"Oh, please don't stand on that!" I urged the passersby. As the guard turned his back on me to redirect the group, I hurdled the lower turnstile meant for access and hurriedly made my way to scoop up the papers. "I should get them back into order before I go up there. Do you mind if I just sit on those sofas there and regroup?"

"Let me see your badge," the guard responded as he made his way to silence the now beeping gate sounding the alarm of circumvention a little obnoxiously for my liking.

"Here!" I snapped, pushing it in his hand. "I need to sort these," I asserted, one last time.

"I have to look at this. Do you have ID on you?"

"Of course—one second," I explained, reaching into my pocket. I handed him my ID. Thankfully we are allowed fake ones for the job—although it should be noted that they are sanctioned, and if they showed up as being used on an airline or in a traffic stop (which would be my two preferred uses), I would probably be ejected from this country. "I will just phone up to James, I am sure he can come down and sort this." As I said it, I continued sorting the paperwork back into its proper order.

"Don't go anywhere. I will be at the desk checking into this."

Literally the minute he turned the corner, I darted into the elevator. This move was my least brilliant idea of the operation. Of course, you needed a card to get the elevator to move so much as an inch. My saving grace was that the security guard probably wasn't at his desk to see my idiocy on CCTV. As I sat back down, though, resuming my position as a hurried lawyer, now dialing her boss, luck came rolling through the turnstile in a three-piece suit. As a six-foot, brown-haired, shiny-shoed man made his way to the elevator bank, so did I. "Yep, I am on the way up!" I said into the phone.

We stood in the elevator with me praying social norms would prevail. After what in hindsight was probably 5 seconds, but at the time felt like 3 weeks, this elevator hero said, "35 as well?"

"That's the one," I said back as smoothly as I could.

It was not the one. It was three floors short of my intended destination. But it seemed close enough to the target and far enough from the security guard.

After some small talk, the elevator doors opened, and I was greeted by yet another set of turnstiles that I most definitely did not have a fake card for now. I let my elevator companion go ahead as I stayed back, again pretending to be on the phone. "Hey, James. I won't be long. I just have to make one call out here, and I'll be straight in . . . yeah, I know. I'm sorry, I will apologize profusely when I get in. See you in a few!" After correctly assuming the coast was clear, I did what any respectable female social engineer would: I sucked in my belly like I was expecting to get punched, tilted my pelvis, and slid through a rather tight gap between the turnstile and the side gate.

It wasn't ideal, but I was at least able to move about somewhat freely now. I darted 30 feet down the corridor toward a sign beckoning me with its little stick figures. The bathrooms. I took out my phone and, for the first time that day, attempted to make actual contact with someone other than my imagination. When my teammate picked up, I offered him what I thought was a fair solution to a potentially growing problem 35 stories beneath me: "You're going to have to spoof an internal number and tell that security guard I am up here and that 'you' will escort me down later for my badge and ID." After a little back and forth on the details, he agreed. Now I was left with finding the solution to my newest problem: getting three stories up without a key card for the elevator.

There was one thing that would definitely help me: continued persistence.

Skills and Common Sense

There's generic common sense, and there's professional common sense. A good measure of both is often advantageous. However, it's somewhat a dual modality for an ethical attack. Let's consider what "professional" common sense is.

Professional Common Sense

Professional common sense diverges from traditional common sense only slightly; the latter dictates you use practical judgment concerning everyday matters or have a basic ability to perceive, understand, and judge—this is *common* to nearly all people. Professional common sense dictates that we do that all of those things, but at work.

Professional common sense is essentially a collection of buzzwords that are meant to transcend personality types. Most organizations would list trustworthy, competent, respectful, courteous, dependable, cooperative, committed, approachable, accountable, steady—the list goes on and on. However, much of this is the antithesis of our jobs as attackers, right? How can we be trustworthy, competent, respectful, courteous, dependable, cooperative, and steady when our jobs boil down to being dishonest, not having a clue about our pretext's job, influencing another human for our own gain, and pivoting at any given opportunity? Well, there's another way to look at common sense: from the viewpoint of the attacker. It starts with a hard-and-fast rule: stick to the scope of the job as given by the client. You apply the rest to yourself as follows:

Trustworthiness   When you are hired to do a job, there is an expectation that you will not take advantage of your power. It's such a fine line for a client to trust you to take advantage of their disadvantage. You cannot exploit it for your own personal or selfish gain.

Maturity   Being an EA is not a license to act however you feel or carry out dangerous or daring activities on a whim. You should never overreact when things go wrong or use high-stress situations to cover for a poor attitude or inability to deal with pressure. Maturity means you act responsibly and respectfully at all times.

Respect   Respect must be conveyed not only in your actions but in your attitude. Maintaining a respectful tone and nature is twofold: you must apply this against your targets as the attacker in motion and apply it against your teammates and the client.

Competence   Since every attack may require something different of you, there is a self-driving incentive to learn new techniques and tools. Learning to pick a lock, write exploits (code that takes advantage of a software vulnerability or security flaw), and carry out surveillance are legitimate and valuable skills. If the route you've planned requires something of you that you are not familiar with and that could prove damaging to the attack or to your target and their environment, you should reconsider your approach.

Dependability   As an attacker, you must be dependable. You cannot flake out on jobs. It's not just a matter of your reputation being diluted or chipped away. You may be headed for serious legal proceedings if you fail to execute as expected.

Cooperation   As a professional attacker, you must be able to work with the client's fears. Working hand in hand with a client, even after you've offered advice to better a campaign or operation, is needed and needed often. Not all clients want a full attack mounted on them, and some don't want their most valuable assets gamified. However, you should remain accommodating and willing to work with the environment given.

Approachability   Being approachable is one of the highest value skills you can offer your client. I urge all of us as attackers to stay away from buzzwords and industry terms when talking to someone outside of our field. As an EA and a professional, communicating with someone on their level will generally serve your needs more expediently.

Compartmentalization   Compartmentalizing helps stress management as it can reduce anxiety as well as tension. Sometimes being able to mentally compartmentalize means being able to avoid mental discomfort. The act of mentally compartmentalizing is singling out an issue and applying all your energy and attention to it. In psychology, compartmentalizing is considered a defense or coping mechanism. Put simply, it's how our minds deal with conflicting internal standpoints simultaneously, and internal conflicts can be plentiful as an attacker. There are a few steps you can take to help ease the mental burden of the job though:

1. Isolate the issues from all the other challenges you are dealing with—personal and professional.
2. Focus on each isolated issue, moving forward in incremental steps.
3. Accept that you can go between isolated issues if progress in one area cannot be made.
4. Do not ruminate if you are not solving. Thinking about something, replaying a moment or situation or reimagining an

internal narrative over and over is a catastrophic thought pattern. Learn to apply solutions (typically for future events) to what you are thinking about.

Finally, to compartmentalize, you have to be able to stomach the idea that, no matter what you do, you are not the only person who can do that job. There are literally backups for brain surgeons. That's not meant to make you feel lesser; it's not to say you won't do the job better or differently, but sometimes compartmentalization means isolating yourself from the project when need be.

Summary

- Curiosity is on a spectrum but is most often persistence's driving force.
- The best way to bait curiosity is to ask questions and then persist in the pursuit of satisfactory answers.
- You will need persistence at all stages of a job and to have it as a cornerstone of your own mindset. Giving up easily is not a good trait for this industry.
- Mental agility forms part of the holy trifecta, too. You have to be able to use information multiple ways for multiple outcomes, especially when you need to pivot because something is not panning out as you'd expected it to.
- Common sense, both in the traditional sense and the professional sense, are prerequisites for the ability to perform well.
- Ethics are not abstained from simply because of the nature of our jobs as attackers. They are a fundamental feature of the mindset.

Key Message

Curiosity is a strong driving force of any attack—ethical or malicious. It serves as a driving force in the pursuit of information and knowledge. Persistence cannot exist without a goal. Morals are at play for the sake of the greater good, and they influence each moment in your intentions as an ethical attacker.

Chapter 6

Information Processing: Observation and Thinking Techniques

A long habit of not thinking a thing wrong, gives it a superficial appearance of being right. . . Time makes more converts than reason.

—Thomas Paine

Processing information to weaponize and leverage is a necessary cognitive skill to get into the attacker mindset and use it to its greatest potential. To process information, you have to collect it. You can *collect* information four main ways: by obtaining, observing, theorizing, and inferring. If you choose the latter two, you will then have to search for information to validate your thoughts.

After you have collected the information, you have to parse it. You will then put it in one of these three buckets:

- Recon: Made up of information that familiarizes you with your targets and their environments
- Pretext: Consists of information that you can directly weaponize in order to disguise yourself as a threat
- Disregard: Consists of items that aren't useful in either of these ways—information you simply dismiss

Once you've decided which bucket the information should go in, you have to weaponize it *within its limits*, which means not stretching the information for more than it's worth. For example, knowing a company uses Splunk doesn't permit you to call up impersonating a system administrator, security engineer, or Splunk administrator. You will likely not have enough information to fulfill your call objective if you hope to learn more than just how the organization reacts to your advances. For example, you cannot infer from a company's use of Splunk which other software it uses. Splunk itself is a software platform that can search, analyze, and visualize machine-generated data gathered from websites, applications, and so forth. It is helpful enough to go into the recon and pretext buckets, but you will need more than that information alone.

You have to collect information to process it, but in many instances, you must observe information, too. In this chapter, we will deal primarily with observation. Observation is not just passive viewing—it's an active mental process. French physiologist Claude Bernard (1813–1878) distinguished two types of observation: (1) spontaneous or *passive* observations, which are unexpected, and (2) induced or *active* observations, which are deliberately sought. Effective spontaneous observation involves first noticing some object or event haphazardly. The thing noticed will usually become significant only if your mind either consciously or unconsciously relates it to relevant knowledge or remembered past experience. However, consciously choosing to think about something that you know nothing about might lead you to reasoning, further research, or inference—which will require a healthy dose of curiosity and persistence.

Observation is a tricky subject, though. Simple observations can be computed in multiple ways. Through the lens of observation, we'll discuss intuition and heuristics, rationale, and reason, all of which we will have to, at some point, rely on as attackers. This is why picking apart observation is so vital; with the ability to observe your surroundings and targets accurately, you can process information with more confidence and a higher likelihood of effecting real influence.

Observation's driving force is attention. I once worked on a job that required detailed and "in the weeds" type of observation to achieve any meaningful facts. In this case, I was passed 10 or so images that were seemingly benign. They were images that I hoped would reveal the location of someone being tracked due to their criminal activity. Figure 6.1–Figure 6.4 show some of the images.

Figure 6.1   Photo A

My observations of Photo A started with an unfair disadvantage; I live in Los Angeles and recognized right away where that photo was taken—this went from observation to inference quite quickly.

There were three other facts I was able to identify, the first almost immediately, although the rest took some research. The first thing I noticed was that a woman's bag is pictured and potentially taken from her point of view. The image also shows pre-tuned radio stations; 102.7FM is KISS FM, and 101.9FM is KSCA, a commercial FM radio station licensed to Glendale, California and broadcasting to the Greater Los Angeles area. It is also a Spanish-speaking broadcast. The audio system console shown strongly resembles that of a Ford, possibly a Ford Focus, although that took some further research to find. An ExifTool metadata probe of these images also showed that they were taken on a Motorola phone.

Photo B contains a bit of a gift as far as investigations go: a receipt.

From here, you can see that the image must have been taken on or after 05/18/2020. The time is printed as either 14:48 or 14:46.

Photo C shows a mask, from which I can infer this picture was taken no earlier than 2020 due to COVID 19—not many of us in the West were wearing masks prior to that, and there is no evidence to support either of the people (the driver or the picture taker) were in the medical field. The mask also has what appears to be makeup transfer on it, further leading me to believe that the man I was tracking was with a woman. The one other thing to note is that the cable doesn't appear to be an iPhone cable. I cannot say for certain, since I don't have that expertise, but I would say that the ExifTool data I found supports this theory.

Your Brain vs. Your Observation

Your brain isn't wired to see everything. It focuses on specific things—such as the fact that Photo A and Photo C are two completely different cars—and filters out everything else. Some of you

Figure 6.2   Photo B

may have neglected that detail, whereas others noticed it. That level of observation is to your benefit most of the time because, if you paid attention to everything, you'd often miss what's important.

Because your brain is hardwired to disregard details and you are, essentially, incapable of appreciating more than just a sliver of your surroundings, you must train your brain to reconsider what it sees as important. To train yourself in this way, it is extremely helpful to understand why our brains function the way they do. In every sensory moment, our brains are swimming in a deluge of input. The information that you are aware of or can recall later is relevant to you at that specific time. Let me explain: If you're a tourist in a new city, the type of stores you notice (and later recall) will differ

Figure 6.3   Photo B zoomed in

depending on your interests and needs at the time. If you are hungry or thirsty, you'll most likely notice cafes and restaurants. If you are interested in architecture, you will likely notice buildings and be able to recall them in better detail than someone else, say, just looking for a cab. If you're scanning a guest list for your name, you are not likely to notice names with configurations different from your own. If you're looking for a friend in a crowd with brown hair, you will not focus on people with any other color of hair.

If I am walking into my friend's house for the first time, I don't need to know what color their front door is—that's rarely served me before. Thankfully, society went with using street names and numbers as a way to identify house positions and not the color of the houses and their parts. If we'd have gone the other way, my brain would've been taught that color and hue were the important details to observe and remember as they relate to homes, which is the key here: you can re-teach your brain what is important to notice, especially relating to engagements. In other words, you must use your limited resources wisely and to attend to those features that

Figure 6.4   Photo C

are most important. It might sound counterintuitive that the best way to train yourself how to observe efficiently is to learn what to ignore. But you must build up this skill over time.

In building observation as a skill, and a sort of "muscle," there is good news: you literally can't do it wrong. Observation is in the eye of the beholder, after all. However, the areas that may serve you best to build up and train on, specifically for AMs, would be as follows:

Walking and "Talking" Walking and listening to other people talking is a skill—and quite a hard one. Try to walk past people talking and pick up what they are saying. Better yet, pretend you are on the phone talking, and see if you can still pick up what they are saying. It's quite a hard task, but a very useful one.

There's every chance you end up doing this in a building as you enter or try to remain within it.

Listening I don't mean *listening* in the same way a therapist does, but listening to your surroundings is a massive skill to have, and it's a skill that so many people lack. That is not meant in a pejorative way; it's just that this is rarely a learning curve for most people: finding the origin points of sounds makes surveying your surroundings—especially on jobs where you must be aware but act disengaged—easier. It also trains the ear to listen for new things and, over time, recognize more of them without having to analyze. This skill will play into your ambient listening skills, too. It is especially useful for vishing calls—being able to ascertain where your target is will increase your level of insight and chances of success.

Looking Detail for the sake of detail is our enemy. It can be inefficient, creating problems instead of creating results, and it can lose you time in the field. There are jobs where details are the bulk of the daily tasks that will be carried out—accountant, journalist, proofreader, editor, and data analyst are all examples. Parts of any attack will require attention to detail. Details for the good of a task or an operation should be lauded. Design can also be important in social engineering. Designing items in replication requires a detail-heavy approach at times. Things like typography and font size can be crucial because the security guard to whom you give your faked employee ID badge will recognize it as such in what science says is less than a second. After visual input hits the retina, the information flows into the brain, where information such as shape, color, and orientation are processed. It has been shown that the human brain can detect an image in as little as 100 milliseconds. A security guard might be able to tell your badge is a fake in about 0.9 seconds if it's got the wrong typography or font size. So, details can be important. Observing them as best you can and as often as you can will go in your favor overall.

Surveying All right, this one is different, but it truly will serve you. The idea is pretty simple. Pick a place, sit or stand still, and take a "mental photo." My method includes what I call "story sentences"; if I were staring at a building, I would describe it as if

I were writing the world's blandest novel. "The eight-story building glistened as the glass reflected the sun." Is this a bit weird? Probably. Does it work? Yes. It makes recall a lot easier. Recall will serve you two ways: it will help you with reports, and it will help you with recon—ultimately "recording" information will help you throughout the entire life cycle of an engagement.

Observation vs. Heuristics

If information is what forms intuition, there must be a heavy connection between observation and intuition. However, there's another variable in how we calculate information and come to a conclusion: enter *heuristics*. Heuristics are mental shortcuts; they aren't guaranteed to be logical or rational, but they help a person reach a decision. They reduce cognitive load and can be effective for making immediate judgments. The downside is that they can result in irrational or inaccurate conclusions.

Heuristics

Heuristics are quite useful in making quick decisions. Heuristics are based on simple logic that is self-evident. But self-evidence isn't always accurate and comprehensive. For example, imagine your doctor used only heuristics to diagnose you. You go in with symptoms that include fever, chills, headache, fatigue, muscle and joint pain, and swollen lymph nodes—these are symptoms all pretty common with the flu. But actually, you have Lyme disease. Your doctor cannot (and hopefully does not) use only what is empirical evidence to reach their diagnoses. Other types of information are also critical—the observation of data, like blood tests, for example.

In the early 1970s, an alternative theory proposed that people use heuristics instead of rationally weighing relevant factors to make judgments much of the time. An example of a heuristic-based judgment is the now famous case of "Linda," originally documented by Amos Tversky and Daniel Kahneman (1982, 1983) in their paper, titled, "The Conjunction Fallacy in Probability Judgement," published in the Psychological Review in 1983, volume 90, number 4, page 229). When participants read a paragraph about Linda (in italics below), the vast majority fell prey to an error.

Behold Linda

Linda is 31 years old, single, outspoken and very bright. She majored in philosophy. As a student, she was deeply concerned with issues of discrimination and social justice, and also participated in anti-nuclear demonstrations.

1. *Linda is a bank teller and is active in the feminist movement.*
2. *Linda is a bank teller.*

Around 80 percent of people thought that the first statement that followed the paragraph was more likely to be true than the second. This cannot be, though. The first statement cannot be more probable because it includes the second. The supplementary information is not aligned in any way with what we first read about Linda. The probability of the first statement is ranked higher than the second simply because it is more similar to the given description of Linda. This is what is called the *similarity heuristic*. Most of us use this sort of method to judge, rather than our knowledge of probability. It turns out that statistical analysis is a mysterious thing to most folks.

However, this is not to say that heuristic diagnosis is not valuable. Using heuristics can be an intellectual skill. The ability to determine in environments what is likely, even if you don't have all of the information, can be a massive help. But why do I say this? Why show you that heuristically thinking is flawed only to pivot and show you it actually has value?

Two reasons: The first is that, using any type of heuristic as an alternative to logic and reasoning, should not be tolerated. There is room for this mode of thought, but it should not be your standard. The second is that there are times as an attacker that you will have to rely on heuristics. For example, in the story I told you earlier about the Manhattan bank I was trying to get into, I used the available heuristics to determine that no one would see me sucking in my tummy like a circus performer as I bypassed the security turnstile. The self-evidence I was using told me that no one was around—I heard no footsteps or voices, or any movement at all. And glancing over the upper walls and ceilings made me think that no security cameras would capture me in the act. Using this mode of thinking as a standard can be hard to get out of for some people. Logic and reasoning are not the most natural modes of thought for everyone. However, there's one good exercise to use to learn if you're using heuristics: ask yourself if the evidence you're seeing would stand up in a court of law. I could not have gone into a court and categorically stated that there were no cameras around. I could only say that to the best of my knowledge and based on empirical evidence, there appeared to be no cameras around.

To reiterate, using heuristics is advantageous when finding an optimal solution through reasoning is either impossible or impractical, such as when in a time crunch, or when faced with a decision for which no data is available or the data is thought to be heavily flawed or skewed.

Observation vs. Intuition

Intuition refers to our ability to know or understand something without reasoning or proof, also known as a gut feeling. Some athletes exhibit levels of intuition that are beyond all reckoning. In Major League Baseball, for example, a pitch takes less than half a second to reach home plate, but a batter cannot afford to wait that long to put their body into action. The player's muscles, nerves, and brain manage to work together to hit the ball in an astonishingly short amount of time.

Once the ball leaves the pitcher's hand, it travels at around 85 to 95 mph, taking only 400 to 500 milliseconds to reach home. Information about the pitch—its speed, trajectory, and location— takes about 100 milliseconds, or a tenth of a second, to go from eye to brain. It takes another 150 milliseconds for the batter to start a swing and get the bat over the plate. This leaves about a quarter of a second at most for the hitter to decide where to swing the bat. This is a form of intuition at play.

Malcolm Gladwell begins his book *Blink* (Back Bay Books, Little, Brown) by telling the story of the purchase of a seemingly priceless Greek statue known as a *kouros* by the Getty Museum in Los Angeles. Before purchasing the statue, the museum carried out its due diligence, consulting with scientists and lawyers who all concluded the piece was the real thing after scientifically testing the materials and perusing the documentation. They gave the seller a monstrous $10 million and then took it to show to some art historians and specialists in Greek sculpture. As it turned out, the Getty had been conned. The art experts they'd unveiled this statue to needed just one look to know that it was a fake. An immaculate, giant, smooth, sculptured-to-within-an-inch-of-its-life fake. To confirm, they did not need to test the statue's claim of veracity or spend countless hours studying it. Intuitively, they knew it was a fake right away.

Intuition, reductively, can be seen as the ability to draw conclusions quickly, without the need for deliberation or conscious analysis. High-caliber intuitive conclusions transpire when you can recognize a situation that follows a particular pattern you have seen before, have knowledge specific to previous situations that fit the pattern, or have general knowledge that's applicable to the new situation. So, if intuition is the ability to understand something immediately, without the need for conscious reasoning, how do you get to that point? An art expert didn't exit the womb as such. When was the last time any of you heard of a child who was able to consistently tell a Picasso apart from a Crayola sketch without study?

My position is that keen observation is the underlying and bolstering principle at play in intuition, at least to begin with. An art expert has, for example, seen so much in their specialized field, analyzed, and has given definitive answers on their assumptions so often that they are then able to build that experience into what is recognized as intuition. In other words, years of observing the real thing can make spotting a fake insanely easy.

Another example that showcases the successful use of intuition comes from expert chess players. Chess experts have gone through a process of perceptual learning, allowing them to intuitively recognize chess configurations as units rather than having to analyze every configuration presented during a chess game. Intuition is formed from experience and acute observation.

Because intuition is based on a large number of variables whose relationships are difficult to classify, intuition cannot be programmed, which, in cybersecurity at least, is perhaps it's most brilliant value. Intuition is personal, and it becomes better with practice and experience. It is something that can be used to your own advantage as an attacker. I suspect that a strong correlation exists between time spent ethically attacking and increased intuition. Responses become more automatic as less concentration is required for technique. When needed, an automatic response during a crunch-time scenario will improve your performance. Overthinking due to nerves or anxiety will cause your AMs to slow down, so improving the skills of your offensive attacker mindsets (OAMs) and defensive attacker mindsets (DAMs) will also refine your intuition capabilities.

However, without years of experience or a specialized background, your intuition alone cannot be trusted. You will have to build it up over time. Attackers with a strong mental game are better at quickly dealing with those unexpected moments, disallowing them from detracting from their focus. Again, I arrive at the conclusion that mental games of chess played with information you have about an attack will result in easier successes and improved agility and intuitive moves. Nothing will beat experience itself, of course. You can get this from capture-the-flag events (known as CTFs), lab practice, hypothetical attacks, and real jobs. For a list of known resources, see the notes section of this book on its website (www.theamsbook.com).

Using Reasoning and Logic

Using reasoning and logic above heuristics and intuition is more resource intensive for the brain. Also, most of the problems that you will face in a day are not mathematical or logical in nature. However, reason must be employed when the stakes are too high to rely on using intuition alone and where data is available.

Most recently at Social-Engineer LLC, where I currently work, we intuitively agreed that we faced an insider threat. All of the signs were there. For example, the employee was accessing information without any explicable need and downloading it. The employee had a growing number of devices and locations with access to sensitive data. They were voicing disagreement with coworkers and were performing poorly, connecting with clients out of band and working very odd hours. Intuitively, they felt like an insider threat. It turned out this person wasn't. But it *felt* like they were. To usher the feelings we had to the side, we looked at all the facts, and the person was just not performing. There was no malicious intent or threat. A *balance* has to be struck between intuition and reasoning—guessing and parsing the data—a lesson I later discovered in a revered Manhattan bank. Let's jump back to that New York skyscraper and pick up where the story last left off, first taking a look at something you can never plan for: luck.

No one ever said an element of luck is not involved in attack execution. Two in a row is something to be marveled at, though. That the man I'd hitched a ride with was a bank employee—that's luck checkbox number one. Luck checkbox number two was a direct result of that: as I walked around the 35th floor, nodding to people as if I was their coworker and this was not the very first time they were seeing me, I happened across an empty desk. It had only a few things strewn across it, but among them was a sight so beautiful, wonderful, and surreal that I almost choked on my own happiness. A key card sat there, on its back, looking up at me as if it no longer wished to be alone. I scooped it up, slid it in my pocket, and listened for any sounds that signaled a change in atmosphere. My peripheral vision seconded this analysis; thankfully, no excuses were needed as to why I was hovering around an empty desk, slyly snatching things off it. No one had bothered to look up—which, looking back, is probably luck checkbox number three. I would like to amend my earlier statement: no one ever said an element of luck is not involved in attack execution. *Three* in a row is something to be marveled at, though.

I moved through the office, completing a loop that ended back at the turnstile I'd very recently circumvented. I looked at the gap I'd slid through only minutes before, thankful I didn't have to do it again. Tucking your pelvis in and squashing your own butt down is an odd activity to do once in a day, never mind twice. I simply swiped my way to the 38th floor, never looking back. I stepped out of the elevator onto the floor I'd been assured I'd never make it to. A sense of smugness that should be punishable filled my body. And it was; that feeling was, in the end, my downfall.

I fell into my most used character—comfortable with her surroundings, with the air of "I have a right to be here" about her. A group of men walked toward me, chattering among themselves. Ordinarily I would only nod at them or smile ephemerally. Talking with a group that's all one gender intuitively feels like a bad idea, as the opposite gender in a group of one. However, I was still high on smugness, so I went against my own intuition, reasoning, and logic and talked to *all of them at once.* My apparently new and strong idiocy allowed me to start the conversation with the stellar salutation of "Hey!" I said it to the whole gaggle of men, now only feet away from me, apparently attempting to stop all of them in their tracks. I continued with the equally brilliant "Where's the CFO's office? I have papers for him!" I lifted the briefcase up a little as if it were some sort of proof.

Fail 1: I stopped a whole group of men with no good reason. There are name signs on the doors. I could've looked for the office or asked one person.

Fail 2: I told them what I was there for. They didn't need to know, and I left myself with negative ability to pivot. When already in and *you* are instigating interaction, let people ask. Don't just tell them everything. You will paint yourself into a very tight corner.

Fail 3: Let's pretend the CFO's name was Jeff. Well, Jeff's voice came from within the gaggle and said pretty abruptly, or at least that's how it hit me in the moment, "I'm Jeff. I am expecting no papers."

Gulp. Idiocy and smugness are a bad combination.

Observing People

Inanimate objects and large, mainly unchanging environments are one thing, but observing and understanding people is another skill entirely. When we perceive the stakes as high, most of us zone in on what we believe we should look for—situations like interviews, first dates, first fights, watching politicians on TV or attempting to work out if your other half is lying to you—for these, we wake up, take in more, and base a lot on our *findings*. Unfortunately, most of us also tend to slack off during the everyday interactions. Nonverbal communication, though, is our most honest and reliable way of transmitting information—even that which we might not want communicated. Therefore, having the base knowledge and tools to understand it are of the utmost importance as an attacker. First, let's sort out some myths of body language and nonverbal communication.

A friend, Friend, mentor, and former FBI agent Joe Navarro tells me that there's no standard for catching a lie. A person's eyes glancing to the left, nose touching, and fidgeting are myths of deception. As Navarro says, not all throat-clearing and arm-crossing indicates something. He refers to these actions as *self-soothers*, the things we do to pacify ourselves in stressful moments. In fact, there is no silver bullet for detecting a lie. You can only detect comfort or discomfort, but that can lead to catching someone in a lie. Holistically, though, this topic of deception detection has very serious consequences. Historically and even recently, people have been tortured, prosecuted, and even executed when those in authority deemed them to be lying or complicit purely based on their body language. There's a large price to pay for wronged individuals because of the perpetuated myth that we, as humans, can "see" lies. With that myth now, hope-fully, busted for you, let's look at the 10 commandments Navarro gives for observing people that will ring out the most information. They directly align with observing people as an attacker:

Commandment 1: Be a competent observer of your environment.
Commandment 2: Observing in context is key to understanding nonverbal behavior.
Commandment 3: Learn to recognize and decode nonverbal behaviors that are universal.
Commandment 4: Learn to recognize and decode idiosyncratic nonverbal behaviors.
Commandment 5: When you interact with others, try to establish their baseline behaviors.
Commandment 6: Always try to watch people for multiple tells—behaviors that occur in clusters or in succession.
Commandment 7: It's important to look for changes in a person's behavior that can signal changes in thoughts, emotions, interest, or intent.
Commandment 8: Learning to detect false or misleading non-verbal signals is also critical.
Commandment 9: Knowing how to distinguish between comfort and discomfort will help you to focus on the most important behaviors for decoding nonverbal communications.
Commandment 10: When observing others, be subtle about it.

Another point about observing and making inferences on body language is that patterns are often idiosyncratic, so you may have to observe someone for a while, find their individual tendencies, then make assumptions and predictions based on those. This is known as capturing someone's "baseline." If you're not paying attention and observing, you may miss these baseline behaviors, and so your chance of decoding someone's behavior as it pertains to you and the environment will be gone. To know if someone is showing comfort or discomfort in your presence, consider their baseline before your interaction where circumstances allow. This is where self-awareness can be used as a pliable, powerful tool. Being able to literally see how you are affecting someone gives you the chance to subtly readjust, and they will most likely adjust with you, consciously or subconsciously.

Very broadly speaking, there are two types of self-awareness. *Internal self-awareness* speaks to how you see your own passions and morals—how you see yourself fitting with your environment and your reactions. It also helps you see your effect on others. *External self-awareness* means being able to understand how other people view you. If you can see how you might be affecting someone—what they may think of you and what you have done or are doing to lead them to that conclusion—you can then influence them to your own benefit and for the benefit of the objective.

Self-awareness is a staggeringly complex topic, so I have chosen to lace it throughout this book rather than confine it to one chapter. Self-awareness used with observation is powerful; it will let you see your effect on someone, and it will allow you the opportunity to influence someone subtly through your own body language, non-verbals, and all of your communication. Self-awareness used with observation is just as important as self-awareness used with interaction. You have to be able to look at someone, a perfect stranger in most cases, and accept that you do not know them, that their actions and reactions might not be familiar to you or even what you expect. But you must be able to observe and figure out how you are affecting them and begin adjusting your behavior. This encompasses all four laws of the mindset: you must know your end goal; you must be gathering information, at this point on the person who stands between you and your goal; you must keep yourself disguised as a threat; and you must use the information gained from observing and/or interacting for the good of the objective.

Observation Exercise

I often analyze people based on appearance—after all, you will likely never know if you are right or wrong about someone if they remain a stranger. You can use observation to take mental notes on your target, and it's a good way to build mental stamina, with others as the central focus. It's also a good way to satisfy your curiosity.

The caveat is that for many of the items I'll list, you will need a baseline to be accurate. A baseline is a state of behavior—essentially what is steady behavior for a person as you observe them. It serves as a standard against which to compare changes in behavior. Baseline behaviors include how people sit, where they place their hands, the position of their feet, their posture, and their facial expression. Establishing someone's baseline behavior allows you to determine when they deviate from it. Often sudden changes in behavior can be revealing.

An example of a baseline change might be the stillness that comes over someone as they are asked what they perceive to be a difficult question. If they are normally prone to fidgeting and animation—if that is their baseline—it will be easy to note when they become still.

People often employ pacifying behaviors, too. We use these to calm ourselves—touching our necks and touching our beards may help us calm down if we feel uncomfortable. As you now know, there's no one single behavior indicative of deception; there is no Pinocchio effect. There are only behaviors that are indicative of psychological discomfort or comfort. Someone sitting with their arms crossed doesn't signal anything other than a comfortable position if they sit like that every day. However, imagine a woman sitting on a bench in a park. You are observing her from a safe enough distance, and she doesn't appear to have noticed you. She seems calm and relaxed. However, a man sits on the same bench as her and she immediately crosses her arms tightly at her womb and scrunches up her shoulders. You can assume these are signs of discomfort given her baseline as you previously observed. Now imagine that man gets up and walks away, and the woman visibly relaxes. A few minutes later, another woman sits down at around the same spot the man did, and the woman makes no changes to her seemingly relaxed position. I can't categorically state that the woman doesn't like men or that she has any problem at all with men. But I can make some level of inference. I could infer that the first person who sat down startled her or that he reminded her of someone else. Ultimately, I know *what* changed, but I do not know *why* it changed.

Cultural norms and baselines have to be taken into consideration, too. For example, although the New York accent is really a pool of accents drawn together in large part, from the Italian, Jewish, Jamaican, Puerto Rican, Dominican, Irish, and hip-hop communities, New Yorkers speak very fast and are known to drop consonants (hence "talkin'" versus "talking"). There's a baseline indignation to the talk. And they are often emphatic in their delivery.

Finally, not every observation needs a baseline. You can just look at someone's nails to know they chew them. You don't have to see them stop or start doing it. You won't always know why someone changed their baseline behaviors, but if you are observant enough, you will know what changed and be able to adjust your own behavior if necessary to accommodate the situation and your goals.

So as you've seen, there is value in learning to be a competent observer of your environment.

When beginning this exercise, I look at the person's overall demeanor. Usually, I analyze their stance for this, quickly followed by the general emotion shown on their face at that moment. From there, given the chance, I make notes on their appearance from head to toe, including perceived age, clothing, how engaged they are in their environment, and from there, I can make inferences.

Is their hair well groomed?
Tells me if they are influenced by vanity or if they were perhaps rushed.
Are their pupils dilated?
May tell me if they are engaged and sometimes if they are on medication—not an absolute rule, but it's a telltale sign in some situations.
Have they missed any spots shaving (if male)?
Tells me they don't pay attention to details or they were in a rush.

Are their clothes ironed?
Tells me how organized they are and to what level they hold them-
selves. People often dress how they want to be perceived.

Do their clothes fit?
Tells me if they have recently lost or gained weight, which I can then
ponder over—if they've gained weight, are they stressed? If they
have lost weight, are they stressed or sick?

Are they wearing a wedding ring?
Tells me the obvious—usually.

If they are not wearing a ring, is there a mark?
Tells me if they are recently divorced, or if their clothes no longer fit,
it might signal their ring doesn't either.

Do they bite their nails?
Tells me if they are nervous or if they have this tendency, and then
I look to see if they do it habitually when they aren't using their
hands in a given moment.

Where do they hold their hands—for instance, in their
pockets or on their hips, by their face?
Tells me how engaged they are and can lend some insight into their
psychological state. If they are holding their head up with their
hand under their chin, they are probably less engaged and more
familiar with their job. If they are standing and their hands are
behind their back, they may be analyzing me. Of course, they may
just stand like that out of habit, but time will tell.

Do they have any habits, like biting the inside of their
cheek or tapping their foot?
Tells me if they are fidgety, nervous, anxious, or waiting for
something.

What's their tone of voice conveying?
Often tells me more than their words do. Subtext should not be
overlooked. People will generally tell you what they want to, just not
with their words.

Are they using colloquialisms that suggest they are from
around the area or from another part of the country?
Tells me the obvious or about travel. It is also a good needle to thread
as a conversation starter to find out more and more about them.

Where are their hips pointing, especially if in a conversation?

Tells me again how engaged they are. If their hips are pointing directly toward the person they are talking to, they are at least interested. If they are turning away, they are likely signaling that they no longer want to be part of the conversation. It might be because they need to go to the bathroom, not because the conversation isn't good. Again, sometimes you will know the "what" but not the "why."

Where are their feet pointed, especially if in conversation?

Tells me how engaged the person is in the conversation and if they'd like to continue or leave.

If they are talking, where do they look when they are talking?

Tells me their thought process. A lot of looking over their shoulder, or the shoulder of the person they are talking to, can signal distractedness. Looking into the face tells me they are present and absorbed (in most cases). Looking up and down the body tells me they are judging or looking for more information about the person they are talking to.

At what pace are they talking and at what volume?

Tells me if they are nervous, eager to have the conversation end, dubious, or happy to help. Pace, volume, and even pitch are nonverbal signals, somewhat contrary to what you may think, considering they are carried with the voice. Cultural norms and baselines have to be taken into account. For example, many Scottish people talk very quickly and it's not to do with nerves, but in conjunction with other signs, rhythm volume, speed, and pitch of voice matter and can be telling.

And, my favorite, where are they looking when they are supposed to be listening?

A person might look right at you when they are talking, but what about when they stop and you start? If someone looks away quickly, it may indicate they don't want to hear your reply for any number of reasons, including they think it will be negative, not what they want to hear, or not something they care about. Someone looking away after speaking doesn't have to imply negative connotations, of course.

The speed at which they move their eyes and head away also holds weight. Someone might look away after they've declared their love, only because they are shy. Someone might look away after they've told a joke, and they are waiting to have you judge it as funny. But how a person reacts after you stop talking should always inform the rhythm, speed, volume, and pitch (RSVP) of your own response.

Now, it's important to point out that it doesn't matter if all of these extrapolations hold true or not—it's good for both mental agility and decision processing and making. However, if you are standing in front of a target analyzing these things, some of them may prove vital in deciding your next move—especially the latter four listed. These can show if you have appropriately engaged the target and, potentially, their internal emotional state.

Let's return to the earlier example of the security guard. If he appeared unkempt and somewhat disinterested, I would quickly assume he didn't care that much about his job, and it would help me talk to him. I'd be far more casual than if the opposite were true. But I would absolutely validate him by talking with him in such a way that he understood I was happily giving him my time. This could be accomplished through RSVP: rhythm, speed, volume, pitch. These four things, given only with my voice, could help me build rapport with him on a personal level, hopefully compelling him to act upon my wishes.

However, if the security guard looked straight at me, unwaveringly, without a normal blink rate, with his whole body pointed at me after I've just explained my need for access, I might poise myself to be asked a rather probing question. This sort of follow-up body language could mean he is looking for more information about me: he remains unconvinced. Of course, this is impossible to say without a baseline and should be taken as an example only. But observation over time will help you parse body language and nonverbals proficiently.

AMs and Observation

Observation is a core underpinning of gathering and processing information. Seeing is not observing, and traditional observation is not the same as the type needed for use by an attacker. AMs observation is a rigorous activity. To become effective and efficient at it, you have to train your attention as an attacker, learning to focus on relevant features and disregard those that are less noticeable. Your brain is already taking them in. One of the best approaches is through the old-fashioned practice of taking field notes: writing descriptions of what you see in a given moment. Try taking notes with a limited word count or with limited paper real estate—this will force you to make decisions about what's important and what's not. You might also consider keeping careful records of your observations, quantifying them whenever possible.

As an attacker, you must actively engage your curiosity: organize and analyze what you see. Although we all want to type queries into Google, hopefully getting an answer that aids progression in an engagement quickly, we should all be able to synthesize and interpret the material we find ourselves emersed in. This is an essential capacity needed to navigate attack life cycles and become a brilliant attacker. You might want to Google the exit points for a building, but if you saw a line of employees to the side of the building as you pulled into the parking lot, you could then infer that an exit (or entrance) is close to it.

A high capacity for observation will also allow for the detecting of patterns. Combining that with your experience is what allows you to predict what happens next, which is another important skill as an attacker. For instance, knowing that the security guards' shifts cross over at 7 a.m. allows you to predict the best entry times (between 6:55 a.m. and 7:05 a.m.), the best exit times, and, if burned by one, when the best time to try again. It also brings into play mental agility once more; you might have intel that had led you to believe one thing, like the back entrance is to the back left of the building, only to get there and see a much better ingress opportunity.

Think of it like learning to drive: you get the mechanics of driving down, but actually reading the road is what keeps you safe. You start to understand typical road patterns and on-road etiquette. The more you observe of the world and people, the better you become at detecting patterns. Subsequently, you get better at predicting what will happen next and, invariably, the better attacker you will become.

Lastly, ordinary members of the public, and indeed the typical workforce, use observation to collect information and then move on; AMs urges you to return to observing again and again, engaging in the cycle of observing, recording, testing, and analyzing many times over. It's a lot more work than just looking, but it will help you hone attacker offensives and build intuition for those times when reasoning is too costly.

Tying It All Together

Tversky and Kahneman did not suggest that every judgment we make is made intuitively or via heuristics; they theorized, and arguably confirmed, we have a strong tendency to use intuitive processes to make many judgments. Kahneman claimed judgments are made from two different systems. One is intuition, regarded as quick, automatic, and implicit. It uses associated strengths to arrive at solutions. The second system is reasoning, considered to be exacting and deliberately controlled. If no intuitive response is accessible, then reason will be used to arrive at judgment. Steven Sloman, professor of cognitive, linguistic, and psychological sciences at Brown University, once stated that the systems work hand in hand as "two experts who are working cooperatively to compute sensible answers." You can find more on Sloman in the notes section.

No matter how you train your brain and what happens in any one isolated incident, this observation and analyzation process allows you to pay more attention and witness more of the world. The real challenge is deciding what to explore in observation and what to disregard. To practice, you might choose to observe your immediate surroundings each day—people, too—letting your brain note all the small things you rarely take into consideration and studying them with a renewed sense of curiosity.

There is one other key to observation: how you will be observed as an attacker. You now know as much as I do about how the brain observes its surroundings. You should be able to use this knowledge against your targets. The best analogy I have involves magic. Magicians don't actually make things disappear or conjure changes out of thin air. Instead, they engage in actions that *misdirect* our attention. As an attacker, in phishes, in vishes, and when attacking in person—and this applies to pentesters, too—there is a similar situation at play: you are creating an illusion, which ultimately is your pretext, that redirects the target's attention. You want them to observe the illusion you are presenting, the details you have thought out, and the narrative you're painting for them. You are using their narrow field of observational capacity against them. I will cover this topic further in Chapter 8, "Attack Strategy."

Critical and Nonlinear Thinking

Critical thinking is a rich concept, but because of this, its operational definitions don't yet exist in a concise or cohesive way in literature. It has a definition, of course, but just saying that it is the ability to "use reasoning, applied logic, and to make judgments" is lacking, more so in the context of AMs. This definition, or any slight variation of it, probably won't serve us in taking critical thinking from the abstract into our arsenal. Critical thinking has also become a recognized construct in philosophy, education, psychology, and professional services. Unfortunately, its existence in those fields only serves to more greatly fragment what are considered to be its core functions. But as an attacker, you must have a working knowledge of critical thinking and know how it pertains to your specific field. Information processing is where critical thinking and AMs meet. Information is the lifeblood of the attack; using reason and logic against that information is often all that stands between you and success in an attacker situation. Critical thinking has to go hand-in-hand with mental agility, which is the ability to apply information successfully to your circumstances and objective.

To successfully understand critical thinking as it pertains to you as an attacker, let's return to our chess model. In chess, visual memory, attention span, and the capacity to predict and anticipate consequences are used to evaluate alternatives. That all sounds a bit fancy if you don't play or understand chess, but ultimately it boils down to this: all of that is demanded from each player because of the objective of chess. The name of the game is to checkmate the opponent, leaving them no legal way to remove their king from attack. The same is true when predicting and executing an attack: you must be able to think through your moves and their possible consequences (ensuring you're keeping the end in mind); you will have to be able to maneuver through the conditions set out for you, too (the scope). Just like the objective in chess, you use your objective in the attack to drive your decision-making at all times, aiming to checkmate the target, although typically without them knowing. And never leave yourself at risk, which is most often achieved with a solid pretext.

Sometimes you will have to make rapid decisions where extensive critical thinking is not an option. Other times, you will have weeks or even months to apply critical thinking skills. Critical thinking is an important part of performance. Mentally manipulating information to make effective decisions requires two things: the first is information; the second is the ability to evaluate it and arrive at a decision or result. This makes thinking critically seem like it's just the simple processing of information (found or given) and arriving at a conclusion, and I suppose that covers a big chunk of it. In any case, critical thinking is, to me, ultimately how you as an attacker judge something. It is you who assigns weight to the items you are judging. Robert Ennis, one of the leading researchers on critical thinking, believes critical thinking to be "reasonable, reflective thinking that is aimed at deciding what to believe or what to do."

Deciding what to do as an attacker has two parts. First, you have to know why you're doing what you're doing (or trying to do), which is law one of the mindset. Then you have to decide how best to achieve that end state or goal. So, critical thinking is applicable whenever you're trying to decide what to believe or what to do. Thinking critically about a question or problem is likely to lead to the right answer or solution. By thinking critically, you increase your chances that your beliefs will be true and your actions effective. As David A. Hunter says in *A Practical Guide to Critical Thinking* (Wiley, 2nd edition, 2014), "Thinking critically may not guarantee that you get the right answer; but a good case can be made that unless you think critically you will get the right answer only by luck, and relying on luck is not a wise policy." Both Hunter and I are in agreement about the following, too: critical thinking has more significance and substance than just being close to truth. Critical thinking is also freedom. Making up your own mind about any action is essential in every aspect of life and in every aspect of being an ethical attacker.

Here is another high-value benefit of critical thinking: there are times when you find or receive information that is either incomplete or unreliable. Evaluating its quality becomes paramount for competent decision-making. This happens in the OSINT phase of a job and in real time as you enter an environment.

The popular rehashing of Helmuth von Moltke the Elder's concept states that "No plan survives contact with the enemy." Believing this to be true, then critical thinking in the moment is more important than critical thinking in planning. In other words, engagements rarely occur in accordance with the original plan. To be clear, this isn't me advocating on behalf of critical thinking being punted in the primary stages of an engagement; rather it's the opinion that both matter—thinking critically in terms of the plan and critical thinking in terms of pivoting. In other words, in-the-moment critical thinking will matter in any case; critical thinking in planning will only matter if it all goes to plan. It. Rarely. Goes. To. Plan.

It is of the utmost importance to note that critical thinking in physics is different from critical thinking in design or security. The standards and methods differ from one discipline to the next, but there is a fundamental essence of critical thinking that remains the same across all disciplines: you're using reasoning above all else to arrive at your outcome.

Vector vs. Arc

Being able to think through information and taking it in order to analyze it is a skill in which the process is invisible, but for which the outcome is astoundingly valuable and often seen by everyone. This is critical thinking: an invisible process with a detectable outcome.

Critical thinking, for me, goes like this, whether I'm pressed for time or sitting with an abundance of it: I fast-forward to the end goal (spoiler alert: I live for law one). For clarity, that end goal might be just a building block of the overall objective (the vector), like getting into an elevator in a secured building. But it also might be the core objective of the attack (the arc). This is vector versus arc, and both exist in tandem as you are actively attacking a target. You care about the main objective, and you are always working toward it, but you may have to break it down into smaller chunks to achieve it. Knowing both exist and having each matter to you simultaneously will help steer you to short-term *and* long-term success, even if the two aren't aligned completely at all times—like getting out of an elevator on the 35th floor when you need to be on the 38th in a rather secure building.

There is another school of thought that considers critical thinking as the ability to scan the environment and create solutions for complex problems or barriers. Pushing both of these philosophies together is probably the closest to a well-rounded description as is possible to get of critical thinking in conjunction with AMs. Smashed together as such, critical thinking can be thought of as the ability to identify a problem and solve it using logic and creative reasoning. Critical thinking is the intersection of visual memory, attention span, and the prediction of consequences coming together to drive decision-making.

Rounding off this concept of vector versus arc or short-term versus long-term actions and goals, you can think of it like this: similar to seeing the situation from a bird's eye view instead of a path, the arc is the whole picture. The vector is a step to get there. The arc is the focus on the outcome; the vector is the shorter steps to get there. Both are needed to get the job done.

Education and Critical Thinking

Critical thinking, defined as the intersection of visual memory, attention span, and the prediction of consequences coming together to drive decision-making, is lacking in today's world, possibly because information is so readily available to the general population without much need or motivation to check whether it's valid. The same is true of students in large part because of how the education system is set up. Academically, critical thinking as a skill is deficient because education in nearly all forms traditionally relies on the collection of content knowledge. This approach neglects to teach the reasoning skills that can process such knowledge. In short, education and training may not have kept up with changes in skill demand for today's society where problem solving and analysis can often outplay status quo beliefs. Your job as an attacker isn't to collect information—your job is to process it, weaponize it, and leverage it.

Workplace Critical Thinking

This brings us to the overlapping topic of critical thinking in the professional workplace. "Critical thought" is—annoyingly—a trending buzzword in workplaces the world over at the moment. The concept of it is fashionable and desirable in professional offices but almost certainly being conducted in the antithesis of its core role; being told to critically think to reach some arbitrary conclusion under the guise of critical thought by your superiors, teammates, or any other faction within your working environment is the great *suppressor* of critical thinking. What you are being told to do is perform a culturally subjective analysis. I am against this in its entirety. If you have gotten into the habit of this and think that your critical thought should lead you to the same conclusions as those of your peers or coworkers, you may have to work to shed this habit. Organizations can thrive through this sort of cultural shift.

Company culture is a large talking point. Culture is not something that can be designed, per se. A company's culture is the byproduct of consistent behavior; it is what a company's employees (of all levels) *do* consistently. It is not what is written in the company's handbook nor what is touted through the intranet or at staff meetings. It is, simply, how employees interact, are treated, and behave most often. This is important to note if you are an "in-house" red teamer or attacker. You cannot and should not be expected to operate under the same cultural expectations and restraints as a regular employee. You should not be concerned with the company's culture at all unless it serves you in terms of social engineering and aligning your persona with what is typical within the company.

To me, the job of the employer is to give information and be willing to consider your evaluation of it. Your job is to present your analytical findings in a professional way and to take critical feedback that definitively exposes holes in your thinking. All workplaces should foster critical thinking abilities in this way, because alternative thought has the potential to be the greatest defender in environments where individuals, facilities, and critical infrastructure face a heightened risk of attack or downfall due to outdated methodology and ideology.

Self-branded, useful critical thought can make you valuable to those who want to hire you: you do not think like them culturally; you are not predictable because of the organization you work for.

Critical Thinking and Other Psychological Constructs

To get to the bottom of critical thinking and how to use it as an attacker, you might find it helpful to conclude whether you are an episodic or dispositional critical thinker. *Episodic* is a state or process that's limited in time; *dispositional* critical thinking is a tendency to behave in certain ways most of the time. In any case, the same skills are required, but for those of you who identify as an episodic critical thinker, a prompt may be necessary to kick you into gear.

Critical Thinking Skills

Critical thinking is heavily related to problem solving, but that is not its only function. Critical thinking is a process that serves many other cognitive tasks such as inference making, evaluation of information and sources, and reasoning. Also, critical thinking has some connection with heuristic analysis. In cases where there is poverty of information or something is completely novel, critical thought may defer to heuristics. Critical thinking skills also involve the unbiased extraction of information from text done through the dynamic process of questioning and reasoning. Critical thinking also encompasses forming and testing hypotheses. The skills have been categorized into four types: interpreting, reasoning, assessing, and monitoring. One of the greatest uses of critical thought is decision-making.

Critical thought serves decision-making because it allows the evaluation of information. In the applied setting of AMs decision-making, forming models of your own actions in regard to target decision-making, then using those models to develop proactive, predictive, and reaction plans, can improve the accuracy of your assessment of engagement situations. This speaks to the mental model of chess, which we have discussed throughout. In performing this game of mental chess in your mind, making up scenarios based on possible happenings and reactions you might come across on an engagement will help build mental agility and, over time, improve their accuracy.

Critical thinking will eventually turn into a type of intuition. After all, critical thinking is using analysis and evaluation to make judgments, which is the purpose of your intuition. The key difference is that critical thinking is the objective analysis and evaluation to form a judgment, whereas intuition bypasses that, at least on a conscious level.

Nonlinear Thinking

Intuition is not based on linear, logical thinking. It is a momentary gut feeling instead of a logical choice. Logic is encompassed within critical thinking, which we have talked about at length now. Problem solving is also a part of critical thinking. In the field, you will come up against a great many problems, and you cannot force your way through or out of everything. There is another, and at times functionally overlapping, type of thinking that can greatly aid problem solving: nonlinear thinking. A nonlinear thinker tends to have a multitude of separate thoughts that somehow interrelate—a sort of ability to free associate. They can find connections between seemingly unrelated thoughts and things, then present them as if they are completely logical. This type of thinking can be extremely useful and can greatly engender creativity.

In a strategy meeting or planning meeting with your team, brainstorming sessions that result in everyone pouring out their ideas, fueling yet more ideas and solving the problem, is an example of nonlinear thinking. Asking open-ended questions in an attempt to solve a problem is another example. In the field, asking targets of the environment a question like "I'm new here. How do you request a new badge?" is an example of nonlinear thinking. You might not need one, but you will be able to pivot in any case.

By contrast, the thoughts of a linear thinker tend to form a line, meaning that at any given time, it is obviously that one thought leads to the next, then to the next, and so on. The implicit assumption in referring to somebody as a linear thinker is that the thought process is easy to understand, and that the conclusions seem logically sound. There are pros and cons to both. For instance, linear thinkers are good in subjects that work on cause and effect. But there is a danger in relying too heavily on logic. The danger is related to where you start. Once a starting point is chosen, there are reduced numbers of logical conclusions to any given problem. There is immense beauty in logic; it allows us to reach an answer from a given starting point. Unfortunately, relying on one starting point can prevent you from finding a more beneficial answer in some situations.

For example, imagine trying to get over a nine-foot smooth wall with no ladder or ropes. You might try many ways: running, jumping, and aiming to catch the top of the wall. But what if you were so seized by that logic and starting point that you forgot you could probably dig under it? This example is simplistic, but it features what is often a linear thinker's downfall: the inability to be agile once a direction is set. Logic says that you have been tasked with getting over the wall (the starting point), and it pushes you to do so with all the ways you can think of. Rigid thinking isn't always a bad thing, but it shouldn't be used at the expense of creative thinking for long if the results aren't in your favor.

The pros of nonlinear thinkers are that they are good at grasping abstract subjects and, importantly, creatively solving a problem, something often required on an engagement. As an example, on a job in 2020 for Social-Engineer LLC, my team successfully snuck a petite-sized human down a trash chute and into the kitchens, which were one wall away from the SOC, which was accessible through the roof of the chef's bathrooms. I picked up on the scent of that route by pushing my phone camera through the bin hole and filming the inside. The assumption was that they must go somewhere. Upon reviewing the footage, we could see light at the other side of the bin encasement. We had tried to get in the door for hours before that point. Logically it made sense. It was the only door we could get to at that point; we had tools to get past the lock, but we couldn't. We kept trying, though, because we did not want to give up. Trash chutes are unrelated in our minds as access to a room. Nonlinear thinking banishes those restrictive thoughts.

Tying Them Together

Critical thinking is an important part of performance. Mentally manipulating information to make effective decisions is possible with access to information and accurate evaluation of it.

As the name suggests, and as we have seen, nonlinear thinking is not thinking along straight lines or in a sequential manner.

In nonlinear thinking, we make connections among unrelated concepts or ideas. Nonlinear thinking can expand in multiple directions, rather than in one direction, and count on the probability that there are multiple starting points from which to apply logic to a problem in order to solve it. Nonlinear thinking is less constrictive but not wholly less structured.

All of these types of thinking are important. AMs relies on thinking outside the bounds of what is average. The real power is in knowing when to use each of them or when a combination of types might be used. For an attacker, logic is best used when you have time and information. Reasoning should be used wherever you can employ it—either creatively or logically.

Summary

- None of us can observe everything closely, so we have to aim to select the significant.
- To observe in an effective and efficient manner, you have to train your attention as an attacker, learning to focus on relevant features and disregard those that are less salient.
- Intuition is not, contrary to popular belief, something we are born with. Observation and experience help inform intuition.
- Lie detection myths flood the social arena of pseudoscience, but reading people, expressions, and environments stem from the general act of observation. The more you do it, the better you'll get at it.
- Critical thinking dictates that, if need be, any solution can be changed to better fit the current situation and is an important part of performance.
- Being able to evaluate information and arrive at a decision that advances or benefits the situation is the desired outcome of critical thinking.
- Being able to use heuristics when critical thinking fails you or cannot be used is often the difference between fast failure or continued success.

- No matter what, problem solving is a required skill. Most of us can often get there with some measure of critical thinking, intuition, or heuristics.
- Nonlinear thinking is the key component of this ability. However, nonlinear thinking is not akin to chaotic thinking. It's an ability so solve problems from multiple starting points and from different directions.
- Finally, critical thinking and intuition can work in tandem with nonlinear thinking.

Key Message

Sufficient observation to arrive at an outcome is key to a successful attack. One of the challenges you'll face as an attacker is to observe in a way that is not conducive to everyday living. To do this, you must learn how to parse visual and auditory information efficiently.

Critical thinking is purposeful and deliberate cognitive processing and serves other higher-level tasks such as decision-making. You must do so without the burden of cultural pressure from your workplace or peers.

Nonlinear thinking does not equal chaos. An attacker's mind is geared toward precision. Understanding it in this way will pay dividends.

All types of thinking eventually intertwine with mental agility, which is a fancy way of saying "adapting" and means that you take the information and successfully apply it to your circumstances or objective.

Chapter 7

Information Processing in Practice

T o talk about how to process information, we first have to talk about information itself. When I talk about information, I mean facts, figures, knowledge, details, evidence, findings, insight, and intelligence. Finding these sorts of information types is most commonly achieved through Open-Source Intelligence, often referred to as OSINT.

OSINT means many things to many people. Its official definition is the practice of collecting information from published or otherwise publicly available sources. These sources include newspapers, broadcasts, official government documents made available to the public, and most often OSINT is reduced to information available online. Of course, there are other ways to gain information that are either not listed in this book or illegal.

However, just having heaps of information on a company or its asset, as examples, is not the final step in your intelligence gathering endeavors. You, as the collector, must be able to scrutinize information for its value in relation to the objective set out.

Now we can talk about information processing. Information processing is how you perceive, analyze, manipulate, use, and remember information. Processing information is as critical as collecting it, and it must be processed strictly through the use of the laws of the mindset, which are:

1. Start with the end in mind
2. Weaponizing information for the good of the objective
3. Pretext can never be broken*
4. Every action taken must be in support of the objective

If you are too early in the process to have a pretext, this takes the form of being in your attacker mindset—being curious, persistent, and acting on behalf of the other three laws.

In this chapter, we look at what reconnaissance is and, broadly speaking, how it is performed. But most importantly, we look at how to make information agile and the power behind your attacks.

Reconnaissance

Good reconnaissance is critical to great ethical hacking and attacking. Reconnaissance is generally the bulk of an attack, which explains why using the four laws of AMs in conjunction is so critical. All the information you gather has to further your attainment of the objective and help you with law 3 (don't break pretext) in particular.

We can then further reduce part of AMs's second law of gathering, weaponizing, and leveraging information to a type of self-discipline. Given that your mind as an ethical attacker (EA) most often is curious, it's easy to commit to the belief that persistence goes hand in hand with curiosity. Self-discipline will keep you safe from the epic time sink of a rabbit hole that leads nowhere. For example, if your job is to get into a data center whose lock cannot be picked, that is guarded by armed guards, that employs 24/7 surveillance, and that is also manned by drones, you will spend time looking in the most obvious places—shift switch times, distraction techniques, and drone information—in an attempt to replicate the design and get your own bird's-eye view, ways to jam the signal, and ways to take over or stop the other surveillance feeds. But you might also look to the sewers, which are most likely not monitored. Cases like this are currently rare but will become increasingly common as the future unfolds.

In a more likely scenario, if the objective is to gather personal data on an executive so that you can simulate an attack directly on them—now a common occurrence in this industry—you will spend a disproportionate amount of time looking for personal rather than professional items. You wouldn't forgo looking at the target's professional life altogether, but you would let it lead you, when and where possible, back to their personal life. If you had to form an attack on an executive based on their professional life only, you would not follow any leads back to their professional life that you couldn't link back to them personally. For example, you would link them only to peers with whom you could prove they had an external relationship.

As an example, I will use myself. I will not use dorks (AKA "Google Hacks") or too many specialized search terms, but if you are interested, please refer to the notes section on the website where you can catch up on more reading and brush up on more OSINT skills, including dorks. I will move through the example quickly, because it's not an exhaustive show-and-tell of how to search, but merely an illustration of how to stay somewhat disciplined and what information is worth gathering, superficially.

If an attacker were given me as a target to attack, and the scope cleared that attacker to phish, vish, or socially engineer me in person, only using personal information, I suspect it would go something like this:

Google search: Maxie Reynolds

I clicked the first five links on the first page of Google results, as seen in Figure 7.1 and one from the second page of results, as shown in Figure 7.2.

Figure 7.1   First page of google search results

By clicking the third search result (`twitter.com`) shown on the first page of results, I was able to find that I have a dog and a Mac-Book Pro, as shown in Figure 7.3.

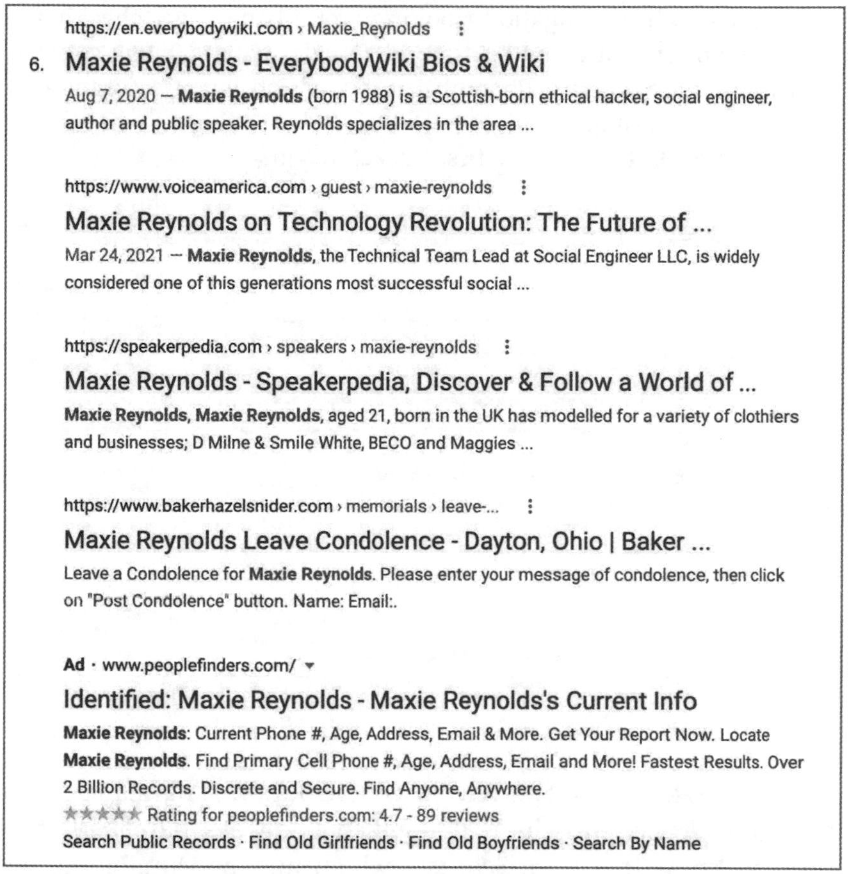

https://en.everybodywiki.com › Maxie_Reynolds   ⋮

6. **Maxie Reynolds - EverybodyWiki Bios & Wiki**

Aug 7, 2020 — **Maxie Reynolds** (born 1988) is a Scottish-born ethical hacker, social engineer, author and public speaker. Reynolds specializes in the area ...

https://www.voiceamerica.com › guest › maxie-reynolds   ⋮

Maxie Reynolds on Technology Revolution: The Future of ...

Mar 24, 2021 — **Maxie Reynolds**, the Technical Team Lead at Social Engineer LLC, is widely considered one of this generations most successful social ...

https://speakerpedia.com › speakers › maxie-reynolds   ⋮

Maxie Reynolds - Speakerpedia, Discover & Follow a World of ...

Maxie Reynolds, Maxie Reynolds, aged 21, born in the UK has modelled for a variety of clothiers and businesses; D Milne & Smile White, BECO and Maggies ...

https://www.bakerhazelsnider.com › memorials › leave-...   ⋮

Maxie Reynolds Leave Condolence - Dayton, Ohio | Baker ...

Leave a Condolence for **Maxie Reynolds**. Please enter your message of condolence, then click on "Post Condolence" button. Name: Email:.

Ad · www.peoplefinders.com/ ▼

Identified: Maxie Reynolds - Maxie Reynolds's Current Info

Maxie Reynolds: Current Phone #, Age, Address, Email & More. Get Your Report Now. Locate **Maxie Reynolds**. Find Primary Cell Phone #, Age, Address, Email and More! Fastest Results. Over 2 Billion Records. Discrete and Secure. Find Anyone, Anywhere.

★★★★★ Rating for peoplefinders.com: 4.7 - 89 reviews

Search Public Records · Find Old Girlfriends · Find Old Boyfriends · Search By Name

Figure 7.2   Second page of Google search results

Figure 7.3   First Twitter find

With enough investigation (looking around the page, checking the comments, or using brute-force Google searches), you could work out the dog is a Pharaoh Hound, which is not a common dog. That information might be valuable, depending on what else you can find. It goes in the first bucket: recon.

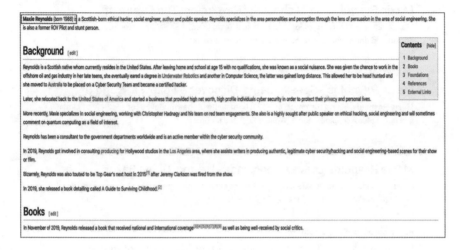

Maxie Reynolds (born 1988) is a Scottish-born ethical hacker, social engineer, author and public speaker. Reynolds specializes in the area personalities and perception through the lens of persuasion in the area of social engineering. She is also a former ROV Pilot and stunt person.

Background [edit]

Reynolds is a Scottish native whom currently resides in the United States. After leaving home and school at age 15 with no qualifications, she was known as a social nuisance. She was given the chance to work in the offshore oil and gas industry in her late teens, she eventually eared a degree in Underwater Robotics and another in Computer Science, the latter was gained long distance. This allowed her to be head hunted and she moved to Australia to be placed on a Cyber Security Team and became a certified hacker.

Later, she relocated back to the United States of America and started a business that provided high net worth, high profile individuals cyber security in order to protect their privacy and personal lives.

More recently, Maxie specializes in social engineering, working with Christopher Hadnagy and his team on red team engagements. She also is a highly sought after public speaker on ethical hacking, social engineering and will sometimes comment on quantum computing as a field of interest.

Reynolds has been a consultant to the government departments worldwide and is an active member within the cyber security community.

In 2019, Reynolds got involved in consulting producing for Hollywood studios in the Los Angeles area, where she assists writers in producing authentic, legitimate cyber security/hacking and social engineering-based scenes for their show or film.

Bizarrely, Reynolds was also touted to be Top Gear's next host in 2015[1] after Jeremy Clarkson was fired from the show.

In 2019, she released a book detailing called A Guide to Surviving Childhood.[2]

Books [edit]

In November of 2019, Reynolds released a book that received national and international coverage[3][4][5][6][7][8][9] as well as being well-received by social critics.

Contents [hide]
1 Background
2 Books
3 Foundations
4 References
5 External Links

Figure 7.4   Further information on Target

Figure 7.4, also shows relevant information. Thanks to it, you now know I was born in 1988—which is always handy information. You know that I am Scottish, which may be valuable used in conjunction with other information. You know that I wrote another book (Would I accept an interview request for this book? Would I accept it via email?) and that I have at least one loose tie to the BBC in Britain. You also know I live in the Los Angeles area (good info for all sorts of attacks). From here you could check Facebook or Instagram to see if you could narrow down an address. If that proved futile, you could check other photos for famous landmarks in the frame and pinpoint my typical movements and even my location.

Case in point, I often run OSINT challenges on my own social media as is seen in Figure 7.5. Recently I posted this photo:

Figure 7.5   OSINT challenge example from social media

From that photo, some 160 people were able to pinpoint my location.

Back to finding an attack avenue: In the case of my workplace's website at the time of writing, as seen in Figure 7.6, which I could then use to reverse search, getting an app or service to do a fair amount of heavy lifting for me. Yandex is especially helpful. Yandex is the most-used search engine in Russia and, in my opinion, is by far the best reverse image search engine, with a powerful ability to recognize faces, landscapes, and objects. At the time of writing, however, there were no valuable leads found with Yandex. So I pivot back to my original find—the page I got the image from.

This is an example of a professional page giving personal information. It also lets you know I have ties to the SANS Institute (Phish from SANS?) and that I used to work offshore with underwater robots (Would I answer a phish from a university or science, technology, engineering and mathematics [STEM] course asking me to take part in an initiative for kids regarding underwater robots? I probably would).

Figure 7.6   Example of professional finding giving usable personal inforamtion

Further investigation into the book could lead you in a thousand different ways. You could contact me looking to do a follow-up for a podcast. For a vish, you could pretend to be a reporter, aiming to get information for an article. You could ask me to verify myself, which isn't the strongest move, but it might work. By getting some security questions out of me, you might gain some valuable information. You could also use this information to approach me as an aspiring author looking for tips (which wouldn't be believable—I'd know you hadn't read the book) and ask for my address to send a copy of your own manuscript to. The podcast's description mentions that I've dabbled in stunts; this is another avenue to explore. You can make certain inferences: I must be pretty fit or must have been quite fit at that time. Was there a specific place I was training? A few searches would tell you that I trained at a popular private gym in West Hollywood. There's another avenue to explore.

You could use this information in a number of ways against me. Picking one would depend on the objective, whether it is to find details, discover sensitive information, or perform a long attack.

So, in under two minutes, with one search and by scanning a few finds, you could've identified three potential phishes and a good amount of detail: my year of birth, nationality, computer type, and ties to large establishments. Most of these, especially the last, have good jumping-off points in which more information could be searched for and tied back to the objective.

This is a light take on what AMs is capable of; it's thought-provoking for the newest members of the community or those who are just interested, and it's probably too superficial for the veterans among you. However, the purpose of the search is not to showcase deft skills that you can learn and perform for your own work; instead, it is intended to show that information can be found anywhere, and nothing precludes a result from being useful—only the objective does.

It's your self-discipline as an EA that keeps you from going down the rabbit hole of "Technical Team Lead" or searching for more information on my consulting with government agencies, because it doesn't follow the objective and you may not have ruled out the possibility of more information that better fits your objective. Only when all else had failed would you resort to those sorts of searches in case there was a hint of a personal artifact.

We return to thinking when there's no hard data. We can make inferences when information lacks definite answers. For example, imagine you could find no personal information on me: I had no social media, not even a LinkedIn profile. All you could find was that I worked for Social-Engineer LLC, but using profession to attack me was against the rules. You could piece together some other information based on my profile. For instance, it looks as though I lived in Australia. A quick search of "Maxie Reynolds Australia" (without quotes) yields the following results as shown in Figure 7.7:

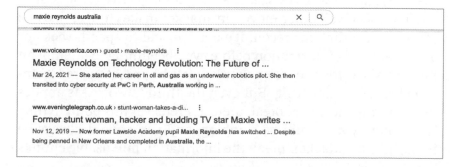

Figure 7.7   Results of a simple search

By clicking in the first link shown in Figure 7.7, you would find that I lived in Perth, Australia, as shown in Figure 7.8. That's noteworthy. You could also infer this by combing through my LinkedIn connections.

I studied at Cranfield University. You could go down that rabbit hole looking to see if they have alumni or speaker events. Reverse-searching the image from the site on Yandex, Tin Eye, or even Google reverse image search will also yield some interesting results.

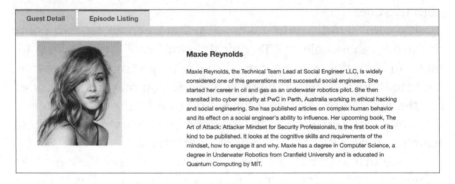

Figure 7.8

Honing back in on the original book result, you could find I was promoting it at somepoint and, as a result, was on multiple podcasts and was part of multiple interviews.

You will often have to break information down into bite-sized chunks and probe deeper.

As the fourth law of AMs teaches you, the objective is the central point from which all other moves an attacker makes hinge. In cases when you have time for recon, it's not unusual to spend weeks or months gathering information before even beginning to attempt an exploit, as is true for network pen testing, web app testing, red teaming, and social engineering. But even the third law of AMs applies here, the pre-game: never break pretext. Pretext at this point in time refers to how you should be thinking, and you should always be thinking like an attacker. Break the information into usable chunks to gain more information. Always keep in mind that the attacker mindset is nothing more than taking information in and applying it to an objective. Information is everywhere. Gathering it and applying it through the lens of your objective is the intersection of having an attacker's mindset and using it.

Recon: Passive

In network pen testing, passive recon does not rely on direct interactions with a target system and is therefore far easier to hide. This technique involves eavesdropping on a network in order to gain intelligence, with pentesters analyzing the target company for partner and employee details, technology in use, and so forth. This technique isn't too dissimilar to how passive recon is executed in social engineering and red teaming.

Passive reconnaissance is when you gather information about the target without actually "touching" the target. In social engineering, passive reconnaissance would include searches like the one I just described and move all the way to the other end of the spectrum, whereby you would comb accounts and movements, piecing together the life—or at least one aspect—of the target's life. There are no direct interactions with the target when you are passively gathering information. This includes using accounts that do not belong to you and attempting to stay anonymous online. There are many reasons people want to remain anonymous online. Some people want their personal details to remain unknown; some people want to voice opinions that would perhaps negatively affect them if they were to voice that opinion freely as themselves. Whatever the reason, anonymity online is important to many people for many reasons.

Working with the Innocent Lives Foundation, an organization that attempts to bring pedophiles to justice, and the National Child Protection Task force, which focuses on time-sensitive cases around human trafficking, child exploitation, and missing persons cases, we often use passive information-gathering techniques. Here, staying anonymous is of the utmost importance. Virtual private networks

(VPNs) and virtual private desktops are employed; using my own accounts would be catastrophic. I apply the same principles to my day job at times. Passive recon means not touching the target, but it also should mean not leaving a trace. I like to take the opportunity to act like a malicious attacker whenever I can, and a good attacker rarely wants to leave a trail of evidence pointing toward themselves. This means employing a sock puppet, or sock, account. It's a pseudonym or persona used for some sort of deception. Some sock accounts are developed and hard to spot. Others are pretty transparent, as if not trying at all to be inconspicuous. But a sock account doesn't have to leave someone believing it's real; it just has to stop them from finding out who is behind it. There is much you must consider when trying to navigate the Internet anonymously.

Creating these covert accounts is indeed becoming harder on many popular platforms, such as Facebook and Instagram. However, there are some loopholes left, but possibly not for long, so my advice is to create as many sock accounts as you can now.

My least favorite platform to create a new account on is Facebook. You will be prompted for a cell number, among other information) and VOIP numbers will not work. The best way around this, at the time of writing, is to clear your cache and log out of all accounts; connect to Facebook without the aid of any IP address masking service employed, but instead of surfing to `facebook.com`, instead head to `m.facebook.com` (the mobile version of the site) and create an account from there. As we browse the Internet, we "leak" information. When it is vital that we remain anonymous, there are certain things we must hide:

- External IP
- Internal IP
- MAC address
- Internet service provider (ISP)
- General geolocation
- Operating system
- Browser type and version
- Language we use

There are many steps you can take: you can employ sock accounts, turn off tracking, change privacy preferences, make use of VPNs, turn off logging, or buy servers and services around the world with prepaid credit cards or Bitcoin, for example.

You must also make sure that, even when you're on a VPN, your computer doesn't contact your normal DNS server. Your ISP could leak your host IP if they deploy a proxy to redirect your traffic back to their DNS server. Newer Windows operating systems have a built-in feature called smart multihomed name resolution, which makes it very easy for DNS leaks to appear. To protect yourself you can choose among a multitude of solutions, but they must be applied against the corresponding issue. For example, if your ISP deployed a transparent proxy, its job is to hide in plain sight and intercept your traffic, leading DNS requests back to the ISP's DNS server. The only way to avoid this leak is to block the proxy on your VPN's side.

You may employ your own proxy. A proxy is a widely used solution to attempt anonymity online. It is meant to hide the IP address. Various proxy solutions are available, such as web proxies and software proxies. Basically, a proxy will redirect traffic to the destination from some other IP address.

Interestingly, a search engine can be used as a proxy. Google has a feature called Google Translate that allows users to read web content in many other languages. By browsing a site through this feature, you can use Google as a proxy. This is often not applicable to day-to-day OSINT investigations, but it's worth mentioning for those rare occasions where you'd find it helpful.

Finally, for OSINT operations, I choose Firefox. It is a browser that has enhanced security and a feature called "add-ons" that are often critical in making investigations easier—add-ons like Firefox containers that isolate your searches. These containers are similar to normal tabs, except that each one has access to a separate piece of the browser's storage which means you can be logged into multiple Facebook accounts at once, as an example, because data between the tabs is not shared. The proxy you choose will have to fit your requirements. Check out the notes section of this book for further information. In addition, passive reconnaissance can include DNS and SNMP mining, dumpster diving, a drive-by of the premises, use of social media such as Facebook and LinkedIn, and of course, Google dorking, among other techniques. When considering a drive-by of an organization, you should contemplate their security cameras and things like how your vehicle fits into the area. If you are going to Detroit, Michigan, and into a low-income area, be sure you don't rent a luxury car. Things like this are seemingly inconsequential, but they might matter in the long run. Other things that matter in passive recon are how you are dressed, when you show up, and how many of your team members show up.

Additionally, when creating a covert account to remain anonymous or when you're impersonating someone, you must use a *clean* email address for your accounts. Every social media network requests that you provide an email address in order to sign up for an account, and using one that's already an established email address leaves you at risk of being tracked. Michael Bazzell talks about this throughout his 8th edition of *Open Source Intelligence Techniques: Resources for Searching and Analyzing Online Information* (independently published, 2021). In it, Bazzell notes his preference is to create a free email account at a provider like Fastmail (`fastmail.com`), a unique, established provider that does not require that you provide an established email address in order to set up a new email address. He also notes that these providers are "fairly off the radar" of bigger services like Facebook, and so undergo less scrutiny from them when looking for malicious activity.

Finally, I've discussed at length the degree to which information is the lifeblood of any operation. But it is learning how to weaponize and leverage that information that is the key to this mindset. Information is everywhere and can be valuable if your thought process can make it so. A great way to find lots of information quickly that your AMs can then parse and place into one of those three buckets I often talk about (recon, pretext, disregard) is through *meta searching*. Sending a request to a regular search engine means you are searching that engine's own database. A meta search will allow you to search multiple search engines all at once. Meta search engines send your queries to multiple data sources and aggregate the results. Mamma, Polymeta, and Carrot^2 are all solid examples. Carrot^2 is a cluster engine, meaning it takes the results it finds and (usually) categorizes them for you. Mediainfo is a utility that displays hidden metadata within a media file. ExifTool is an application for reading, writing, and editing meta information in a wide variety of files. It's easy to use from the command line and should not be overlooked.

Recon: Active

Active reconnaissance is information gathered about the target by actually interacting with them or, as we often refer to it, "touching" them. The results of active recon are often much more specific and reliable but also much riskier to achieve. For example, vishing a target within an organization is the equivalent of sniper-style information gathering. If you miss and the target alerts the organization of the shot you took, you risk blowing the operation up or making it harder for yourself later. The same is true if you send a phish to a target and the network catches it or if you aim to socially engineer someone into giving you pointed and valuable information, but they become suspicious—you may make it harder for yourself later. Any time you send a packet to a site, your IP address is left behind; it's the same in person—you will almost always leave a trace.

There's much to think about with active recon. As another example, I would not vish a target directly prior to an in-person attack if I couldn't use an accent. I have a very strong and identifiable accent, and it could be too recognizable. I would use an accent to call, but only one that I was sure I was a natural at.

Many people shy away from active recon, but it has a great value that shouldn't be ignored because of the risk. Rather, the risk should be calculated and analyzed as a cost–benefit—what does it cost to perform, and what's the benefit if it goes right? But also, what's the cost to the operation of performing it unsuccessfully? There are always new, creative collection efforts and exploitation activities bringing data sources, but those efforts and activities can introduce new complexities, too. You have to be able to lend some amount of credence to your findings, especially if the attack hinges on their being true. As an example, finding that a target used Pricewater-houseCoopers as their accounting firm in 2015 by way of a leaked document is somewhat valuable. What would be more valuable is knowing that PwC is *still* the target's accounting firm. As an ethical attacker you can't call PwC to ask, because they aren't in scope, but you might be able to call your target company to inquire using the right pretext. In cases like these, active recon becomes valuable.

OSINT

The real backbone of recon, for most social engineering attacks, and a cornerstone for network attacks, too, is open source intelligence (OSINT). OSINT is intelligence drawn from material that is publicly available. The tools and capabilities you use are ever-changing and evolving. Because of the changing nature of publicly available information, the current period is widely considered to be the second generation of OSINT. Practitioners recognized that the rise of personal computing in the 1990s would change the face, and indeed function, of OSINT forever.

OSINT Over the Years

OSINT began as a defense-oriented enterprise. The Office of Strategic Services (OSS) was a wartime intelligence agency of the United States during World War II, and a predecessor to the Department of State's Bureau of Intelligence and Research (INR) and the Central Intelligence Agency (CIA).

In WWII, the OSS pored over obituaries in German regional newspapers, pursuing news of important Nazis, movements, equipment creation, and deployment. Images of new battleships, bomb craters, and aircraft were fastidiously gathered and, when assessed together, allowed the OSS to measure the state of its enemy, which is exactly how we use it, too.

It's remarkable how similar the OSS's behaviors are to modern-day OSINT investigation behaviors, notwithstanding computer usage. It's possible to argue that the roots of open source intelligence stretch back nearly a century. Moreover, you could argue that William Donovan's quote, made decades ago, in which he stated, "Even a regimented press will again and again betray their nation's interests to a painstaking observer," is truer today than ever.

Prior to fighting in World War I, Donovan went to Columbia Law School, where a young Franklin D. Roosevelt was among his classmates. After the war, Donovan had a successful career as an international lawyer, and scarcely missed out on becoming the US Attorney General. During the period between WWI and WWII, Donovan traveled the world as a lawyer, interacting with influential foreign figures and subsequently writing up reports for the US government. It was Donovan's connection to Roosevelt that led to the creation of an intelligence agency in the United States. And his quote still holds up today, among the billions of posts, uploads, shares, and likes, that individuals again and again give away valuable, actionable information to painstaking observers.

At the end of WWII, the Foreign Broadcast Information Service (FBIS) was taken over by the War Department on January 1, 1946. One year later, it was transferred to the CIA under the National Security Act of 1947. By then it was a systematic organization. From this time until the 1990s, the concerns of open source analysis were mainly the monitoring and translating of foreign-press sources.

There are important differences between the first generation of OSINT and the second (current) generation. With the first generation, the collection of material was the bulk of the effort. The FBIS operated 20 worldwide bureaus to allow it to physically collect material. The other function of OSINT at this time was the facilitation of trend analysis.

Today, open source intelligence is defined by the RAND Corporation as "publicly available information that has been discovered, determined to be of intelligence value, and disseminated by

a member of the IC [intelligence community]." https://www.rand.
org/content/dam/rand/pubs/research_reports/RR1900/RR1964/
RAND_RR1964.pdf. OSINT is information that can be accessed without
specialist skills or tools, although it can include sources only available to subscribers, such as newspaper content behind a paywall or
subscription journals. The CIA says that OSINT includes information gathered from the Internet, mass media, specialist journals and
research, photos, and geospatial information and social media.

Events such as the Iranian Green Revolution in 2009 illustrate how using fresh practices of social media data collection can
provide a real-time intelligence picture in an otherwise inacces-
sible environment. Sometime in 2009, Iran was on the brink of a
"Green Revolution"; many of its citizens were protesting against the
regime and millions of young Iranians took to the Internet to coor-
dinate their activities, share viral content, and encourage others to
join in the revolution. For the first time, the Internet was awash
with citizen information about a major political event. Internet
use in Iran skyrocketed, as did mobile phone subscriptions. During the first week of the protests approximately 60 percent of all
blog links posted on Twitter were about Iranian politics. Networks
like Twitter have played a great role in attracting people's attention
to this user-generated content. All of this meant that for the first
time, any individual with access could mine social networks for
intelligence-grade content. Although the protests were ultimately
fruitless, it is prudent to look back and regard the Green Revolution
as a seminal event in the history of open source intelligence and
indeed the pinnacle of second-generation OSINT.

Barely a year after the Green Revolution, revolutions spread
across the Arab world. The combination of public anger, smart-
phones, and social media rocked dictatorships across North Africa
and the Middle East. However, the CIA OSINT Center was unable
to predict the precise evolution of Internet-based social activism in
the Arab world, arguably because government intelligence was con-
sumed with collecting intelligence from the powerful elite.

However, in recent years the United States, United Kingdom, and others clearly have taken notice. According to

Cameron Colquhoun in an article on `bellingcat.com`, titled "A Brief History of Open Source Intelligence," published July 14, 2016 (`https://www.bellingcat.com/resources/articles/2016/07/14/a-brief-history-of-open-source-intelligence/`), the US military "destroyed an Islamic State bomb factory a mere 23 hours after a jihadi posted a selfie revealing the roof structure of the building, which is perhaps the most powerful example of the military using OSINT for targeted operations." In the private sector, you and I most likely and most often use intelligence for corporations that require a predatory eye on the information available on them. Ultimately, whether a civilian or otherwise, the realization that OSINT can make or break operations is a fundamental way of thinking.

Finally, as well as the challenge created by the sheer magnitude of information available, and the limited computing ability and other resources we have to parse in real time, government agencies, police and spies, and OSINT practitioners face the growing trend for users to livestream content. This presents very real challenges for all of us. Machine learning, virtual and augmented reality, and artificial intelligence will eventually transform OSINT into its third generation.

Intel Types

I feel it is prudent to also list in this section the types of intelligence, or intel, and some subcomponents. Again, you will have to go hunting for more information on each type to satisfy what information this book must skip over.

Perhaps lazily, I call it all *OSINT*, but that is not strictly true. Here are all the types of intel that are relevant currently and likely enduring, with broad descriptions:

- **Human intelligence** (HUMINT) is the collection of information from human sources. The collection can be done openly, such as a police officer interviewing someone, or it may be done through clandestine or covert means (spying).
- **Signals intelligence** (SIGINT) refers to electronic transmissions that can be collected by ships, planes, ground sites, or satellites.

Communications intelligence (COMINT) is a type of SIGINT and refers to the interception of communications between two parties.

- **Imagery intelligence** (IMINT) is sometimes also referred to as photo intelligence (PHOTINT).
- **Geospatial intelligence** (GEOINT) is the analysis and visual representation of security-related activities on the earth. It is produced through an integration of imagery, imagery intelligence, and geospatial information.
- **Open source intelligence** (OSINT) refers to a broad array of information and sources that are generally available, including information obtained from the media (newspapers, radio, television, etc.), professional and academic records (papers, conferences, professional associations, etc.), and public data (government reports, demographics, hearings, speeches, etc.).

One advantage of OSINT is its accessibility, although the sheer amount of available information can make it difficult to know what is of value.

Alternative Data in OSINT

There are four popular types of alternative data, which can be defined as data that is drawn from non-traditional sources. Alternative data is useful when used in conjunction with traditional data sources, like those we've already talked about throughout this book.

Web Scraping   This is the most widely used form of alternative data, according to research firm Greenwich Associates. Types of web-scraped data in high demand include job listings and employee-satisfaction rankings, which can offer clues to a company's growth prospects and internal activities.

Satellites and Aerial Surveillance   Satellite images can be used to count cars in parking lots, a potential source of insight into activity and peak periods. Satellite and other types of aerial surveillance data are best supplemented with other types of data able to provide more detailed estimates of actual foot traffic when it comes to gauging retail sales. Satellites are also used to track ships, monitor crops, and detect activity in ports and oil fields.

Sentiment Social media feeds, newsfeeds, corporate announcements, and other items are monitored and analyzed for clues to the sentiment of the company and its employees. Watching who in the company unfollows ex-employees on their social media gives insight into how the employee left. This is sometimes very useful information.

Financial Intelligence (FININT) Information about the financial capabilities of a target is gathered. Detecting financial transactions is a rich source of information. Even if you find out about a transaction weeks or months after, if it is big or important enough, it may not be out of the realm of what is normal for a company to communicate about, such as services, tax, and refunds.

Tech Intelligence (TECHINT)   Intelligence on equipment and material is gathered to assess the capabilities of the targets.

My last note on alternative data is controversial, only insofar as there is disagreement on whether or not FTP data is *alternative* or not. Either way, it is useful, so I don't want to get caught up in the taxonomy. FTP stands for File Transfer Protocol, and searching FTP servers is one of the most underutilized, underrated activities undertaken by investigators. There are simple Google dorks that exist that will allow you to perform a search. Most often I use "inurl:ftp –inurl (http | https) [company name]" without the quotation marks. Another option for searching for FTP servers is Global File Search (www.globalfilesearch.com).

Signal vs. Noise

The word *signal* is a representation of the patterns and meaning that are hiding in data that is transmitted. In electronics, signals must be separated from noise to be useful. In OSINT, it's no different; the signal is the information you should follow. The noise is the tidbits of information that will not be useful to you. In the age of big data, there's often more noise than ever when investigating a target and so more challenges in isolating the signals.

With that in mind, how do you go about filtering the signal from the noise? First of all, there's no "cheat"; you have to bear in mind—*always*—that no stone can go left unturned. The separation of signal from noise is often used in vetting the myriad sources available and evaluating them efficiently. There are categories that should be staples of your searches, like these:

- Data breaches and leaks metadata search
- Search engines
- Social media
- Online communities
- Email addresses
- Usernames
- People search engines
- Telephone numbers
- Online maps
- Code search
- Documents
- Images
- Videos
- Domain names
- IP addresses
- Government and business records
- Geospatial research

Much of this is easily verifiable, which is the first step in knowing when to stop. If you come across something that is not verifiable but that you think matters, you must "add things up," or infer, as we talked about earlier. In doing this, information will become more than the sum total of its parts in cases. You must then try to verify your inferences, but it's the quickest route to putting information into one of our three buckets as is shown in Figure 7.9.

To truly separate signal from noise, there are a few steps you can take that should become second nature. Stephen Few wrote a book called *Signal: Understanding What Matters in a World of Noise* (Analytics Press, 2015). Few has written more than a couple of books (some would say he's written a *few* books, pun intended) on harnessing visualization to help in analysis. In *Signal*, he takes a broader viewpoint, focusing on the idea of "sensemaking," which

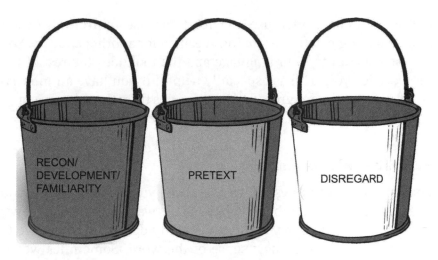

Figure 7.9   Buckets: Categorizing OSINT Findings

is different from analytical thinking. Sensemaking involves imagination and a healthy tolerance for taking leaps where there is no information to support your route. Upon taking these leaps, you will eventually land at a theory you can then assess and research. The two types of thinking—sensemaking and analytical—are necessary for separating signal from noise where some items remain unverifiable. One will help you navigate a cluttered information landscape, and the other will stop you getting lost down one track. It is easy to think of these as lying at opposite ends of a spectrum of thinking styles, but a blend is often a good way to approach OSINT inference. I typically start by using an analytical approach and then move to sensemaking, although the sequence doesn't matter if the outcome ends up being the same.

You should keep in mind that everyone great started out as someone new. It's imperative that I do not further the false narrative that only people "gifted" with some set of intangible skills will be good at untangling signal from noise. This is not the case—I am merely stating that experience helps.

Finally, OSINT relies on search terms plus the information available. If you don't change the language to suit your country, state, city, or demographic, your searches will not be as effective and efficient as they could be. I often use I Search From (isearchfrom) if I want to search Google within a version specified for another country. You choose the country and language and the tool does the rest of the leg work for you. This is especially helpful if you have an international target. It is also great for news articles from the selected country that would otherwise be buried in US Google results.

Weaponizing of Information

There is one more question to ask about vulnerabilities: can you really create a vulnerability where there was none? Good news: in short, the answer is yes. A vulnerability doesn't always have to be identified in the firmest sense of the word. Sometimes we, as attackers, have to turn information into a weapon to fully form a vulnerability. We can weaponize information.

Note that the word *information* here is that of visual and sensory as well as data or typical information (data). The attack surface is all the ways that an attacker can affect the target. If your target has not been able to map their surface and defend against it wholly, there your true value as an EA lies.

As you have seen, OSINT has evolved with speed and power, and it will not stand still now. Technologies will continue to expand and ultimately enhance OSINT practices. With billions of posts, images, streams, records, and data uploaded to the Internet every day, an abundance of intelligence is available. As previously described, individually, this data would be of little value, but collectively it can lead to important insights. The open source intelligence cycle contains four key steps: collection, processing, exploitation, and production. What you can infer and analyze from data is often as important as the raw intelligence itself. Social network analysis, geospatial context, and often metadata to create meaningful intelligence are of the utmost importance. This process will require your curiosity and persistence if it is to pay off, though, given how cyclical the process can be. However, the payoff is often high—for instance, the intelligence community has been able to use geotagged social media posts to track down Islamic State fighters; the messaging itself was secondary.

The information environment can be generally categorized along both technical and psychosocial dimensions. This is why cybersecurity's primary concern with purely technical features—defenses against denial-of-service attacks, botnets, massive intellectual property thefts, and other breaches that typically take advantage of security vulnerabilities—is lacking and precisely why we need more critical thinking and AMs for defensive measures. The technical view is too narrow. As an example, the April 2013 Associated Press Twitter hack was performed with very little technical prowess and a lot of attacker mindset. In this attack, a group hijacked the news agency's account, putting out a message that "Two explosions in the White House and Barack Obama is injured." With the weight of the Associated Press behind it, the message caused a drop of roughly $136 billion in equity market value over a period of roughly five minutes. This attack exploited both technical (hijacking the account) and psychosocial (understanding market reaction) features of the information environment.

Another attack, exploiting purely psychosocial features, took place in India in September 2013. The incident began when a young Hindu girl told her family that she had been verbally abused by a Muslim boy. Her brother and cousin reportedly killed the boy. This action prompted clashes between Hindu and Muslim communities. Fanning the flames of violence, a video was posted of a gruesome act in which two men were shown to be beaten to death. The video was accompanied by a caption that identified the two men as Hindu and the mob as Muslim. It took 13,000 Indian troops to put down the resulting violence. It turned out that though the video did show two men being beaten to death, it was not the men claimed in the caption; in fact, the incident had not taken place in India. This attack required no technical skill whatsoever; it simply required a psychosocial understanding of the place and time to post to achieve the desired effect.

With AMs, if something can be used for good, it can be used for bad, and vice versa. There is nothing good or bad, but your attacker mindset will make it so. As an attacker, you can weaponize information for the good of the objective and, ultimately, for the good of the target, who can then attempt to de-weaponize it and gain a new and helpful perspective for how information is gathered and can be used.

In any case, what should be clear by now is that information is the lifeblood of the attack. There is no attack without information. Behold the two stages of open source intelligence through the lens of the organized, ethical attacker: there's OSINT *before* the objective, and there's OSINT *after* the objective. There is no single playbook for OSINT; most pentesters have their own methods and preferred tools. Most often, though, OSINT starts with manual reconnaissance and reading up on the target subjects, including using nontechnical sources such as an organization's annual report, financial filings, and associated news coverage, as well as content on its websites and YouTube and similar services. How this unfolds is a mechanism of the second law of AMs, which states that everything you do (and collect) must tie back to the objective.

Tying Back to the Objective

In Chapter 3, "The Attacker Mindset Framework," I talked about two categories of development. The first, recon development, involves looking for information that can bolster your objective. If the objective is to get to the target's SOC, you look for information on what kind of security doors were in the building; search for building blueprints; meticulously go through social media accounts to see if there's ever been a photo posted from within the organization; and comb through LinkedIn, searching for the people who work for the organization and for job titles, locations, and schedules.

The second category I talked about was pretext development. Pretexts are dependent on the obstacles you have to get around and the type of establishment you are going to. If I were to build up OSINT to pose as an elevator maintenance person, I'd have to find information to support the pretext. I would need the elevator supplier/manufacturer uniform and ID badge, and I would need to know about offices the maintenance company has. I would also want to show up with seemingly legitimate paperwork to support my pretext.

This is all OSINT heavy.

These are two separate avenues of OSINT that eventually converge but ultimately need separate collection and analysis. In both cases, all information must tie back to the central objective.

We've now looked broadly at OSINT, taking into consideration its roots and evolution. However, honing in on OSINT and its everyday functions is the start and lifeblood of every operation. Every campaign and engagement I have been involved in, with every company from the United States to Australia, has started with OSINT. Our team does not go on a job without extensive OSINT, and we go through that OSINT with a fine-tooth comb daily on the run-up to make sure we've missed nothing and that everything we are using from it is in scope. We allow that OSINT to be ripped apart with no form of ownership attached to it. There's no room for personal emotion in OSINT on this level. If the intel isn't good, then it needs to be scrapped. This means that the collector has lost time and the engagement has lost time. That's the nature of OSINT. If there was a perfect way to perform OSINT or any type of intelligence technique whilst ensuring you were on the right path, then companies probably wouldn't need us.

OSINT is our most valuable tool; it often has no cost but that of time, which, overall, is well spent. The thing that non-attacker/members of the public often don't understand is that information doesn't have to be secret to be valuable. What most of us in the information security community call *operational security*, or *OPSEC*, the public deems almost valueless as private information. People publish dates of birth, hobbies, interests, and vacation times as if they can't be used to help break into their bank account, house, or other accounts. Businesses publish updates on their sites constantly in a bid to keep their customer base informed, not always realizing that an attacker with a finely tuned AMs is easily able to use that information against them. Given how many of us use the Internet and, in particular, forums, online communities, and social media sites, we can cheerfully and optimistically approach outlets confident there's an employee within our target company who has posted something valuable. But do note that not all online communities and forums gets indexed by search engines, so you may have to independently search these types of sites based on previously collected information on your target to see if they have posted there.

Taking advantage of information found can be as simple as asking for help for a product they use. Searching job postings from a company may also be advantageous. Such postings may ask for candidates with special skill sets, such as "expertise in Python." None of this is groundbreaking stuff. You can read more about this topic in many books dedicated to OSINT (see the notes section for some of those books). What's novel is looking at OSINT through the lens of AMs.

There is a technical pursuit of OSINT, too. I recommend tools like SpiderFoot, Recon-NG, Google Earth Pro, and Sherlock and Maltego.

In addition to scanning web page content, SpiderFoot looks at HTTP headers, which can ultimately produce OS and web software names and version numbers. This information can prove vital, should you find out that an older version of Windows, Apache, or PHP is being used and exposed on the Internet.

There are many OSINT databases, which makes it possible to search a software version against a known vulnerability database, and then work out the details of leveraging the security hole. Recon-NG is a favorite of mine. It's a full-featured web recon framework. It has plenty of features, such as domain name discovery and credentials gathering, to repository scrapping with additional integrations like Masscan.

Maltego is both a data management and visualization tool as well as an OSINT tool. It's quite complex and cannot, in my experience, be learned intuitively. It is extremely powerful, though. It offers two types of recon options: infrastructural and personal. Infrastructural recon deals with the domain, covering DNS information such as name servers, mail exchangers, zone transfer tables, DNS-to-IP mapping, and related information. Personal recon deals with information such as email addresses, phone numbers, social networking profiles, and even mutual friend connections. It is a very sophisticated tool.

Sometimes, even a technical pursuit can start with OSINT and will maintain a pure level of AMs throughout. This is why OSINT pays off. I won't say you need to devote weeks to OSINT, but even a few minutes can count when you don't have much more time than that to spend.

Finally, there will always be people who leave the rest of us in the dust when it comes to searches, dorking, and using the tools. Being able to collect OSINT proficiently is a valuable skill to have. However, anyone can learn to do it. That sort of technical technique can be taught if you want to learn. The bulk of AMs, as applied to OSINT, however, lies in one area: the ability to analyze information for its value. This can only be done by applying everything you find to the objective and evaluating it through that lens. But more than that, applying AMs to OSINT means the ability to twist that information to fit the objective. How a piece of information gets you closer to an objective won't always be clear, but with a finely tuned AMs, you can see the value in most information. In other words, you must learn to critically evaluate information and apply it (or disregard it) based on your objective. Instead of being burdened by the amount of information you will collect, you will be able to rank it as you come across it. This concept may seem abstract, so I will supplement it with an example.

Let's start with an easy task. Say I want to write a spearphish and all the information I have on the target is his email address and that he went to Colgate University. I can write a phish from the university asking him to give a commencement speech or citing something about the alumni, or even asking him to be part of a mentor program, which I could tailor to his job if I knew it. It's a spearphish, so it would have to be quite warm and personal, using his name, injecting it with any other relevant details, or using a sense of familiarity.

Even easier, if his CV (curriculum vitae) is online, whether it be on LinkedIn or on his own site, it will likely list his "expertise," which I can bend to my objective. It might have metadata attached that will give me insight to the type of system he is using, which I might be able to leverage in a seemingly technical phish.

If this target has no information available online but a family member does, I would potentially be able to use this. For instance, knowledge about a vacation might allow me to email as the hotelier about the bill or items left behind if the scope permitted and if it was aligned with the objective.

Another thing that will need careful analysis when considering information directly from the target is the use of language. I can extract information from social opinion to emotion by studying his use of language, i.e., how articulate and balanced his communication seems, as well as intensifiers and indications of his stress level. I can thus begin to build a picture of my target that I can work with. This last point illustrates one of the shortcomings of OSINT: misinformation. Operating off false information is harder than operating off no information.

OSINT is valuable and becoming more so every day because now everyone is interested in the findings and has learned to apply them to their role and business interests from IT and security to boardrooms. This is because OSINT is effectively the start of the foothold. The beginnings of gaining access to a company is gaining information about it, and if you can gain enough information to list assets, operations, to profile a company accurately or to circumvent security and other defenses, then you come that much closer to achieving your final objective—whatever that may be.

Figure 7.10   Determining the location of my target by photo
Twitter: Julia Bayer / @bayer_Julia 1

Let's move to a slightly harder task. Imagine just having one photo with little information, but it places a target at a location. The poster of this image, Julia Bayer, simply asks that you work out where the photo was taken (see Figure 7.10).

Let's say I know the target lives in Berlin and looking at her online profiles, this seems easy to infer. I queried Wikipedia and "churches in Berlin." Without knowing if this image was that of a "former place church" or a current "place of worship", I clicked on the latter and got to what turned out to be the correct list (Figure 7.11).

The spire from the first picture (Figure 7.10) strongly resembles one from the Wikipedia page. The name given for it is Sophienkirche.

			building					
Şehitlik-Moschee en: Military Cemetery Mosque	Neukölln	Berlin Türk Şehitlik Camii (i.e. Berlin Turkish Military Cemetery Mosque)	Şehitlik-Friedhof (i.e. the Ottoman diplomats and military cemetery) Columbiadamm	E: before 1983 N: 1999–2005	Isl. Sun.	DİTİB	Neuk.
Silas-Kirchsaal en: Silas Church Hall	Schöneberg	–	Silas Großgörschenstraße	E: 1961	Luth.†	EKBO	T-S
Sophienkirche en: Sophie's Church	Spandauer Vorstadt	Spandauische Kirche (i.e. Spandau bound Church) till the 1740s	Sophia Louise of Mecklenburg-Schwerin Große Hamburger Straße, Sophienstraße	E: 1712–1713	Luth.†	EKBO	Mitte
Sri-Mayurapathy-Murugan-Tempel en: Shree Mayoorapathy Murugan Temple	Britz	–	Murugan Riesestraße 20–22, Blaschkoallee 48	E: 2006–2013	Hind.	BHM	Neukölln
Kirche Staaken-Gartenstadt en: Staaken Garden City Church	Staaken	–	Staaken Gartenstadt Kirchplatz, listed building	E: 1922	Luth.†	EKBO	Spand.
Stadtkirche Sankt Laurentius en: St. Lawrence City Church	Köpenick	–	Lawrence of Rome Alt-Köpenick / Kirchstraße, listed building	E: by 1239 D: 1837 N: 1838–1841	Luth.†	EKBO	T-K
Stephanuskirche	Gesundbrunnen	–	Stephen the Protomartyr	E: 1902–1904	Luth.†	EKBO	Mitte

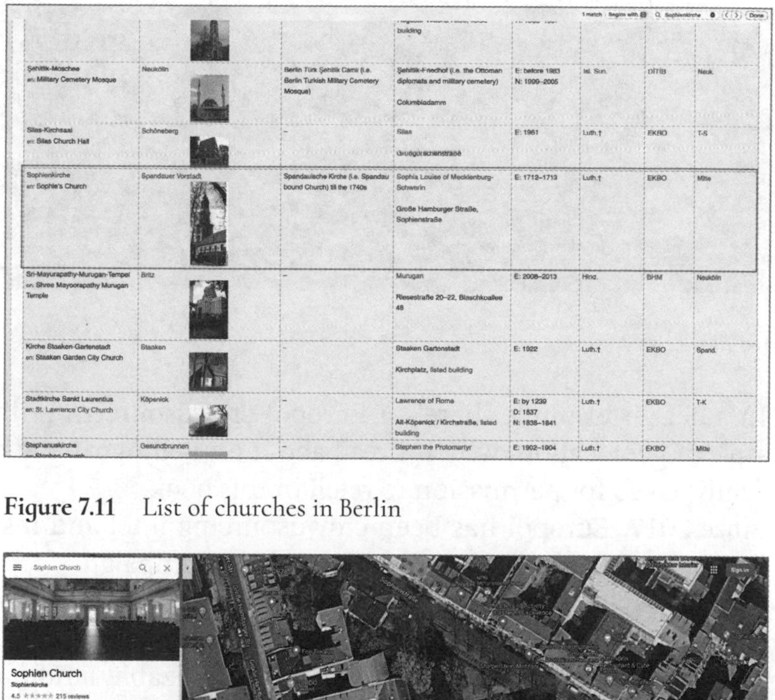

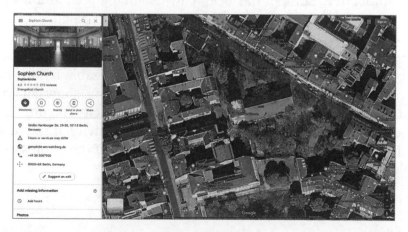

Figure 7.11 List of churches in Berlin

Figure 7.12 Result of Google Maps search

A quick Google Maps search shows trees and surroundings (Figure 7.12).

This gives me hope I am on the right track.

Then I try Google Street View but have no luck. Probably user error. So, I return to the Google Image search. I've found photos of the church, which are a match for the one posted by Julia (Figure 7.10). I can match the photos by the windows, spire, and roof color from Figure 7.10 with Figure 7.13 (below) for a quick pairing.

Figure 7.13

In a darker example, here's a Europol crowdsourced, brilliant example of geolocation, which I read about on Bellingcat and subsequently asked for permission to retell in this book.

Since 2017, Europol has been crowdsourcing intel and insight for their "Stop Child Abuse—Trace an Object" campaign.

Europol shared new images via their website and Twitter on October 15, 2018. A few photographs were taken outside and made it possible to use geolocation because of recognizable landmarks. Two of these photos, taken from a roof of a building, show concrete buildings and were presumably taken in an Asian city (Figure 7.14). The photos are heavily censored due to the sensitivity of the material. Europol's investigators needed the location of the photos to be able to trace a child abuser and save the victim.

The photos don't seem to contain many recognizable land-marks. There's no text or signage displayed on the buildings, and the concrete structures don't reveal much of anything.

Twitter user "Bo" contacted Bellingcat and mentioned the architecture showed similarity to the city of Shenzhen in southern China. Bellingcat responded to Europol's tweet with this information and included a photo of similar architecture and an overlay image of the two photos, noting the blue road sign and a structure similar to a satellite receiver on top of a building shown in the photos.

Figure 7.14   Two photos from an Asian city

A short while later, Twitter user Olli Enne from Finland geolocated the exact location of the photos in the Bao'an district of Shenzhen. According to Olli, the images were taken from the roof of a building with coordinates 22.722917, 114.053194. He showed several buildings and a hill in the photos that matched the buildings visible in satellite imagery. Also, a view line across a building with a blue roof to a building with arch shaped windows in the distance lines up with the view line in satellite imagery.

Figure 7.15   Map showing satellite imagery

In later tweets, Olli explained that he searched in Shenzhen and other major cities in China for several hours (note the timeframe—not everything you search for will take just minutes of work). You will need curiosity and persistence in abundance at times. Over this time period, he was looking for little green hills and road shapes, and he drew a map of how the area would look in satellite imagery (Figure 7.15).

The geolocation of the photos could not be immediately verified by Bellingcat because matching the buildings in the photos to the buildings visible in satellite imagery was difficult. However, thanks to Baidu Maps, a Chinese web mapping system, Bellingcat was able to verify that Olli's geolocation was a perfect match (Figure 7.16).

A Google Earth 3D view of the building the photos were taken from shows the same mountains. In particular, the shape of the mountain on the left side of the photos is very similar to the shape of the mountains in the 3D view (Figure 7.17). A smaller mountain with a relatively high peak is more difficult to spot, but following a view line in the photos from the location where they were taken in the direction of that mountain shows the same buildings in the 3D view that are visible in the photos in that view line. Also, the partly visible small green hill at the end of the road is clearly visible in Google's 3D view.

Figure 7.16   Building match

The Bellingcat article goes on to talk about many more interesting and relevant items in its article, including more initial research and how they estimated the year the photographs were taken. You can find the article here: https://www.bellingcat.com/resources/case-studies/2018/11/08/europols-asian-city-child-abuse-photographs-geolocated.

Figure 7.17 Google Earth 3D view

This example steps away a little from the OSINT and type of recon I started out describing, but it demonstrates the power of some of the most important intel types we can use.

Summary

- Good reconnaissance is critical to any operation.
- In general, reconnaissance is the bulk of an attack. This is why the first, second, and fourth laws of AMs used in conjunction are so critical.
- All of the information you gather has to further your attainment of the objective, and it will help you with law 3 (never break pretext).
- There are technical components to OSINT, especially if you want to stay anonymous.

Key Message

OSINT is only as useful as your mind makes it. AMs is taking in information and applying it to an objective. You have to be able to break information down into critical chunks and perform further searches from there.

Part III

Tools and Anatomy

Chapter 8
Attack Strategy

Before we get into the meat of attack strategy, I want to take a moment to round up the mindset. The Attacker Mindset is formed by cognitive skills applied to four laws. The mark of a good attacker is the ability to come into contact with information, weaponize the valuable information and disregard the rest, and then leverage it in an attack. Sometimes the information will come to you already weaponized; other times, you will have to mold and shape it into something to be leveraged. Notably, you do not need the skills to understand the laws. You do not need to know or care about the laws to have or use the skills. It is, however, the use of both in tandem that forms the mindset.

The skills you need are curiosity and persistence, which are interdependent, since one will not pay off without the other. The other skills are information processing, mental agility, and self-awareness. Mental agility is a fancy way of saying you must be able to adapt the information to the situation in which you find yourself. Applying your self-awareness as an attacker results in leaving someone feeling a certain way, which is most often accomplished by your demeanor, your choice of words, your body language, and your general way of being. All in all, it's knowing what you have and how to leverage it for the objective. It's knowing when to push and when to pull when evaluating your own strengths and deficiencies.

The laws that these skills are applied to are as follows:

1. Start with the end in mind.
2. Gather, weaponize, and leverage information.
3. Never break pretext.
4. Every move you make should be in the interest of the objective.

Law 1 means that you are always thinking ahead; you need to be able to think far enough ahead to the end goal, to be able to keep it in your mind, and know what your short-term goals are. Then you must employ laws 2, 3, and 4 to reach the end.

Law 2 states that you gather, weaponize, and leverage information as a means to that end. Law 2 takes practice, but information is everywhere. Used in tandem with curiosity and persistence, you will see results.

Law 3 means you are never yourself. You can switch "characters" or pretexts when it serves you, not just because you are bored or want to show off your acting range. A pretext is a way to disguise yourself as a threat. It's a narrative you're presenting that allows you to be exactly where you are, doing exactly what you need to do. Some pretexts will let you do this overtly, whereas others require a more covert approach. For instance, posing as an office cleaner won't get you in the server room, but it might get you deep enough into the building.

Law 4 states that every move you make after deciding the objective of law 1 will benefit it. Everything you do must get you closer to the objective. If you need to take a new route because the one you tried is a dead end, do it. If you have to sacrifice entry one day due to new intel but wait to try again the next day, you should do so. In any attack, convenience isn't a factor or concern.

Attacks always have a gain in mind. The attacker is only concerned with how to achieve that objective in the most efficient way.

Undoubtedly, there is an element of opportunity that shows up in every attack, but the art of an attack is still formula- and skill-based.

Attacks in Action

Attacking is defined as engaging your opposition with your objective in mind. Some of the art of attacking relies on engaging *and* deceiving your opposition with the objective in mind—keeping them in the dark about the facts that are indeed part of an active attack. Offensively, an ethical attacker (EA) takes on the role of the adversary, and ultimately the most cost-efficient way to perform an attack is under the radar and with as little resistance as possible from the opposition. Concealing your identity as an attacker is always prudent, though not always as easy as you might first think. It's important to know your pretext, and ensure that it gets you all the way to your objective or that there is an opportunity to pivot into a new pretext once inside.

Remember that the third law of AMs is never to break pretext. That essentially means you are never yourself. You can draw on multiple pretexts in one engagement, but they must have a purpose. For example, if your job is to get to the bank's vaults, you will need a finely crafted pretext to get you from the entry point to the vault. The best-case scenario is that you've had time and permission to perform vishing and phishing attacks, gaining enough details to know how to facilitate a good pretext for that endeavor. However, that might not all be within scope. If it is not, then you must be able to come up with an agile pretext. You will have to infer where needed and adapt where possible. Your offensive attacker mindsets (OAMs) will fight to overtake your defensive attacker mindsets (DAMs) in this situation. You must overcome this urge in part. Your DAMs will allow you to look at the risks your OAMs will not care about in the moment.

There will also be times when your pretext will slightly alter depending on who you are speaking to. If you have been tasked with getting into a bank's vaults, you may enter the bank as an auditor, which may be enough to get to into the perimeter, but the deeper you get into the building and its defenses, the more layers you may need. When you reach the bank's vaults, you will, in all likelihood, not get into them as an auditor. If you cannot tailgate in or brute-force your way in with tools, you may have to pivot and ask for assistance as a fellow employee.

Opportunities that arise in the course of an engagement make a one-track offensive strategy impossible. In fact, sometimes pivoting becomes the offensive strategy. There are two ways to pivot: there's a single person adjusting and adapting the deeper they get into their target environment, and there's team pivoting, which is like a team of baton runners doing a hand-off. In the latter case, there may be less flexibility when advancing to the next stage of an attack if it is contingent on one attacker within a group. For example, if one attacker from the team needs to get into the building in order to let another in from an alternative entrance point, then more rigidity is introduced to the setup.

This was the case for me on a recent job. I was to gain entry to one of multiple buildings and test the visitor system. My teammate and I coordinated as I walked through the building, entering from a far-off alternative entrance. Initially I tried to let my teammate in the side door of the cafeteria, but there was a locked gate that prohibited him from getting to it. He could have jumped the gate, but law 4 prevented it. In broad daylight, jumping a gate in a busy professional complex would've stood out. Note that the building was glass on three sides, and the crowded cafeteria looked out onto the gate.

Our plan failed there, so it was on to the next plan. I soon made my way to reception and ultimately signed my teammate in as my guest. It has been one of the few times I have used an authoritative approach on a target. As I approached the reception desk from the side, I waved to my teammate and ordered the desk receptionist to sign him in without much in the way of amiability. I made a point of being brisk with her and yet friendly with him from the other side of the barrier I was trying to remove. It worked. I used all the laws in one moment and they paid off.

We used the same tactic to enter another of the buildings the next day. Two of my teammates made their way to stand with a small crowd of actual employees waiting for service at the food truck in the parking lot. They then nonchalantly walked back in with some people from the crowd, effectively tailgating into the building. Making their way from the back of it to the front, they greeted me and one other team member, again asking a receptionist to grant us entry via the visitor system. Ultimately, and sadly for us, this maneuver got us caught. We got a little cocky and greedy.

We didn't actually have to enter this building since we'd compromised all the others within the scope. But we also had nothing to lose by that point because we were hours from calling the job to a stop. After around 15 minutes in the building, taking photos and collecting sensitive information from desks, as was the objective of that operation, we were escorted out by security. The woman who had let us in didn't fully buy all the way into our scam, and in the end, she alerted security and her bosses. We did not adhere to law 4 here. It was on me, too; I was adamant we could get into that building.

As you can see, a misallocation of the economy of force can increase the complexity of a job. However, it's a fine line to tread; in trying to employ all available combat power in the most effective way possible, you can inadvertently create rigidity and extra work for all. In cases where you cannot enter and remain alone, remaining frill-free is vital. The offensive mentality of the team's AMs must outperform the best or most successful attackers alone; otherwise, too many variables are introduced.

Strategic Environment

The strategic environment that you enter as you perform attacks remains as it has always been—complex. In the book *Foundations of Homeland Security: Law and Policy* by Martin J. Alperen (pp.55-78), the strategic environment insofar as a military definition is described as "a broad range of strategic factors that influence an understanding of the operational environment. . . ." For you as an attacker, strategic factors in your operational environment include a wide range of people inside the target environment, as well as the security protocols it has in place and the location.

Beginning with the people part, you will run into three types of people in your target environment: lucrative, neutral, and opponent. In and of itself, this is not cause for concern if you can easily identify people within their category. However, more often than not categorization will not be possible until you've had that initial interaction and you are left to either steer the interaction to your benefit or be a subject of its outcome. So, for example, you might walk by 10 people sitting in their cubicles with their heads down or walk by one security guard who doesn't look up; these two fall under neutral and lucrative, respectively. However, you might interact with someone you hoped would turn out to be in the lucrative category but immediately begins to challenge you, moving them to the opponent category.

Moreover, these three cohorts will interact in an uncoordinated manner to produce a complex environment for you to navigate. And so, because of this complexity, you must be able to employ a certain amount of mental agility in your approach, either by gently steering the conversation and outcome or by employing chameleon tactics and reacting to any targets you come into contact with in a way that seems favorable to them. This takes quite a lot of AMs's bandwidth, as you will have to subtly adapt to interaction with a target in order to advance. To do so, you will have to read them correctly, which takes a certain amount of active engagement. It's done through information processing, mental agility, and self-awareness. If you can read them, you can adjust in a beneficial way, but you will need accurate self-awareness. The strategic environment thought of this way presents broad challenges. But there are concepts that can control the use of your AMs to meet the demands of the environment, the most important of which is strategic agility.

Strategic agility is the timely application and sustainment of your AMs, and at a speed and tempo that your adversaries cannot match. In other words, you must always aim to be ahead of your targets; you must always be preemptively assuming their next move. Being faster than your opponent doesn't mean always accurately predicting the future. It can mean steering the present to create the future. Typically, people do what you expect them to do. A security guard will try to stop an obvious intruder, which is great if you have a team member to spare as a distraction—in this case, you're already ahead of your opponent.

In network pentesting, if you are noticed, the incident responders work to take the impacted applications or systems off the network. They will also check for backdoors or block associated accounts.

Your targets may know how to stop one style of attack, but your AMs allows you to see what is invisible to them and to exploit those unknown (to them) variables. This is attacker agility, and it creates opportunity and momentum in the moment from target reaction, which takes definite social skill. Attacker agility is an important skill that will help you combat the uncertainty you face given the three types of people you will come across. Offensive strategy allows an attacker to see vulnerabilities and valuables invisible to the organization and exploit them in plain sight, such as the visitor system, which is any process that helps an organization keep track of the people that visit their location. Some businesses and buildings simply collect the visitor's name, but others have higher security standards, such as badges, legal documents, employee escorts, and sign-in systems.

The Necessity of Engagement and Winning

As an EA, you advance the fundamental and enduring security needs—the protection of livelihoods, information, and data—of businesses, institutions, and governments. Effectively, your goal is always to enhance security. You are an instrument for ensuring it. Accordingly, the primary purpose of an EA is to deter threats against an organization and its interests, and to help them defeat such threats should deterrence fail, by empowering them with awareness of what an attack looks and feels like. As an attacker you stand with the other instruments wielded by these organizations—typically technology which can be a deterrent.

Deterrence via technology focuses on forcing bad actors to consider the costs of doing attacking, as well as the consequences that might come from a counterattack. There are two main principles of deterrence typically at play. The first is denial, which (hopefully) results in bad actors being convinced that they won't succeed, at least not without enormous effort and cost. The second principle at play is punishment, which focuses on making the bad actors believe that there will be a strong response with serious consequences.

Of course, deterrence doesn't always work. Threats such as those posed by nation-states. Some criminals are simply not afraid of the law or consequences and often are affected by other mitigating factors such as greed or abject behavior tendencies.

As an attacker, your immediate task is to attack and win against a client. To do so well, you will have to be well organized, trained, equipped, and work against the deterrence in place and note where there none. However, attacking to win isn't your overarching goal. Ethical attacking is a structured process that seeks to better understand the capabilities of an organization to secure itself against malicious threats. It's safer to do this process through simulations rather than waiting for the real thing to occur. You test defenses and identify blind spots in the hopes of hardening your client's defenses. Winning at all costs doesn't teach an organization. Sure, you could scale the building, use a glass cutter, and escape down the trash chute from the 20th floor, but that's really the absolute last sequence you should try; otherwise, you leave them vulnerable because the least resource-intensive, least costly ways are left open—visible to malicious attackers, invisible to the future victims of them.

Certainly, there are some jobs where you will have to resort to extreme measures; the higher and more advanced a business's security, the more advanced your attack will have to be. In any case, your job is to attack and identify vulnerabilities that are invisible to the client but that put them in grave danger. The EA's job exists because of the necessity of engagement.

The essential nature of engagement lies in its ability to enhance security through integrated approaches, such as network and physical pentesting as well as awareness. This allows organizations to structure their environments, deal with the full spectrum of threats, and prepare for an unclear and ever-changing future. By using all tools and tests that are essentially instruments of destruction, including physical and network-based engagements, as ways to strengthen security, one-by-one the national landscape is made less penetrable. Ethical attackers play the key role in this effort. As an EA able to think maliciously but not become hostile, you form the foundation of mutually beneficial alliances and security partnerships, bolstering security stability in the long run for the organization you serve. But perhaps more importantly, you bolster and stabilize the security of their customers, which are typically the public, our families, communities, and the wider socio-ecological networks. Short-term malicious activity for the greater good makes the world safer for everyone, and in any attack strategy, there are asymmetric dangers. Thankfully, as an attacker with an offensive strategy, they are often to your benefit.

As an EA doing what is necessary, you will often resort to asymmetric means to counter the target's defenses. This might include unconventional approaches that circumvent a target's strengths, exploit their vulnerabilities, or confront them in ways they cannot match. For example, a target environment's location can severely go against them—if they are the only buildings on a street, then waiting until everyone is home for the night and entering (scope permitting) is probably a good idea. If your target is located on an extremely busy street, diverting and (mis)directing traffic can be of great use if you have to lock pick your way in. You should look at how adjacent neighborhoods are connected, ensuring that you can take the most efficient low-key routes as it's valuable information for your client. Surrounding landscape is a huge variable in how adversaries pick and execute attacks. Robbing a bank in New York would be easier due primarily to a lack of aerial views—deep "canyons" created by the tall buildings make getting away a little more likely than in say, London, where there aren't huge skyscrapers lining every street. Now, I am not condoning robbing banks anywhere, but this is how criminals and other adversaries think. They look at the whole, and so should we.

Circumventing a target's strengths and exploiting their vulnerabilities extends to network attacks, too. Let's say your target company has a bring-your-own-device (BYOD) policy in place. Targets have the freedom to choose whatever device they want to work with, which makes the process of keeping track of vulnerabilities and updates considerably harder for system administrators. It also makes being prepared for an array of potential malware attacks on different devices quite difficult.

An average hacker can make quick work of creating a hotspot to trick targets into connecting. If credentials are available to them on the connecting device, there's no reason they couldn't soon find themselves on the target network. Viruses are also a big problem when implementing BYOD strategies because potential targets can access sites or download mobile apps that would otherwise be restricted.

We have discussed information weaponization in a few chapters, but touching upon it now seems prudent as giving out information is most often a function of something most businesses need to do: A company must be able to market itself and perform its core functions; if these are inherently vulnerable, you are at an unfair advantage as an attacker. In other cases, the media will report information for general consumption that, with AMs applied, results in the identification or creation of a vulnerability. For example, I was able to enter that bank's Manhattan headquarters by piecing together information from the items placed in news articles and inference via off-the-cuff comments made by top-ranking employees on social media and in articles.

These sorts of risks have the potential to threaten most organizations directly, and it is important to use this against them so that they are no longer blind to seemingly innocuous information's potential for weaponization. Other challenges your targets generally face are things like denying them access to their own assets and owning their defenses, rendering them useless. Your target's environment is best protected through deterrence. For this to happen effectively, you illuminate what must be deterred.

The Attack Surface

Every attack surface varies slightly. But generally speaking, the attack surface is the full and integrated area of an organization (or system) that is susceptible to attacks. It is everything from the boundary of a system, some element of the system, or environment where an attacker can attempt entry. It includes all systems, all locations, all physical and digital assets, and for us, as attackers, everyday information about the company/operation.

For every defense a company or system has in place, like infrastructure, network security, endpoint security, building location, asset location, physical security, surveillance, human resources, policy understanding and execution, there are conceivable and proven breach methods for those defenses. Things like phishing, vishing impersonation, social engineering, malicious insider, physical theft, recon, unpatched vulnerabilities, zero day exploits, unpatched systems, DNS leaking, IOT attacks, breach data, network attacks, and covert entry methods—some overlap in execution at times.

This is a good way to gain an understanding of an attack surface (broadly speaking), which should ultimately translate to the identification or creation of vulnerabilities.

Vulnerabilities

. . .or as I like to call them: *FUN*erabilites. See what I did there. . .?

Vulnerabilities are where the security provisions employed do not properly defend against the hazards of their counters. As stated by Ross Anderson, professor of computer security at University of Cambridge, in his book *Security Engineering* (Wiley, 2008): "Vulnerabilities are where a property of a system or its environment, which in conjunction with an external threat, can lead to a security failure." Vulnerabilities are like magic to you as an attacker; they are your means of achieving the objective. You can find them; you can also create them. You have the unfair, asymmetrical advantage. A studying of the attack surface deserves your full attention throughout any job.

AMs Applied to the Attack Vectors

As you have noted by now, attackers exploit businesses and people through a variety of means—phishing, vishing, impersonation, physical, and smishing—all of which require a custom solution for each client. They also all require AMs to be executed well. We haven't explored phishing or smishing in this book because the examples used to illustrate points from my career haven't often included them.

However, to ensure you have a view of all the means available to you in which to execute your attacks, we will discuss phishing, looking at the subcategories of spearphishing and whaling as well. We will also look at smishing and impersonation. Viewing each of these through the lens of AMs requirements, we can break them down and see how we can garner enough information through each of these vectors to steal, change, or destroy information, one of which is typically the objective.

In the notes section of this book, you will also find other books and materials to read if you want to learn more about each of these vectors, beyond what is relevant for this chapter.

Phishing

Phishing may have been what gave social engineering its rise to fame—it's prevalent and easy to understand for most of the public. I would go as far as to say, it's basically the common pigeon of Internet attacks. We've all seen one, we've all recognized one, they are all too common now. However, phishing makes headlines because, try as we might, the infosec community cannot seem to quash the veracity of which phishing campaigns conquer.

Most typically, phishing relies on a simple method: emails are sent under false pretenses, like Amazon wanting to update your payment information or your bank detecting unusual activity with a link straight to the evidence. The emails are often sent to multiple targets at a time, although spearphishing sees them heavily customized and extremely convincing for most.

The goal of a typical phishing attack is, most often, to get a target to reveal their logins, passwords, and payment information. Viruses are sent that gather sensitive logon information, and others that recruit target machines into botnets that are used to send illegal spam through networks. Others can be used to obtain intellectual property. Deciding which one of these to use doesn't truly matter from an AMs perspective, because generally the scope is the deciding factor.

There are two important components of a phish for your AMs to consider. The first is messaging and the second is how that is malicious, although the latter is beyond the scope of this book. A single phish can often do most of the heavy lifting for you as an attacker, which is both anticlimactic for most people and deliciously empowering to know (and use). The next few sections will look at the various types of phish and which AMs features they should employ.

Mass Phish

Arguably, a mass phish is the easiest phish to write because it benefits from the Barnum effect, but with a twist. The Barnum effect is a common psychological phenomenon that allows people to be convinced that the developed statements are personal to them. The statements are so vague or broad that people can interpret them in their own way, finding their own meaning and sometimes feeling in awe of their accuracy. A good example is a horoscope. Mine today, from Astrology.com, says the following:

> *This time of year is all about getting out of your comfort zone. Don't be afraid to stretch yourself and refresh your perspective. This story is highlighted today, as the creatively rich Pisces moon aligns with your ruler, action-taking Mars. Use this energy to push ahead with personal projects . . .*
>
> *. . . You could have a new idea, spark of inspiration or work on a project that allows you to tap into this side of yourself. Even if your job is quite analytical, today will require you to flex a different mental muscle.*

There's not a single sentence in there that cannot be applied to one of the tens of millions of people who believe in horoscopes and partake in pseudo-spirituality.

Now for the simple twist: although the Barnum effect allows individuals to give high accuracy ratings to descriptions of their personality, a phish plays on generalities specific to an environment—if you work for a bank, you may well be expecting an email about HR updates in January. If you live in the United States, you might expect to be contacted about your vote in an election year. If you have an email account that was active before February 2020, you definitely got email about COVID-19.

As far as AMs is concerned, a lesser amount of effort goes into these types of phish. They have to be themed for their audience and sent in a way that makes sense (e.g., time of day). They don't have to be 100 percent believable; they just need to have enough believability to pique the target's curiosity. For example, the target might not need to know about "Changes to Capital Gains Tax" for their current bank role, but it's a familiar term, and here is a general call from—*seemingly*—the right department telling them that they must sign this acknowledgment. They may not need to know about "WFH Policy Updates," but they might click anyway, because the email has made it sound important, has given them a call to action (the link, usually in disguise), and has made it easy for them to follow that line of action.

Almost all AMs here is channeled into making it believable for the masses and not too specific, overbearing, or long. No one enjoys a long email.

Make it short.

Make it pointed.

Make it clear.

Give it a call to action.

Give it believability.

Tie it to the objective you've been given (through its theme).

Spearphish

A spearphish targets specific people or specific positions within organizations. Whereas most phishing attacks implement a "throw

1,000 daggers in the water, and see if you can hit a fish or two," spearphishing is often carried out with some knowledge about the target. Spearphishing emails will often be personalized by name and appear to come from someone the target knows. Some recent studies, including one from TrendMicro (https://www.trendmicro .com/vinfo/us/security/news/cybercrime-and-digital-threats/ spear-phishing-is-the-favored-targeted-attack-bait), suggest that up to 91 percent of data breaches within organizations start with a spearphishing email.

Where mass phishing expeditions typically use broad strokes to create a malicious email, spearphishing attacks are slightly more sophisticated. They involve documents containing malware or links to credential-stealing sites, including cloned sites, to steal sensitive information or valuable intellectual property.

But what do they require of you as an attacker, you may wonder? Spearphishing is a campaign built with a goal of penetrating an organization, not often the individual themselves. The research needed is mid-level; you will have to know names, as spearphish attacks are most typically addressed to the recipient; roles and job level are also things you must research for this type of phish.

The message itself will have to be believable and centered on the target. You will have to theme it according to your objective— meaning you should give them a reason to click the link or open the file that makes sense *and* that they can't resist *and* it can be personalized.

It will still have to be short, although I typically allow for a sentence or two more in a spearphish.

It will still have to be pointed.

It will still have to be clear.

Whaling

Whaling is somewhat similar to spearphishing but directed toward upper management and C-suite positions at an organization. There's no immunity from whaling within an organization, and that's a pretty good position to start off in as an attacker. Even Facebook and Google have been scammed at the highest levels—they were scammed out of $100 million in 2019 according to CNBC (https://www.cnbc.com/2019/03/27/phishing-email-scam-stole-100-million-from-facebook-and-google.html). Whaling emails were sent to some *whales* that had some authority and ultimately got counterfeit invoices paid.

What do whaling phishes require from an AMs perspective? They require research, as you want to hit the right whale or whales, taking into account susceptibility, vulnerability, and scope.

You will be required to investigate three categories:

1. First, you explore the company landscape in two ways:
   - You will have to learn about the company—what do they do, what their reputation is from a client/consumer point of view, and what it is from an employee point of view.
   - You will also benefit from getting a sense of what things look like on the inside—you'll want to know how they communicate as a company both in terms of vernacular and technology-wise; you may benefit from learning the distance between the C-suite and the D-suite, for example, or how casual the corporate culture seems and how busy upper management is.
2. The second thing you will have to investigate is the individual you want to send the email to. You won't need everything you come across, but you might note it in case the track you decide to follow ends up fruitless. For example, you might find that the CEO you are targeting was divorced, usually an emotive topic that could override most logic, ultimately allowing a reply or otherwise inadvisable action. However, you might also find out that although the news outlets are marking the occasion, he was actually divorced 20 years prior and his ex-wife is actually now his late ex-wife. There would be little point in emailing him as her attorney, and even if she were alive, typically most things have been taken care of 20 years after a divorce in terms of legalities, so it's a somewhat fruitless track. It would take up too much of your time to bend this information into a believable story, so you'd be better off to look elsewhere.

Not every company will allow this style of an attack. You can always list it as a potential avenue, even if you can't carry it out due to scope or your own ethical boundaries.

However, if you've gotten to know your target and company and you've arrived at a dead end with one attack, you hopefully have enough information to lead you to another attack.

To execute a whaling attack well, your AMs—specifically your curiosity, persistence, and law 2—is best applied to the following areas: public records, legal subpoenas, news sources, and social media accounts. Friends of the target's social media often provide information, too, even if they don't have much of a presence themselves. This is because people like to know people deemed important. If you are targeting someone with any level of celebrity (micro or macro), it's likely that someone, somewhere is talking about them on social media, talking about the good times, commenting on photos, and so forth.

Research of any kind will aid you on your phishing quest. For example, a malicious attacker was able to successfully attack Mattel—a multinational toy manufacturing company—using research. Through investigation, the attacker learned there was some internal turmoil in the company. The attacker researched the company's organizational chart and found that Mattel required signatures for payments. The attacker also used social media to learn the names of key individuals sending requests for funds. On top of this, the attacker also recognized the company had just hired a new CEO and was looking to expand into China. A request for a wire transfer to the Bank of Wenzhou seemed like a good bet for the attacker and authentic from the target's perspective.

3. It is the level of sophistication of the whale that matters most. You cannot afford generalities; everything must be targeted, including who it comes from, which should be a trusted source. Usually, a trusted source is someone with whom the executive

expects to communicate, which is the third branch of a whaling phish you must investigate.

You have to look for information on the source, whether you are sending the phish from inside or outside the organization, so that you can replicate their communication style. Whale phishing attacks are successful because they are well planned. You must seek to find the behavior of the target, their patterns, and business headlines relevant to them. This level of deception will make it hard to tell the difference between a whale phish and a real email.

In all honesty, the thing that makes whaling hardest for me is that I cannot gauge who they are, what they are like, or how they operate. I often find myself navigating to YouTube or some version of it where I can see them, whether it be in an interview or in a casual conversation.

Whaling requires a sort of *superiority* that some of the other types of phishing can lack and yet still be successful. Whaling will require more of your AMs than the others.

Make it high-level.

Make it relevant.

Make it pointed.

Make it clear.

Lend it credence through investigation and research.

Vishing

I enjoy conducting a vishing call. They are often similar to a phishing attack, insofar as they are typically used as a way to extract information, but a vish is conducted over the phone. Unlike a phish, you have immediate data on the target—many things can be conveyed through a voice, which means that AMs can be employed in one of its most natural states: as agility in reaction. If the target answers, you can infer a lot from their voice. If you are right—great, proceed. If you are wrong—great, pivot. It's the same in the field.

Vishing can be used to learn many things, but it all boils down to either gathering information or using the vish in conjunction with a phish. I will break these two methods down so as to be clear.

When gathering information, you might vish a target belonging to the organization you've been hired to test in order to ascertain how much information they will willingly hand over. Typically, banks employ people to vish their workforce this way. I will call up as a member of the HR team citing the "recent company changes," which, even if there are none, tends to work. Before long I will ask them to confirm some items on their record, such as marital status, the best contact number for them outside of work, their Social Security number, and so forth.

Another pretext often used is that of IT, usually calling about a database that was cloned incorrectly and thus leading to discrepancies in the data. If the target doesn't wish to answer and they are low enough on the rung, I will pivot and ask for their email and their manager's name so that I can gather the needed information from them. People are usually willing to oblige—their manager will, after all, know what to do and be pleased that they themselves did not give out information, only that of someone else within the organization.

The second reason to vish is to use it along with a phish. My favorite.

When vishing, it's the three first laws of AMs that have the most impact. The first law states that you start with the end in mind. It is a way of taking information in and applying it to an objective, and in this case steering the call through the information you provide in order to get to the objective. The second law states that you must weaponize information for the good of the objective. The third law states that you never break pretext. I tend most often to focus on the hardest flag to get. (A *flag* is a piece of information or asset you are aiming for. The objective can consist of multiple flags or just one.) I do this because it informs my pretext well. As an example, if my objective is made up of three flags—getting the target's full name, their job title, and their Social Security number—I will focus

first on the Social Security number because in doing so, I immediately take the threat out of the scenario. *Of course*, I, posing as
Tina from HR, shouldn't be asking for your SSN over the phone,
but I do so only after I've "proved" to you that I am who I say I am
by reciting your name and job title (which you will confirm for me).
That counts as two of my flags. In doing this, I build up some trust
and lend myself some credence. These are the cornerstones of rapport building. Rapport is a Swiss army knife for the attacker, so to
speak. It can help you persuade people to take actions they ordinarily would not if the request came from a perfect stranger or from
someone they did not feel comfortable around. Rapport can divert
or misdirect the attention of an individual, too.

Misdirection itself is a form of deception in which you draw the
target's attention to one thing to distract it from another. For example, there are temporal misdirection's of attention whereby you can
walk into location or start a call and be clear with the target that you
are under the pressure of time to get *something* done. The *something*
could be getting the database fixed, which you might need their
assistance with or it could be performing checks around a physical
location. As a network pen tester, it might simply be a diversion.
Whatever it is, it's a lengthy departure from the real reason you are
making contact. Add rapport to the equation and you are even more
likely to find success.

Rapport can be struck up with something as seemingly insignificant as creating a (false) shared experience: "I know we are all
flat out just now, so sorry to call this late..." or, my favorite, "I love
your name. My mum's name is [Christine]." This works for me
specifically on the phone because I am quite soft-spoken and can
sound young, especially when I make you think of my mom, who is
definitely not called Christine or any other target names I've had to
date. Rapport can be developed many ways, but the level of rapport
is actually decided by the other person, not by you. If the other person doesn't really care that she shares the same name as my mom,
then I don't get to act like she does. In vishing, developing a worthy

pretext, is the first step required of your AMs, but your AMs's staying power should emerge during the call. It must never let you break from the pretext, and everything you say must be steering the way to the objective.

This technique doesn't require that you should get down to business and forgo all small talk. You can use rapport-building techniques, and often rapport is the result of small talk. To get someone to like you, you have to allow them to believe you like them (no one ever said being an EA was a clean game). You might employ an air of authority, but your pretext will have to be pretty airtight to pull it off.

AMs applied to vishing relies most heavily on two things. The first is agility for the good of the objective. Think through the call; play that game of mental chess whereby you imagine all the scenarios you can—it will warm you up for the real thing, including the chance that the target asks you details about yourself or your job. The second thing is to never falter in the pretext you have chosen. You must be acting exactly as your chosen character would in a real-life scenario.

An average vishing call for my team lasts three minutes. They are clear and effective in their approach. They get through hundreds of calls in a day this way. I, on the other hand, have had calls that last 25 minutes.

I got my target's number from our internal list and dialed her number, spoofing my own so that it appeared I was calling from her workplace rather than my own. When she answered and, I'm not being facetious when I say, she had the voice of an angel. I explained who I was and was happy to hear her reply each time. A minute or two into the call, I asked for the first flag, her user ID. The tone changed immediately, and she tried for 20 minutes to verify who I was.

The real story of the call is that she asked me who my manager was. I made up a name, which obviously didn't pass her internal checks; then she asked who my manager's manager was, which due to its fictitious nature also did not pass her internal check. Then she asked me who my manager's manager's manager was. When I again pulled a name out of my fake name generator, it was, in fact, the name of a manager of a manager of a manager.

My target said, "Oh, *Bob Smith!* I know Bob, hold on." She typed his name into the internal database, and sure enough "Bob Smith" existed but he was off this particular day. "I can't verify with Bob," she told me with a hint of disappointment, given that we were now about 20 minutes into the call. "He's out of the office."

"Really!" I exclaimed, feigning disappointment but feeling relief. I really did not want to speak to Bob. Eventually, after her following all of her internal procedures and doing so as a professional, we went our separate ways. I marked her name as "Shutdown" so that when we sent the data to the client for the day, they would see who within their organization was acting in the exact way they were training them to. There was no need for me to mark it, it turned out.

Mere hours after the call, I was sitting on my living room floor trying to get a kink out of my back when my cell rang. It was my boss. Surely, he was calling to congratulate me, given I had heroically stayed on a call about eight times longer than our average in order to gain a couple of flags. Negative. He was calling to let me know our client's substantial and prominent legal team had given him a call to threaten ending the contract as one of his employees had name-dropped a point of contact, an action that was strictly forbidden within the terms of the scope. Not the most comfortable conversation we'd ever had.

We were going to lose a very large contract—and I'd probably lose my job—thanks to my using a very dad-like name. In picking a common dad's name in Scotland, at random, and giving it as the third name I had made up for the call, not including my own made-up name, I had unfolded all of this mayhem.

The next few minutes were spent getting my boss to believe I had made up the name, which was an easy start given I had never seen the contract, and didn't know the name I'd inadvertently spat out was actually a C-suite employee.

And I spent the next few hours trying to convince the legal team that I had made the name up. We went through the call what must have been 10 times, listening to me making up names and letting legal ask questions about how I could've possibly arrived at such a name at the drop of a hat. We also listened to what might be the most epic response to a declaration of country, too. The woman who had the voice of an angel also had the ear of a rubber chicken. She was basically in need of a translator—she could not get her ear around my Scottish accent, no matter how much I slowed down or annunciated. About midway through the call I said, "I'm Scottish," as if that was somehow an excuse for my not having any presence at her organization. Her reply: "I am sorry." This, mixed with the fact that I had no real way to know who was listed on our contract, allowed the bank to forgive us, and we lived to vish another day.

However, the point remains: never break pretext, and stick with the goal until you've exhausted every option and you've won or been defeated in a valiant effort.

Smishing/Smshing

Smishing stands for SMS phishing, and it's executed via the target's mobile phone. Many social engineering methods associated with phishing are implemented here, too. You will typically still pose as a representative or as someone familiar with the organization. Smishing works best on individual targets, but there are times when the organization at large can be targeted, too, as famously occurred with the alleged hack of Amazon CEO Jeff Bezos's phone via a link sent through WhatsApp.

I find these sorts of attacks to require short, sharp jabs of AMs. An SMS phish need only inform the target of something, like an account that is not operational, or give a call to action, typically in the form of a link.

Smishing is largely seen as the least creative form of social engineering, but getting a target to believe their bank or organization or delivery service is legitimately texting them takes a fair amount of AMs, for hardened targets, at least. Smishing, by all accounts is an underrated vector, and they matter in the world of security Smishing matters so much, not only because each time one is sent in an organization's name their brand is diluted and trustworthiness is chipped away from a consumer point of view, but also because each Smish puts their customers and employees at risk. Businesses should be taught to think of Smishing the same way they do phishing: a real threat with real consequences.

Make it personal.

Make it urgent.

Make it clear.

Make it concise: Because of *this,* do *that* for *this, more optimal and solution-based* result.

The sheer number of variations on the term phishing may seem extreme, but each represents a potentially catastrophic threat to businesses and their data. But they also represent a way to show an organization how easy and effortless it can be to circumvent their defenses. As I said previously, defensive measures often lag behind offensive measures because it is hard to tell the future accurately. Even if security professionals could see how the future would unfold, how their measures would be circumvented or brute-forced, they would not be able to see how the countermeasures would be exploited. So, yes, defense lags offense. As an EA, your role is to exploit the current shortcomings of a client's defenses and allow them a speedier, smoother road to defense and deterrence.

Impersonation

Impersonation is one of several social engineering tools used to gain access to a system. Most often, impersonation tactics make use of the human tendency to trust or obey. Impersonation can require a lot of preparation and, depending on the person you want to impersonate, you might have to get permission. It will have to be clear, unambiguous permission, too.

I recently led my team on an exciting vishing engagement in which we were targeting a prison service company. We were allowed, per the scope, to impersonate internal employees below the C-level, but one of the flags was a copy of some counterfeited inmates' criminal records placed within the system. For this particular engagement, we impersonated civil servants—nongovernment employees—a technique that was somewhat effective. We also used the title *lawyer* for our pretexts, which yielded good results. Apparently, people will give lawyers a fair amount of information, which seems reasonable—a lawyer may need a copy of a criminal record. However, when we were planning the engagement, we reached out to a friendly contact within law enforcement to ask if we could impersonate one or two officers. We were, in no uncertain terms, told no. However, a real attacker will have no qualms about impersonating an officer or anyone else who would help them achieve their goals. Just like us, they use all the laws of AMs without the rules of engagement.

Ubiquiti Networks, a manufacturer of technology for networking, lost almost $40 million in a 2015 attack. After sending a phishing email, the hackers used the technique of employee impersonation to request fraudulent payments, which were, rather unfortunately, made by the accounting department.

A lawyer, Richard Luthmann, chose a different course of impersonation. He created social media accounts in the names of politicians. He created fake Facebook and Twitter accounts that impersonated political candidates and power brokers and set a myriad of small, figurative fires. For example, he created a page about city councilwoman who talked about "SRO Welfare Hotel Full of Criminals and Drug Addicts" that "she" planned to develop.

Luthmann was apparently unaware that any of this came close to what could be recognized or classified as a crime, stating that he was only engaging in "dirty tricks." A special prosecutor disagreed, and he was indicted on 17 misdemeanor counts, including identity theft.

You can play many roles as an impersonator. The ones I most often come by are repair or maintenance, auditors, fellow employees, and system manufacturers. The list goes on; it's only as short as our imagination. Impersonation works best when you come in full character, so to speak. If your chosen pretext wears a uniform, you should make every conceivable effort to have that uniform. The same goes for an authentic-looking ID badge. The less tangible things you will need are knowledge that appears to be insider information, such as jargon, technical data, and industry-insider terms; names and details about employees; and details on the skills needed to do the job of your chosen pretext. These tricks work because we all regularly interact with people we don't know. It's commonplace and acceptable to trust credentials—a badge or a uniform—and, thankfully for you as an attacker, these things can be forged.

As a network pentester working in Australia, I was part of the team that got to venture out as what I can now identify as social engineers, but what at the time seemed like an inherent part of being a network pentester. I got into a small industrial complex as instructed, but my pretext was based on what would become one of my best fails. My pretext was that I was Swedish, there to inspect the machinery. The co-founder of the business was Swedish, and I was acting as his ambassador.

To the culturally untrained eye, I suppose I could get away with saying I am Swedish. However, as a man with stark white hair and glassy blue eyes approached me yelling what seemed to be exclamations of joy at seeing one of his countryfolk, I noted internally that I could not fake knowing Swedish. Alas, it did not stop me from trying. As our paths collided, he held out his hand, saying, "Hej trevligt att träffas!" I replied, "Ya!" and quite enthusiastically, too. (I know this because my whole team watched this scene on repeat for about a week after thanks to iPhone's recording possibilities.) He then asked me some follow-up questions, also in Swedish, which was not ideal for me. Soon thereafter, he switched to English and eventually had me escorted out.

He'd started out with, "Hi, nice to meet you!" and had quickly moved to, "Okay, well, she does not work for the company, we should call the police."

Your pretext should be slightly more airtight than that.

Physical

In performing physical social engineering assessments as an EA, you are a company's capability in defending against unethical attackers. A walk-through of how you executed your attack and how you achieved the objective, or at least partially achieved it, gives organizations a wealth of knowledge about just how secure they really are, what issues they can fix, and what measures they can take to fix those issues.

However, you also have to be aware enough to observe the paths you *didn't* take. For instance, on one engagement I could have gained unfettered access to the facility where my client's production took place by jumping up onto the loading dock and walking through the fire door that was propped open, taken the physical keys left on the office table, and then enjoyed unrestricted access to the facility thereafter. And I for sure had a look at that route, even photographing it. The reason I didn't take it all the way to its fullest potential was, and this is not to sound arrogant, but it would have been too easy. This client would have learned nothing of the actual dangers. In just telling them of this observed one, they could easily remedy it. Proving it seemed unnecessary and like taking a liberty.

Physical assessments are often seen as specialized, but they are a growing trend, with many businesses seeing them as the next "must-have" service. My hope is that these assessments are not treated as special ops missions in all cases. As an attacker, you must be able to confidently tread the thin line of what's a substantial find for your client and what is essentially special-operations theater. There will be cases when you will have to get extremely tactical and creative with your attacks. However, those types of attacks should be reserved for the clients who are extremely well protected and who will benefit from such extremes and creativity. Underwater data centers that require physical testing is an example of this. Protected government buildings are another.

In a related, but different, topic, keep in mind that attacker mentality doesn't always point outward; it can also be introspective, protecting us from doing things that will ultimately work against our interest, such as taking illegal, dangerous, or unprofitable actions. Such actions include stopping an entire group of people as they walk toward you, who were almost oblivious to your presence, in a bank you aren't supposed to be in.

Back to the Manhattan Bank

As the words, "I'm Jeff and I'm not expecting any papers" hit me, I got what is surely evolution's way of punishing me for my trade—a nerve rash that spread all the way up my neck and pushed out into patches on my cheeks. I could literally feel my face heat up. I had no contingency plan for this.

"Jeff. Hi. Diana. Sorry for turning up on such short notice!" I said in my best impression of an apologetic lawyer and not an imposter. I held out my hand for him to shake. "I've brought papers from Sullivan's for you to look over."

"This is very unusual," he said, not raising his hand to shake mine. The group he'd been walking with dispersed around us, grunting their goodbyes to Jeff. "My office is just down here; let's take a look."

As we headed to his office, I barely had the confidence to make small talk. I'd agreed to put a brief moratorium on calling myself an idiot internally, but it hadn't immediately kicked into action. "Good day, so far?" I struggled out, feigning a nonchalant spirit I did not feel.

"Yes," he replied tartly, without looking away from our current course. I said nothing in reply; I just nodded. As we reached his office, I committed to the only rational path I could think of at the time: the fourth law of AMs: never break pretext. "Let's see these papers, Diana," he said, looking me dead in the eyes, hunched over his desk and giving off an air of being inconvenienced.

"Sure thing!" I slammed the briefcase down on the desk. At the time, I did so mainly to show him I was not scared of his tone; he seemed to want to intimidate me. Looking back, my action was a bit weird. He was just a little abrasive, but my adrenaline was too high to work these things out in real time. Fighting fire with fire just makes a bigger, hotter fire, it turns out.

I clicked the case open and inside was what looked like the whole of the Amazon rainforest scattered around it. "Ah! Yeah, there was an incident downstairs. I might just take a minute to reorganize these, if you don't mind?" I wasn't really asking as much as saying, "I am going to make up a new plan in my mind behind the lid of this case. Please allow me to sit here and do that."

"I actually don't have all day, Diana. You've interrupted me on my way to a very important meeting."

Jeff was becoming a very good target.

"I am so sorry! How about this? I have all the papers on this USB. It will be faster to reprint them than to reorganize them. Do you mind?" I asked as I looked from the USB to his computer a few times to make my point.

"I do mind! What are these papers about? Why are you here today? Why have I not been told about this?" His face flashed anger like a blinking light.

"All good questions. Listen, maybe I've caught you at a bad time, but I am just going to step out now as you obviously have a lot going on and I don't want to frustrate you further." I gathered the case and placed the USB back into its safehouse: my pocket. Unceremoniously, I opened his office door; before stepping out and walking down the hall like a bat out of hell, I said, "I'll have the firm reach out to you for a better time," and then I crossed the threshold to what seemed like freedom from the indignation of Jeff.

"As you should!" he spat back, his words chasing me down the corridor.

"That did not go to plan at all!" I said half-jokingly to myself. Back to the bathrooms. Upon sitting on the very uncomfortable throne of porcelain shame, at the end of the cubicle line, I thought about two good things I'd learned from my brief time with Jeff: he did not lock his office door, and he definitely had a meeting to go to. I let 10 minutes go by, slid out of my top layer of clothing, folded it down and slid it into the briefcase, tied my hair up, and made my way back to Jeff's office.

The good thing about the setup in the office was that the middle of it was like a large pit for people, with the peripherals only offices. There was one sort of tunnel that shielded some of the executive offices from pit view. Jeff's had a partial view of the floor, but his space was private enough from most angles that few people would likely see me parading around his office as an unwanted guest for the second time in a day. There were also a few communal hubs splashed around the huge floor. I made my way to the closest and smallest hub that was currently unused. Slid in, pushed the brief-case to the far end of the table, and waited a beat. I pulled out a sheet of paper from it, placed it next to the case, and left it there, hoping that people, for a while at least, would just think the hub was occu-pied and keep on walking. I didn't want to carry it into Jeff's office again and leave it in the bathroom; that would have been far more suspicious. I slid out from the table and chair and walked toward Jeff's office. As I approached, keeping my body pointing forward as if I my intention was *not* to go into his office, I could tell he had vacated it. I pivoted on the spot and raced into it, flipped the light switch off, plucked the USB from my pocket, and shoved it into his computer.

Jeff also had not locked his computer. I snapped a picture and was just about on my merry way when his phone lit up the room like a '90s disco. The caller's number appeared in big, bold, black digits and, what's more, I recognized it. Without having to double-check, my gut told me what I absolutely did not want to know. It was secu-rity. "Dammit, Jeff, why!" I whispered to myself. I retreated from the office and made my way through the pit of people paying little atten-tion to me, thankfully. I got back into the little hub and gathered my things. Sitting there for a second, I pondered my best move. I had absolutely no way to predict how long Jeff's meeting would take, but I did know I did not want to be on the floor when he made his way back to the office, lest he see me.

Back to the toilet cubicle.

Summary

- As an ethical attacker, you advance businesses', institutions', and governments' fundamental and enduring security needs: the protection of livelihoods, information, and data.
- Effectively, your goal is always to enhance security. You are an instrument for ensuring security. Accordingly, the primary purpose of an ethical attacker is to deter threats against an organization and its interests, and to help them defeat such threats should deterrence fail, by empowering them with awareness of what an attack looks and feels like.
- There are asymmetric challenges in being a target and an attacker, often skewed to the attacker's benefit. This is a legitimate concern for businesses the world over. But, alas, just worrying about it won't do.
- As ethical attackers, you are to increase your targets' capabilities to counter these threats and adapt to them defensively via training.
- Much goes into attack strategy, including all the AMs Laws. Furthermore, to defend and protect your clients after they've been your targets, your objective must become the promotion of stability and the ability to defeat real adversaries.

Key Message

Attackers always have a gain in mind—also known as the objective. The attack strategy is only concerned with how to achieve that objective in the most efficient way.

Even in this data-driven era, many people can be tricked by mass emails and calls that seem to apply to their environment—an important point to consider in an attack.

Chapter 9

Psychology in Attacks

The job isn't always just to "get in." Usually there's work to be done after the initial breach. Access is just the first hurdle. Following an initial compromise, you will try to gain traction and maintain your place within the environment. For example, after entering into a system, a pentester will try to increase his privileges to administrator level to install an application, modify, exfiltrate, or hide data. A physical pentester will attempt a similar endeavor, typically by getting deeper into the building, penetrating it until the asset, location, or data has been reached. It starts with what is called *gaining a foothold*, and this chapter looks at the tactics you, as an ethical attacker, can use to gain a foothold and some tactics that will help you establish a firmer one.

Setting The Scene: Why Psychology Matters

We've looked at the process of gaining a contract or other legally binding correspondence, specifically the scope and how that directly affects what you can do as an attacker, while noting it does not hamper the mindset; rather, it should make your AMs perform at a more creative level. We've also looked at what makes OSINT important and what your AMs should provide you with in regards to OSINT finds and searches, routes, and rabbit holes—specifically weaponization and leveraging through the tie-back method.

Now, though, I want to turn to the things you as an ethical attacker (EA) must do to gain a foothold within an organization and how to maintain your position and then increase it. In network pen testing, access can take various forms, and the prosperous attacker will often creatively come up with multiple attack vectors. Once they have completed comprehensive recon and know all the ports, services, and apps, they may turn to the vulnerability databases to look for known vulnerabilities and exploits. Their attack methodology will differ based on whether they have remote access or local access and if they have physical access to the network. But in any case, it's widely accepted that if an attacker can circumvent security, all bets are off. This last point is why your job as an EA is so vital – in the physical or network category; they are not mutually exclusive. They can be complementary or extremely potent when used together. Of course, sometimes your client, your skill, or your objective means that both options in tandem aren't available and so only one type of attack will be performed. In any case, gaining a foothold and penetrating further into the organization (or operation) has some identical tactics, regardless of the mode used.

My experience and conversations with people in the community tell me that gaining access physically as an attacker is no more anxiety-inducing than testing the network—it's completely dependent on the person executing the attack. This is where offensive attacker mindsets (OAMs) and defensive attacker mindsets (DAMs) come into play (see Chapter 2, "Offensive vs. Defensive Attacker Mindset"). Contrary to popular opinion, it is advantageous to plan something that might rely on seizing an opportunity in the moment, which sounds utterly absurd at first, but bear with me.

As in football, where a team trains, practices things that might never happen, such as an intercept, passing, and possession play, all the time knowing that the games they train for won't necessarily turn into the games they play, you too must plan this way. You must strategize how you will get access and gain more—this type of planning is one of the most fundamental and vital steps you will take as an EA, even if the actual event(s) are nothing like your imaginings. Planning leads to flexibility. This method goes all the way back to one of the first mental models I talked about and have threaded throughout this book: a game of mental chess. Think through all the options you may have based on the information you've collected. Imagine the situation unfolding in all directions, and envisage your reactions to all the good and bad, positive and negative scenarios you can come up with (keep them based in reality of course) because here's the thing: your reactions matter most. People will do, say, and act however they *feel* they should most of the time. You must react how you *think* you should. Going through the motions in your mind will help you react in a way that's best for the objective more than any other type of preparation. More than how important your reactions are is how important your reaction time is. This is the key to attack psychology, because as a social engineer, for example, you are already reading a person's non-verbals, assessing and analyzing them. It's part and parcel of the job. Having your reaction manufactured and ready in the nick of time may seem like a big ask, but I proffer we do this much of the time in social situations: we get ready for the laugh when someone is telling us a colorful story enthusiastically; we get ready to be outraged when our friends tell us a scandalizing story; we get in line with someone else's happiness as they are telling us the reason for it. It's not always logical, but it's part of the human condition. Therefore, it's not as big an ask as you may have first thought to be ready with a reaction when testing.

It can be applied to network pen testing, as an example, too. Your reaction time matters as it plays heavily into the "thinking on your feet" approach that is so critical in that sort of testing. For example, password cracking is great but it can take anywhere from minutes to years to perform; a hacker with the ability to problem solve and react quickly might work out the easiest thing to do it to move around it. Spoofing attacks are a great example: you may be able to take advantage of misconfigurations of workstations on the internal network in order to collect password hashes, which can then be taken offline and cracked, but you could also search for admin consoles with default credentials.

Lateral movement techniques are definitely not lacking in number or diversity, and they typically follow the same process: gain access to a low-privileged asset with low protection, escalate privileges and seek out targets of interest on the network. The type of lateral movement may need to be decided on quickly—you will nearly always have to do internal recon after initial access, and that can be noisy.

From another perspective, unethical hackers process information and use it unnervingly quickly. According to research by the Federal Trade Commission, it took only nine minutes before the hackers tried to access the information from a fake data breach (`https://www.consumer.ftc.gov/blog/2017/05/how-fast-will-identity-thieves-use-stolen-info`). First, they created a database of information of about 100 fake consumers. To make it seem legitimate, the Financial Trade Commission used popular names based on Census data, addresses from across the country, phone numbers that corresponded to the addresses, intuitive email addresses based on the information, and they provided payment information, too. They then posted the data on two different occasions on a website that is used to make stolen credentials public. After the second posting, it took only nine minutes before the information was accessed. We have to think like this, too. This is how we, the ethical hackers, get ahead on both the offensive and defensive curves.

You must have a plan in mind for both ingress and egress but take the opportunities when they arise. It's also vital to note that access does not equal privilege escalation. You can have limited access both physically and on the network. However, it can be a little harder to cover your tracks if you have limited access on a physical job. I once entered a building through the back entrance. A very helpful man (a lucrative target within the environment) held it open for me as he left, presumably for the day. It feels pretty good when getting in is that easy.

Continuing this account, upon getting inside, I saw the only room open to me was the cafeteria, and the only open exit led back to the street. There were two more doors inside, but both were locked. One was a solid door at the top of a staircase, but the other had a small window. Through it I could see all the way into reception, but I couldn't get there because I didn't have a card. Worse still, it was quite late in the day when I gained access, so I had missed the lunchtime folk passing through. The building lacked security personnel, so I did what any respectable social engineer testing physical security would do: I made myself a cup of coffee and sat at the closest table to the connecting door.

I did this for two reasons:

- If someone came in, I could swiftly get up and catch the door before it closed behind them.
- Coffee tastes better when it is free.

Eventually someone did come in, and I managed to make it look like I was just getting ready to leave anyway and got through the door before it slammed shut. However, what is most notable is that my initial access did not guarantee privilege escalation; it merely upped the odds. I did not know the layout of the building because there was no OSINT or outside observation to tell me that, so I couldn't plan for a better route in. The back entrance seemed like the most attractive and least bold entry point. However, it was only on-the-spot thinking that led me to sit with a coffee, which is a very inconspicuous thing to be doing in a cafeteria, and remain close to the door so that I could catch it—which in the end permitted me access. I didn't plan it, it's not particularly brilliant, but it is a way of thinking; it's a way of anticipating progress and waiting for the payoff.

However, with a bit of planning and a few games of mental chess beforehand, I might have concluded that was the best route forward, or I may have chosen to leave and then try to gain access through the front door at a better time.

Ego Suspension, Humility & Asking for Help

There is something else that complements the planning and execution. It will be one of the most significant and powerful tools in your AMs arsenal: ego suspension.

Ego suspension is the ability to suppress one's own wants, needs, and motivations and place priority on the other person. I consider it one of the most powerful techniques for building rapport, and in terms of AMs, it falls under the fifth skill of self awareness. Oddly enough, as an attacker, you will likely find that you want your targets to perceive you as humble. This trait is often associated with honesty in my experience and a way to fly easily under the radar. Effectively, ego suspension can ostensibly neutralize your threat shadow (your threat shadow refers to the activities, actions, contributions, and communications taken as an attacker even though you are acting through a pretext).

Ego suspension is easy in theory. It's the act of intentionally placing the focus on the other person, which often serves to further increase your own trustworthiness. The ability to suspend one's ego leads to overall likeability. This alone increases the probability that people will be more open to your requests and appeals. There are other ways to get people to comply with your requests. For instance, you could use authority. However, not everyone can be intimidated, and even if they were, it's not always the most effective way to get what you want. If you can make people like you, then you have created a path in which the fruits of your labor may last longer. This all sounds great, doesn't it? All you have to do to gain access to a secured building or network, by my reckoning, is to not let your nerves get the best of you, use your OAMs and DAMs, employ critical thought and heuristic prowess as needed, gather some intel, walk in and place yourself in a lower position than your target, and watch them bend to your will.

Alas, no. That would be a pretty good outcome, but this book would then be more akin to a novel.

Ego suspension is a difficult beast to battle. That's because ego, no matter what flavor of it you have, is linked to who you are.

It's a large chunk of your identity. The solution is not quite as simple as I'd like. Because ego is inseparably connected with who you are, the act of suppressing it is often in direct conflict with your mind's autopilot goals. Our ego lets us believe that people see who we are projecting ourselves to be—this is the ego's great delusion. Whether it be intelligent, intellectual, sharp-witted, reasoned, composed, competent, nice, moral, attractive, easy-going, etc., we all want to present ourselves in a certain way. As humans, we know that any time we speak or engage with others, judgment typically follows, which impacts how we are treated.

It is a natural tendency to want others to think favorably of us, because this impacts our self-esteem. Most people have been in a situation where a conversation has escalated to wild claims of understanding and skill in a domain—where no matter than you say, the person you're talking to knows what you know but knows it *better*. Perhaps you have even been this person. The stronger we feel about a subject, the more difficult it is to maintain an air of neutrality or ignorance. So, when you are standing in front of a top executive in their headquarters, asking to place a USB drive into their machine, and they say that they couldn't possibly allow that but that you could talk to their assistants, it can be hard to suppress gloating and a sense of smugness, which is a form of ego.

This is why ego suspension can be so difficult—it's your sense of self-esteem or sense of self-importance, and it can be at odds with someone else's. Law 4 of AMs says everything you do is in favor of the objective. Someone standing in the way of what's important to you might make suspending your ego and sense of importance difficult. But, despite how hard it can be to suspend your ego, learning to do so is a critical skill for an EA; you will be much more effective in your interactions.

Ego suspension is also the base for many other tools you can use as an EA, ultimately leading to rapport and the target liking you, or at the very least viewing you as nonthreatening. The bottom line is, help people feel valued and they will help you; that starts with ego suspension.

Ego suspension falls firmly under self-awareness. In *Ego Is the Enemy* (Portfolio, 2016), author Ryan Holiday explores how ego hinders our development more often than not. Our ego makes us say, "It was just a mistake" when in fact, your ego is attempting to protect itself by playing down your mistakes. Mistakes aren't patterns. They are typically made a couple of times, with the person making them learning from them. Mistakes that continue to happen are flaws. Record the mistakes you make most often on jobs, and note the reason. You can generally reduce the reasons down to a lack of attention or focus, poverty of information, impatience, or non suspension of ego (lack of humility).

This level of introspection will take a certain amount of self-awareness. Self-awareness itself is the ability and tendency to pay attention to the way you think, feel, and behave. It is understanding our own emotions and moods as well as how we behave and act. Making the changes to become and stay self-aware will take humility and more self-awareness.

Remember, self-awareness is invisible; you cannot see if someone is self-aware, but you will know if they are or not because they will leave you feeling a certain way. Think of the "friend" who doesn't stop talking, doesn't ask you how you are, isn't interested in whatever is happening in your life at all. They only talk about their own life, their own circumstances, and they give you their own thoughts on matters, never asking for your input. They are most likely *not* very self-aware. When dealing with someone like this, I often am left feeling drained and sometimes dejected.

Increasing your self-awareness will allow you to adapt to your circumstances, adapt to your opponent's ego, and leave them feeling the way that's most fitting for your objective and your circumstances. Most often, it's to your advantage to make someone feel as though they helped you, not that you won. But increasing your own self-awareness is two things: the first is difficult and the second is never-ending. But, fear not, there are a few steps you can take to start the journey: ask for feedback on yourself and take it well! Choose a solid relationship in your life and start small.

Identify your cognitive distortions (essentially how we lie to ourselves). By diagnosing the irrational thoughts and beliefs that you unknowingly reinforce over time, you can free yourself of them, pruning them out of your psyche. Some of the more common ones include the *Nothing Thinking/Polarized Thinking* also known as *Black-and-White Thinking* which results in you seeing things in terms of extremes—you are either perfect or a total failure, etc.

Another is overgeneralization that makes you view a single event as an invariable rule, so that, for example, if someone lets you down once, they will always let you down. Another is Jumping to Conclusions, also known as *Mind Reading*. This distortion manifests as the inaccurate belief that you know what another person is thinking. Whilst you might have an idea and be able to infer from time to time, this distortion is tied to the pessimistic and unfavorable interpretations that we jump to.

Magnification (Catastrophizing) or Minimization, also known as the *Binocular Trick* can skew how you see reality, too. This distortion involves exaggerating or minimizing the meaning, importance, or likelihood of things. A pentester who is generally savvy and sharp but makes a mistake may magnify the importance of that mistake and believe that they are actually not good at their job (which could lead to or stem from imposter syndrome), while a pentester who always performs, is agile and quick, and that can live off of the land when tools cannot be used, may minimize the importance of their skill and continue believing that they are simply lucky.

There's also Emotional Reasoning which refers to the acceptance of your emotions as fact. For easy understanding's sake, I can reduce it to "I feel it, therefore it must be true." This is common, but as is logical, feelings are not facts and they often change with nothing more than time.

Should Statements imposed on yourself (what you "should" do or what you "must" do) are damaging because they introduce stress, which can lead to increased anxiety and avoidance behaviors. They are also notably damaging when applied to others because by making these statements, you are essentially imposing a set of expectations that will likely not be met, which can lead to anger and resentment, which is toxic in a professional or personal setting.

Control Fallacies are another category of cognitive distortion. This distortion can manifest one of two ways: (1) that you have no control over your life, no agency at all, and that you are a helpless victim of fate, or (2) that you are in complete control of yourself and your surroundings, the latter one being a distortion I am prone to.

Whichever way you lean, both are damaging, and both are equally inaccurate. No one is in complete control of everything happens to them although I'd like to believe that we are. And no one has absolutely no control over their situation.

The final one I will list is my least favorite and most recognizable from a self-awareness point of view: Always Being Right.

Those struggling with Imposter Syndrome or those with an anal retentive personality may recognize this distortion—it is the belief and truly *feeling* that you must always be right. Being wrong is absolutely unacceptable, and you will fight to the figurative death to prove that you are right.

There's another benefit of self-awareness and ego suspension that should be noted: your ego will tell you that you have to be the best, you have to play your best character and role to date, you have to *best* the client so that they are on their knees by the time you depart. This is not accurate. You have to assess the client and outwit them. That's a game of data analysis and then acting based on the answers. You do not have to be James Bond. You don't have to play complicated openings or closing moves. Don't let your ego or your DAMs win in those moments.

Ego will also tell you that you don't have to go through the sewers, that you will find another way in. . .or that you don't have to hide in the bathroom for hours on end. . .or that you won't be the one to get shot on the engagement where the security guards have guns. . .or that you can pull off that southern accent. . . or that no one else could do what you do. Don't let ego do this to you. Use your DAMs, not your ego, to calculate risks.

Additionally, chess players study general opening principles, basic tactical and checkmate motifs, pawn structure, strategy, and endgames, too. The best chess players sidestep ego. They have to. You are never done learning chess; you will never know every move. It's not too dissimilar to our line of work as ethical attackers. The landscape will always change; the world will always be changing, and it's not enough just to change with it, we have to be aware of where it's headed, take preemptive courses of action and be okay with being off by a few degrees, but smart enough and sharp enough to fix our erroneous solutions.

Self-awareness in terms of ego suspension forces us to do one other thing: ensure that you are studying material that is appropriate for your level. You might have to study the basics of networks before you start on commands. You might have to study lock picking before you start scaling buildings. Even as you progress, learning things like bypassing alarms and using network security protocols, you will have to be able to recall and be up-to-date with the latest techniques for the basics.

Moreover, you will have to constantly find ways to test your knowledge. Doing so will help you know when you can move on to studying and practicing more complex concepts and skills, and it will keep you honest with yourself insofar as what you retain. I recommend performing OSINT challenges, taking capture-the-flag and red team courses, writing phishes and getting feedback, and gathering OSINT on yourself and your loved ones.

Ego suspension and self-awareness means that before you can get really good, you have to be comfortable being bad. It also means that you should not be afraid to make mistakes. Get the basics, move forward as you need to, and refresh whenever possible.

Humility

Humility isn't just a virtue but also a trait. It heavily relates to the degree to which we value and promote our interests above others, and this is why it's such a powerful weapon in an attacker's arsenal: it helps you adhere to the fourth law: every move made is for the good of the objective.

Humility is also an important factor in knowing jurisdiction over a situation does not always have to be conspicuous or explicitly said to be felt. If you are impersonating someone who is above your target in the hierarchy, the target will know that. You may not have to do anything more than tell them "your" name. Explicitly making the point that "you" are their superior is often moot. Allow them to do some of the heavy lifting for you.

Humility also allows two other things that aren't synonymous with *attacker* but that are powerful when used by one:

- An ability to acknowledge mistakes and limitations
- Low self-focus

The last in that list ties back to law four, also. Your focus is the objective.

Asking for Help

Sometimes, in order to influence others, you will find it prudent and rewarding to begin with what appears to be vulnerability and openness, which then helps your play into assistance themes. The success of this technique relies on the human desire to help when asked.

Mutually beneficial and altruistic behavior is common throughout the animal kingdom, especially in species with complex social structures. Across many studies of mammals, from mouse to man, data suggests that we are profoundly shaped by our social environments, and we are biologically inclined to help others. Each of these motivates people to engage in what is called *prosocial behavior*. So simply asking for help can be effective, but you will need to have at least temporarily muted your ego to ask for help and approach the person you wish to ask with a level of humility that is moderately conspicuous. In other words, you cannot show them your expectation of help just because you are aware helping each other may be a natural instinct. The good news is that as humans, we're generally not good at suppressing instincts (helpful when considering targets): the bad news is that as humans, we're generally not good at suppressing instincts (not helpful when considering what we have to contend with internally as attackers).

Another Chess Parallel: Opening Selection

Your opening is where self-awareness matters most in terms of what is critical to the operation. If you have low self-awareness in the recon and OSINT stages—where you don't know what you aren't good at—you will fail to collect sufficient information to construct a good attack. If you have low self-awareness in the actual execution of the operation, you run the risk of ruining it. Unlike with OSINT, you likely won't get any second chances.

When it comes to your openings, three things matter most: mental agility, self-awareness, and your pretext. There will likely be several options on most jobs. Your opening is based mainly on how you approach with your pretext. The pretext is the narrative in which you are the detail. You will need self-awareness and typically some degree of ego suspension to pull your pretext off. You will also need mental agility, in order to bend incoming and already known information to fit the circumstances in which you find yourself. Remember, you are always working in the best interests of your objective.

Introducing the Target-Attacker Window Model

As I've shown, it matters more what the target thinks of you than what you think of the target. You have to be able to read the target, but you don't have to be sold on their story, mainly because you are approaching them. Their story is likely to stand. To be honest, I don't know if there's a brain in the world with enough bandwidth to run mental games of chess all the way to the moment you walk into the target environment only to find out it's a front.

The target for you is your obstacle—how they perceive you matters immensely. The Target-Attacker Window Model (TAWM) addresses this. Specifically, the model focuses on why snuffing out ego is often difficult. The egotist may not know that ego exists; they may have a skewed self-perception or be deluded by ego and false entitlements. Not being able to identify your own ego at play is common and often invisible to the bearers. This would fall under the "Known by target(s)" pane, which is covered in the next section, "Four TAWM Regions."

TAWM is based on the Johari Window model, devised by two American psychologists named Joseph Luft and Harry Ingham. The Johari model was produced in 1955 whilst the two men were researching group dynamics at the University of California, Los Angeles. TAWM is made up of four panes and is a simple and useful tool for illustrating the attacker's vantage point as well as the target's. It can be used for much more than just identifying ego and, by extension, identifying ways to suppress it. This model can be used to assess and improve an attacker's ability to further disguise themselves and to gain the upper hand through knowledge. The model can also be used for understanding and training self-awareness, development, and target-attacker dynamics.

Four TAWM Regions

The TAWM window is a technique that helps ethical attackers better understand their relationship with themselves and their targets. It's made up of four quadrants that visualize the attacker's known or unknown information.

Known by All What is known by the attacker about themselves and is also known by others

Known by Target(s) What is unknown by the attacker about themselves but that others know

Hidden   What the attacker knows about themselves that others do not know

Unknown by All   What is unknown by the attacker about themselves and is also unknown by others

The TAWM window, depicted here, is based on a four-square grid.

In the field tactics of an attacker, the two on the left are the most advantageous, whereas the two on the right are the most problematic and the exact reasons why you cannot predict outcomes but only stack the odds in your favor, which I will circle back to in a moment.

For now, let's break the categories down. There are certain things that are apparent as you walk into a building. Unless you are disguised, the first person or people you meet, most often the first line of defense within an organization, know that you are whichever gender you are and how you look physically. These two things are known to you, too. They are "Known by All." There's nothing magical about this category. Everything you know and that is also known by the outside world (upon interaction) is represented in this category. Known by All includes factors like accent, health status (broadly speaking), and confidence level. As an attacker, you want the faux reason you are there to be in this category, too. If you show up as a mechanic, look like one. If you show up as the boss, look like one based on that company's culture.

The pane directly below Known by All is Hidden. Hidden is both your objective and what your pretext conceals. Hidden is why you are there in the first place and the basis of the attack; it is also your AMs as applied to the attack. The Hidden pane is perhaps the most important set of things you are in charge of. It's everything you don't want revealed about yourself; it's the bolstering cause and effect of the operation and should be protected at all costs. It is the employment of every skill and law of the mindset.

Known by Target(s) is my least favorite category but perhaps the most important to play around with mentally. How your target thinks of their job, feels about their role, and what they know about their environment and perceive of you are all contained within this category. Those are all things that can go either for or against you. Scary, right? Well, I do have one piece of good news: the previous figure misrepresents the size of the panes. They are not all equal, because some have more influence than others. Realistically, the categories should be represented by their impact on the whole engagement. If I had started out like that, they would've looked more like the following graphic, give or take, based on the skills of each attacker and the security culture in each individual environment.

Ego suspension is a huge part of what I teach in my Advanced Practical Social Engineering course and is a fundamental skill. You can have every other facet of an attack down, but if your AMs can't handle the suspension of your ego, all bets are off. If you know your ego is at play, you will have an easier time of subduing it where and when advantageous. If you don't and your ego falls within the Known by Target(s) pane under Not Known to Self, you may find many of your interactions and engagements going awry, even if they are meticulously planned.

There's a simple reason ego suspension is so important. It boils down to the fact that you cannot appeal to someone else's ego if your own is in the way. And most of the time, you need to appeal to your target's ego in order to influence and steer them in the direction you need them to take. Your ego will always want you to do and be the best, but it will help you resist doing some of the less glamorous things that you might have to when executing an attack, like dumpster diving or entering through sewers or cargo bays. It might stop you from starting your vishing calls toward the bottom of the organizational chart because your aim is to get to the CEO, and you shouldn't waste your time with those lower in rank. Big mistake. Your job is to gain information and weaponize it. No target is too big or too small.

Target Psychology

Many attacks exploit psychology to a larger degree than technology. As computer security professional Bruce Schneier once said, "Only amateurs attack technology; professionals target people." However, that's because it's easier in many ways than dancing with technology—attacking a person will yield a far greater payout than targeting technology most of the time. I would go as far to say that the most brilliant yet most terrifying attacks we have seen in our lifetimes, whether it be those that threaten the global supply chain, like the Maersk debacle, or those like Frank Abagnale's Pan Am pilot jaunt, contain a hefty element of AMs that rubs up against technology only slightly.

With Maersk, it is understood that the NotPetya malware got into corporate networks via a hijacked software update for a Ukrainian tax software tool. The attack was executed via phishing emails, which helped take down the world's largest shipping corporation.

At the peak of infection, almost all connected assets owned by the corporation were touched directly or indirectly by the phish. Some of the computer screens affected read "repairing file system on C:" with a simple warning not to turn it off. Others were a little more menacing, reading "Oops, your important files are encrypted" accompanied by a demand to pay $300 worth of bitcoin in order for them to be decrypted. This onscreen messaging included a single kiosk in a gift shop stationed within a basement in Copenhagen. People reportedly ran into conference rooms and unplugged machines in the middle of meetings, and hurdled over locked keycard gates, which had also been rendered useless by the malware.

Disconnecting Maersk's entire global network took the company's IT staff about two hours, but the phish likely took far less time to formulate and definitely less time to send. Employees—rendered entirely idle without computers, servers, routers, or desk phones—were left without work. Maersk ships operated normally throughout the ordeal, but for roughly two days, affected terminals couldn't fulfil their function and move cargo. NotPetya affected Maersk's global business, too, and IT costs weren't insignificant either.

As I pointed out earlier, this all started with phishing. But it's something more general that's the true point of reference here: as humans, when one party believes the intent is pure, a vulnerability is created. Your AMs must use this as its compass for doing bad (for the sake of good of course). It must be able to create a vulnerability with that principle in mind and be able to use it to your advantage time and time again. You create the vulnerability; you yourself are the exploit.

This rule applies to every vector I talked about in Chapter 8, "Attack Strategy"; with phishing, vishing, smishing, and in-person, you only need the other party to believe that your intent is pure to allow a vulnerability to be created. You may not always be able to exploit it, but creating it is the first step in any case, and it stems, of course, from your pretext and committing to it for as long as it works for you.

Committing to a pretext in and of itself is powerful. Fairly recently a Malaysian bank robber who used social engineering as his primary weapon in a string of thefts successfully gained $142,000 by pretending to be a fire extinguisher maintenance technician. He never broke his pretext, and what's more, he never bothered to make it more convincing than the words coming out of his mouth. Where you and I would typically dress the part of our chosen pretext, this man approached his target environment carrying a backpack and dressed casually in a T-shirt and shorts. He walked into the bank with a single document that he claimed was a floor plan for the building. According to local reports and CCTV footage, he simply displayed the paper to a bank manager and requested permission to do an inspection. He was refused access by the manager upon being incapable of producing any sort of identification to corroborate his story. But, even a bank manager needs lunch. While the manager was away, the attacker continued to check extinguishers and the whole environment continued as was normal, with staff assisting customers and keeping business rolling. Working quickly but discreetly, the attacker got closer and closer to the safe room, needing only one thing to happen—for the head cashier to access the area. And when that happened, he essentially tailgated his way to quite a bounty.

Niftily using a magnet on the door's lock, preventing it from shutting fully, he waited until the coast was clear before entering. Once inside the secure area, he pushed a hefty amount of cash into his backpack and walked away. In a bid to make a convincing escape, the attacker approached a security guard and explained that he was leaving to get additional staff to help with the inspection. All told, he was inside the bank for less than 20 minutes and walked away with $142,000.

In a final short example, we look to Frank Abagnale, maybe my favorite social engineer of all time. He predates the industry in terms of security, and he's been on both sides of the law. His AMs is sharp, and when combined with his instincts, he created precise conditions that allowed vulnerabilities to be created, which he exploited in plain sight. Frank Abagnale is most often associated with the Steven Spielberg movie *Catch Me If You Can*, with Leonardo DiCaprio portraying a handsome, charming young man using somewhat ingenious crimes as paydays. Abagnale is a famous check forger, imposter, and con artist. He was between the ages of 15 and 21 when he committed most of his crimes. He was arrested multiple times in multiple countries, spending six months in a French prison, six months in a Swedish prison, and finally four years in a US prison in Atlanta, Georgia. That's generally the extent of what people know about him. But Abagnale escaped prison in 1971 in one of the most agile and AMs-centric methods you could ask for, and unlike with many of his other exploits, Abagnale had help this time.

Abagnale was transferred into prison by a US Marshal, who inadvertently forgot to give the prison his detention commitment. This struck the administration as odd and caused the guards to believe that he was a prison inspector sent by the FBI. Frank Abagnale was a sharp observer by this point, so he quickly took in the information and used it to create a vulnerability to be used against the prison. He used his one phone call to speak to Jean Sebring (as she was named in his book), a friend of his, and asked her to forge a business card to back up the story the prison administrators had told themselves. Once the card was delivered to Abagnale, he donned the pretext they'd created for him and finally told the guards the "truth" that they wanted to hear—that he was in fact an inspector sent by the FBI. The guards believed him and even bragged about how they knew all along. Ultimately, they allowed Frank to leave the facility.

Social engineering, for good or bad, when used in tandem with AMs is a powerful force to be reckoned with, and the best way to wield this force is to understand elements of psychology, the traits we have in common, and the best way to exploit them. So, with that in mind, let's look at target psychology, beyond what was discussed in relation to TAWM, and find out which human pressure points your AMs is best applied to. You should know by now that AMs has its benefits and that having a strong AMs puts you at the top of the food chain. But to truly have a well-rounded AMs, you will need two things, both of which all the examples in this book have incorporated:

- Empathy
- Knowing the pitfalls of human behavior as they pertain to security and, specifically, to you as an attacker

Empathy is important because it allows you to place yourself in the shoes of the target. This ability to empathize, even if it's just cognitive empathy, is strongly related to the ability to use human nature against those you are attacking. This is even beneficial to those of us that only attack digital assets; knowing how to hide your tracks is often linked with knowing how to disguise them to humans. Being able to place yourself in the shoes of someone else allows you to be able to exploit the individual more easily.

Empathy is the birthplace of the principle I've been talking about in this chapter. As humans, when one party believes the intent is pure, a vulnerability is created. Every breach occurs because someone did something they weren't supposed to do, or somebody failed to do something they were supposed to do. This is the perfect counterpart to knowing that the basic premise of social engineering is that people have certain predictable characteristics such as an innate desire to be helpful, and that, when put under time pressure from someone they believe to be genuine, they will be prone to bypassing basic security protocols.

Given this, I will look at three of the most potent and prevalent biases we can use to our advantage as attackers:

- Optimism bias
- Confirmation bias and motivated reasoning
- Framing effect

Optimism Bias

People tend to overestimate the probability of positive events and underestimate the probability of negative events happening to them in the future, as author Tali Sharot says in her book, *The Optimism Bias* (Vintage, 2012). For example, I may underestimate my risk of getting hit by a car and overestimate my future success on the stock market—that's optimism, right? I really don't want to be hit by a car, but I really do want to see my stock prices go up. Another example is that of most newlyweds underestimating the likelihood that their marriage will end in divorce. According to the American Psychological Association, it is estimated that 50 percent of all marriages end in divorce in the United States (https://www.apa.org/topics/divorce-child-custody).

People are optimistic. Because people are optimistic, they tend to underestimate risks. Therefore, they engage unnecessarily in overtly risky behavior, and you can capitalize on that as an attacker.

When a target receives emails designed to infect their machines with malware, they don't necessarily treat them with the suspicion they deserve. Adding to this, somewhat counterintuitively, is that the security communities have actually done a good job of raising awareness about the perils of clicking links in phishing emails. Countless resources explain how to spot a phish. To most people, the danger of falling victim to a phish is reduced, which is paradoxical, of course. But it stands to reason that the victims think the criminals must've found another way by now because phishing is overdone, overused, and too easily recognized. The criminals think the targets will fall for their phish in spite of those things. The loop continues and is likely an infinite one.

Optimism goes beyond the measures of technology, though. Thanks to people's inherently optimistic nature, they expose themselves, and the companies they work for, to threats they could easily avoid. The illusion of invulnerability, either of self or of the organization, is something that will often present itself to you as an attacker in the form of security by theatrics; a placebo effect, or rather a nocebo effect transpires. Targets within the environment will simply go through with the process they've been instructed to without much critical thought. The very consideration of you being a malicious actor either does not occur or washes over so softly that it is basically useless. If you are presenting your pretext correctly,

leveraging your mental agility and self-awareness and never breaking pretext, people will tend to believe the narrative you present
and look for signs that it is legitimate. They will most often assume
that they are not standing with a real-life threat in front of them disguised with nothing more than a seemingly good reason to be there.

A number of factors can explain this optimism bias. The two
most important that I have investigated are perceived control and
being in a good mood.

With perceived control being a bolstering effect of this bias, you
can see why ego suspension is so important, as well as committing
to pretext (typically a non-authoritative one). Leaving the target
with the misconception they are in control is enormously important if you are to count on optimism bias in an attack.

And though other forms of positive illusions have been identified in psychology, including self-serving bias and wishful thinking,
the illusion of control matters most to you as an attacker because
of what it is: an exaggerated belief in one's capacity to control inde-
pendent, external events, which I tie into one with optimism. This
is the tendency for people to believe that compared to others they
are less likely to experience negative events and more likely to experience positive ones. It's like the gambler who thinks they have a
better chance at winning than everyone else at the table, with everyone else at the table thinking the same thing.

When it comes to mood, people tend to be more optimistic in
safe settings, but when it becomes critical to recognize threats and
danger, even the greatest of optimists are prone to revising their
beliefs when faced with negative information. This is why pretexts
in combination with commitment are so important: you must present the narrative in such a way that the target never has to think
about it as anything else other than what is being presented. If this
is not an option, you might try circumventing the target altogether
by applying AMs to neutralize technological defenses.

Although it is a hard argument to make that all people suffer
from optimism bias, it's safe to say that many do and on many dif-
fering fronts. As an attacker, your best bet is to use optimism bias
for yourself and against the target. Ironically, you must believe that

your target suffers from this psychological phenomenon and act accordingly; adopt a well-rounded, comprehensive pretext and treat most people as if they are not expecting to be approached, influenced, and circumvented by you.

Confirmation Bias and Motivated Reasoning

Confirmation bias is the predisposition of searching for, interpreting, favoring, and recalling information in a way that confirms or strengthens your prior personal beliefs or assumptions. In other words, confirmation bias is why people see what they want to see.

Here's an example: You search online to back up what you think is true, like "Area 51 Aliens," and take into consideration the press release in which the US Army Air Forces (USAAF) announced they'd recovered a "flying disc" from a ranch near Roswell, *but* you ignore the one after, in which USAAF stated it was actually weather balloon debris.

Some believe Area 51 is researching and experimenting on aliens and their spacecraft. Others theorize that the moon landing was staged at Area 51. If you search, you will find. Confirmation bias keeps you steady as you wade the murky waters of information—it keeps you looking and agreeing only with information that reinforces what you already know.

Another example of the confirmation bias is someone who forms an initial impression of a person and then interprets everything that this person does in a way that confirms this initial impression—for the good and the bad. Consider the debate over gun control. Let's say Alice is in support of gun control. She seeks out news stories and opinion pieces that reaffirm her beliefs. When shootings occur, she looks at the *facts* of the situation in a way that supports her existing beliefs.

Bob, on the other hand, is as against gun control as any one person could be. He too seeks out news sources that fit his viewpoint. When shootings occur, he looks at the *facts* of the situation in a way that supports his existing beliefs.

These two people have polar opposite positions on the same subject. Even if they read the same story, their bias will likely shape the way they perceive the details, further confirming their beliefs.

Now imagine they meet for the first time and in a place where gun control was the main issue—each of them passionately advocating on behalf of their own side of the debate. They share a tense and dramatic conversation and part ways. But, oh dear, something else happens. . .they meet again the next day as they are walking into work. Bob just started working where Alice does and, worse still, she's going to be his buddy for the next few days to get him settled in.

Most likely, they can, at least ostensibly, put their differences aside to talk about the protocols that need to be followed. Alice will be able to show Bob how to get to the cafeteria and how to clock in, but there's a slim chance of her trusting Bob, wanting to be friends with him and wanting to know more about any of Bob's other beliefs. The same is true for Bob when considering Alice. They are each operating on the belief that they are opposed on one major front and will start looking for other *facts* to build their cases against each other. When Bob sees Alice drive out of the parking garage in a Prius and Alice looks over to see Bob's pickup truck, they will each build more beliefs about the other.

Confirmation bias can trick the mind into only looking for specific patterns based on a person's previous experience and understanding, instead of considering each event as isolated. The use of this cognitive shortcut is easily fathomable: evaluating evidence requires a great deal of mental energy, so our brains select to take shortcuts. This saves us all time and prevents us from feeling overwhelmed with the constant bombardment of new information we surround ourselves with every day.

Biases are, after all, a wonderful vulnerability to tap into. You can most easily put this bias to good if you are fully dedicated to your character and have assumed the role before you've even walked in the door. This is because as you approach a person, they look for information that supports, rather than rejects, their preconceptions, typically by interpreting evidence to confirm existing beliefs while discarding or discounting any incompatible data. If you are about to enter an art gallery as a very wealthy person looking to buy a piece of art, with some hidden objective (hopefully set by the client), then you cannot simply assume this role as you talk with the target inside. You would have to be in character upon arrival on the street. Personally, I would arrive in a car, with a driver, I would be dressed the part of my wealthy character, and I would be fully in the role before I even stepped out onto the pavement. In taking pretexting this seriously, you help the confirmation bias in your target and over the whole environment bloom, which is only to your benefit.

With motivated reasoning, the tendency is to assign weight to information that permits us to come to the conclusion we want to reach. Accepting information that confirms our beliefs is far easier and less energetically consuming than reassessing and relearning. Contradicting information causes us to withdraw cognitively. Although confirmation bias is an inherent tendency to observe information that matches our established beliefs and ignore information that doesn't, motivated reasoning is our tendency to readily accept new information that agrees with our worldview and critically analyze that which doesn't. Using both against a target and environment effectively is a very powerful force.

Using the two in tandem against a target is easier than it first seems. Confirmation bias occurs from the direct influence of desire on beliefs. When people want to think a certain idea or concept is true, they end up believing it to be true. Once someone has formed a view, they embrace information that confirms that view while ignoring, or rejecting, information that casts doubt on it. Confirmation bias suggests that most of us don't perceive circumstances objectively. This is why, when performing attacks in a team, you must most often play to what is typical within society, not what is politically correct. For instance, it's more likely that an older man with me is my boss than I am his. Neither AMs nor social engineering cares about what is politically correct. Neither does confirmation bias. Using confirmation bias as attackers demands we use whatever is typical for the environment.

Motivated reasoning is actually suffused with emotion. Not only are motivated reasoning and confirmation bias often inseparable, but the positive or negative feelings about people, things, and ideas arise more rapidly than the target's conscious thoughts—in a matter of milliseconds, in fact. Many people, and so many targets, want to push threatening information away and reel in nonthreatening information. In our modern society, people have instinctual reflexes, not only to tangible threats, but to information, too. And although we are not only driven by emotions and biases, reasoning often happens later. So for the sake of not making the target "think" too much, it is often necessary that I show up as the assistant or the employee and not the boss if culturally and traditionally that's more fitting.

Framing Effect

The framing effect is a cognitive bias that impacts our decision making when something is said or presented in different ways. In other words, we are influenced heavily by how something is presented. There are many subtypes of this bias, but I will concentrate on positive and negative frames.

At first glance, the framing effect doesn't seem much different from the other biases presented throughout this book or even throughout this chapter, but this bias is a little special. Whereas with the last three biases I've covered I have painted an all-or-nothing type of situation—stay in character or you will get yourself caught; don't do what is politically correct, do what is expected, or you will get caught, and so on—the framing effect teaches you presentation because this cognitive bias occurs when the outcome between the two options is the same. When the options are framed differently, they result in us choosing the one that is favorably framed.

There are different kinds of framing, but I will concentrate on positive and negative frames. We've all been subject to marketing strategies such as 'Don't miss out' or 'Get it before it's gone'. The frame is simple—make people feel like they are losing out on something. People tend to fear losses more so than gains and take action to avoid losses. Negative frames are effective in certain scenarios too, because they can create urgency. For instance, telling the front-line of a building that their "audit" will be delayed three months and that "headquarters" won't be too pleased if you are turned away now might be enough to make them reconsider allowing you entry then and there.

Our fear of loss is strong, but we tend to seek out positivity. Posi-tive frames often work better in convincing people. For example, "I can be done and in and out of your hair in 30 minutes if I get going now. You won't see an auditor again until next year." This also brings into play the use of an artificial time constraint, which also results in the illusion of a positive frame. An artificial time constraint is manufactured restriction on time—using made-up time constraints can result in the neutralization of discomfort for the other party.

In an everyday example, how many times have you been sat next to someone on an airplane, on public transport, or in a public place and had them try to start a conversation with you? This can make many of us feel uncomfortable and not because of the interaction itself, but because we don't know how long the intended conversa-tion will last for. . . the whole flight? The entire length of the line at the DMV? This is why artificial time constraints work so well with positive framing—they create the illusion of a positive outcome in a short amount of time.

However, the result is the same either way: the security guard or receptionist can choose to let you in for 30 mins now so that they don't have to wait months for their next turn an at a safety audit, which may have broader effects on the company (audits are often mandatory), or you can have a teammate spoof a senior personnel's number and corner them into allowing you access. The results are the same. The framing is different.

Looked at this way, even when you know you will get what you want, you should frame it to the target to get them to feel one way or another about it because getting people to *feel* a certain way about something often allows them to react a certain way, which you can often count on.

Framing, when used positively, is about covering your tracks at a zero-distance range by giving the target the illusion of control: you're using a bias against them that results in them feeling good or in charge. The other way to do this is to create a problem and then offer a positive solution straight away, and it can be "personal" to you rather than contingent upon the target environment: "This is my first weekend with my kid in a month, and if I don't get out of here in 30 minutes I am going to be late and his mom/dad will make a big deal of it. You can really help me out if I can just get this job done." This again gives someone a choice to make (and the illusion of control over the situation), and if they lean in and help you out, they also get to feel good about their choice.

As a note, I generally do not use negative framing, but I am not in charge of every attacker looking to implement AMs by reading this book, and they can be effective.

Thin-Slice Assessments

A successful attack depends on a target's perception of the attacker's personality, motivations, trustworthiness, and affect. Person-perception research indicates that reliable and accurate assessments of these traits can be made based on very brief observations, or *thin slices*.

Thin slicing is a term that means making very quick inferences about the state, characteristics, or details of an individual or a situation with nominal quantities of information. It is a type of social cognition that proves beneficial in AMs and works both ways. You can and should get comfortable performing thin-slice assessments on your targets, and you should be aware they are doing something of the same to you, whether it's subconscious or not.

Thin slices of behavior is a term coined by researchers Nalini Ambady and Robert Rosenthal (https://tspace.library.utoronto.ca/handle/1807/33126). They discovered that very brief, dynamic silent video clips, ranging from 2 to 10 seconds, provided sufficient information for people with no special skills to evaluate a teacher's effectiveness, which was measured against the actual students' final course ratings of their teachers. Thin slices can be assessed from any available means of communication, including the face, the body, speech, the voice, or any combination of these. Notably, static photographs would not qualify as thin slices.

Thin-slice judgments have been shown to accurately predict the effectiveness of doctors treating patients, the relationship status of opposite-sex pairs interacting, judgments of rapport between two persons, courtroom judges' expectations as to a defendant's guilt, and even testosterone levels in males.

Malcolm Gladwell in *Blink: The Power of Thinking Without Thinking* (Back Bay Books, 2007) shows art experts identifying a piece of art as a forgery in the first few seconds of examination. Tennis coaches have known whether the player will fault on a serve in the half a second before it is even struck; a salesperson is able to read someone's emotions and future decisions on the basis of three seconds of observation—these are examples of thin-slice assessments. However, the thin-slice methodology is useful only if relevant and valid information can be extracted from a person's behavior in that given moment. There are many factors that influence the accuracy of thin-slice judgments, including culture and exposure, individual differences in the ability to decode information accurately, differences in accuracy based on expertise, and the type of judgment being made. This is where AMs comes in, and it works both ways.

As human beings, we are wonderful storytellers. We tell stories about who we are, what we're doing, and why we are doing it. To pass someone else's thin-slice assessment of us, we must be such good storytellers that no one could possibly know we are deceiving them. To do this, consider everything visual and auditory about yourself: how you walk, your pace, your posture, your eye contact, your tone of voice, your rate of speech, the words you use, and even your blink rate. You have the upper hand—as long as the target believes your pretext, they are not judging your ability as an attacker; they are judging you as who you have presented yourself as.

Looking at it the other way, you must be able to perform a thin-slice assessment of your target. The more accurate your assessment, the better your chances of success as an attacker. You may need to alter your character's persona once your assessment results are in. You would when you wanted your target to stay or get to a more relaxed state than your intended interaction would allow for. They are judging and reacting to your behavioral stream, which is natural. You are using this against them and using your sampling of their behavioral stream to carve the right outcome for your objective.

What is interesting, and not at all helpful when writing a section of a book on it, is that there's no real guidance on just *how* to perform a thin-slice assessment. We know that they are sampled from a channel or a combination of channels of communication; we know that people segment units of behavior and ascribe meaning to them, even though life is more a continuous stream than isolated segments. People also tend to think that the more they know someone and the more information they have, the more reliable their perception of them is—this is, paradoxically, why the first few moments of interaction under your pretext are so critical. It sets the tone of how the target envisions you as a whole person, not just the person standing in front of them. Typically, we all aim to extend our first impressions of someone and infer from there.

Something else to note is that research has found that people are better at accurately judging targets from their own culture or similar cultures to their own. Similarly, in-group benefits exist for tribes of people, who show an advantage at accurately extrapolating details about others based on thin slices of behavior. An example would be a group of IT workers—they will likely tell if you are pretending to be a sys admin based on a thin-slice assessment. Thin-slice judgments can be affected by people's expertise and competency, which is important to note as an attacker if you need to impersonate someone to fit in at such a granular level.

The type of judgment being made matters, too, which is somewhat helpful to keep in mind (and to take the pressure off). Thin-slice judgments are accurate only to the degree that applicable variables are apparent to the assessor. In other words, it is possible to accurately assess how warm and likable a person appears to be, because these characteristics can be swiftly revealed through behavior. Other traits, depending on the situation you find a person in, are shown over time, such as how persevering someone appears to be. It's harder in one, short interaction to see this in someone or to have them see it in you. This is welcome news for us as attackers. It means that in a short engagement, a solid pretext will afford us enough cover to pass such assessments, with our own personality and traits having little bearing on the outcome.

> People tend to trust uniforms and overall appearance, even though absolutely anyone can wear a uniform or dress as a professional. This automatic tendency for people to trust what they see helps us pass a thin-slice assessment and ultimately leads to success.

Default to Truth

As Tim Levine, author of *Duped: Truth-Default Theory and the Social Science of Lying and Deception* (University of Alabama Press, 2019) ultimately proved, humans tend to default to truth. Let me explain.

Overwhelmingly, our human tendency is to operate on the assumption that the people we are dealing with are straightforward and trustworthy. Although this instinct will always leave us open to deception, and even facilitates it, it also underpins nearly all of our initial interactions with one another and, as such, enables friendships to form, relationships to start, business to be conducted, and society to operate. The consequence of not defaulting to truth is that, if you don't begin in a state of trust, you can't have meaningful social interaction. There are people who do not operate through this tendency. If you have ever met someone who seems to offer up acute analytical inspection at every word you say and every action you take, you will know it is tiring and difficult to build and cultivate any sort of meaningful, symbiotic relationship. The simplest of processes in society could not take place as they do if we all functioned with such conspicuous distrust at every turn and every encounter.

Moreover, evolution should have favored people with the ability to pick up the signs of deception, and yet here we are—still all pretty terrible at knowing whether someone is lying. We are able to pick up signs of comfort or discomfort, but we aren't able to pick out a lie. This is counterintuitive and, upon first inspection, seems to not make any sense at all. Surely suspicion and caution would fit us best in this dangerous world. Alas, we are more inclined to assume someone is telling us the truth. It may be that evolution cannot give us the ability to tell whether a lie is being told because every lie we hear comes with different signage and indicators or because every person's tells are too different. Or it could be that always knowing when an individual is lying is not needed. Catastrophic lies are rare and often told by a very small subset of people, so defaulting to truth makes sense for us in terms of building societies and thriving as a race. Or my favorite theory: the reason we haven't evolved to tell when someone is lying with precision could be many reasons combined.

Knowing that operating under this default to truth tendency is socially necessary, we can begin to look at ways to exploit it as an attacker and also, at the end, stop it from becoming such a vulnerability for businesses and people. We've discussed, thanks to Daniel Kahneman's brilliant work, especially that written in *Thinking, Fast and Slow* (Farrar, Straus, and Giroux, 2013), how we can get by people as long as we don't snap them out of their "System 1" thinking (automatic, intuitive, and unconscious mode) into System 2 (slow, controlled, and analytical method of thinking; uses reasoning). This means we have to operate in a way that is congruent with our presented selves. It means adhering to law 3—never breaking pretext—never uncloaking yourself as a threat. The default to truth tendency, as defined by Tim Levine, is an extension of this. To snap a target out of truth-default mode takes large and conspicuous deviation from what you are presenting as. This is not to say a target won't have suspicions or doubts—they may. It is your job, via the laws and skills of AMs, to win them over. What refraining from snapping someone out of this tendency means is that you cannot do something so egregiously incongruent that they fall out of truth-default mode. People will forgive little incongruencies, because as humans we often rationalize things away. We start out by believing people and we end supposing deceit over truth only when our doubts and uncertainties grow to a point where we can no longer rationalize or explain incongruencies away.

Imagine you had to analyze whether your grandfather was a spy. Let's assume he could speak multiple languages, was very private, did not like his picture to be taken, and did not want to be in the background of pictures, especially if they were going to be posted on social media. Imagine he was against social media altogether, but you often found him perusing it, looking at foreign countries—not as himself, of course. Let's go further and imagine that whenever you asked him what his job was, his answer didn't make sense: imagine he traveled a lot for "an electrician." Imagine you found items that you could identify as ways to bug people—devices that were small and nifty. Now imagine you asked him about all of those things, and he said his expectation and need for privacy was a biproduct of his generation and upbringing. . .that he did not like the way he looked in pictures. . .and that he liked the thought of getting news from locals, a sentiment he remembered his own father longed for as an immigrant but without access to social media. Imagine he said he traveled because there was no work as an electrician at the rates he charged in the immediate vicinity. Moreover, he works big jobs, generally for large buildings that make staying beside the facility easier. And imagine he had a hobby that made him want to dismantle small, wily devices that outdated your time on Earth. Great; truth-default mode says you will rationalize what he says with what he does. But actually, your grandfather is a spy. It's not until he is caught and on the news that you think to yourself,

"I feel like I knew that the whole time." Also, "How much is bail from the Soviets?"

Truth-default mode is a powerful cognitive bias. The only way to stop from becoming a liability to businesses is to teach people, through behavioral security, that defense starts in the brain—that there are no circumstances in which security protocols can be bypassed. If the security protocols are lacking, then these too must be fixed. The people, more pointedly *us* as ethical attackers, are not the target's immediate family. We deserve no rationalization.

Summary

- Humans are vulnerable to dishonesty and strong narratives. An attacker can leverage this knowledge for their own gain.
- Part of an attacker's arsenal is being able to think like the people and businesses they are targeting.
- Building knowledge of fundamental human tendencies and biases is vital.
- You can use many biases against your targets, not only the ones listed within this book. Use AMs to look at them and tie them to your objective as they pertain to the target.

Key Message

Use thin-slice assessments to your advantage in two ways: know how to perform them to get accurate readings, and know that they will likely be performed on you. Be prepared for that, and use every tool and technique at your disposal to avoid exposure as an imposter.

Part IV

After AMs

Chapter 10
Staying Protected—
The Individual

Attacker Mindset for Ordinary People

As we've discussed previously in this book, there's a large discon-
nect for most people—the Internet is still another world, not quite
in the real world. This allows most people to think the bad things
that happen on the Internet often have no real consequences here,
in *this* world. The digital realm as a whole seems to be up against
some modern-day folklore. A failing to bridge this gap for the
individual is cause for concern. I believe our duty as functioning
members of this community—a community built to secure other
communities—is to raise awareness among the masses that have no
insight into our world and to help them also think like an attacker,
just with more everyday utility. Teaching people this way of thinking
will also bolster our efforts from within the community—educating
people so they can more readily identify and respond to attacks.

As an individual, maybe you are very security-conscious and
security-aware. Maybe your cyber hygiene is the stuff of legend. In
that case, you may stop the phish, but will your bank or cell phone
company? If they don't, your data can still be given to an attacker,
and you are then compromised, which is where learning about
security and privacy (separate, but related categories of security) is
helpful, which I will talk about later in this chapter.

243

Moreover some factions are acutely susceptible, such as the elderly, who may not be tech savvy and are often targeted because they tend to have their financial affairs in order, making them the ideal target. Socially savvy kids are also targeted often. Children often lack experience in the world with adults outside of their families and so can fail to understand how quickly and easily they can be manipulated by outside sources. They likely cannot think ahead to foresee the dangers.

Regardless of whether you fall into one of these or another category, the vastness of the Internet and the spectrum of security techniques and advice is often daunting. It should come as no real shock, then, that the thought of an imposter, attacker, or malicious party existing, whose main concern is centered on gaining access to "our" world through the Internet, is outlandish to many people.

Moreover, there are two other things that become increasingly apparent as I talk to people outside of the infosec community. One is that there is a yawning gap between what ordinary people value as information that should treated as sensitive; the other is that privacy is a spectrum, not a standard. Both are cause for concern that require different solutions.

I believe there are a few science-based things we should keep in mind that will make the likelihood of a successful attack mounted against us, either digitally or in person, much less probable. The remainder of this chapter will cover those after briefly setting out why information matters so much and which types matter most.

Let's start with people and data. People are not aware of what constitutes as *sensitive* data, and it can be a hard task to bring many people around to the idea that data, or information that is seemingly benign, poses a threat to them if leaked. I wrote an article (Healthcare: Elite Data, 2020, `https://www.social-engineer.com/ healthcare-elite-data/`) which you can find in the notes section of the book (on the website) in which I stated that health data is elite data and noted that most people can't fathom the prospect of that data being worth anything. People tend not to look past the obvious when it comes to categorizing data as sensitive. Most people would agree that a malicious actor getting their credit card information would be detrimental, and that's because the effects are tangible: someone else having your credit card does stimulate fear—you can guess the outcome of that, even if you still prefer bartering. In other words, you don't have to own a credit card to know its functionality and what a criminal could do with it.

However, asking if it really matters if someone can find out their blood type or weight, or that they have a +3.00 prescription lens does not provoke the same level of anxiety or moment of sudden insight or discovery. Asking people if they should be concerned if the Internet crime leagues know they've been treated for high blood pressure or a broken foot five years ago raises no immediate suspicions or fear levels. Most people don't seem to care if a stranger knows about a recent heart attack or the onset of diabetes. In fact, most people shrug this off, wondering just how dangerous it could be for someone to know this type of information about them. Only after it's pointed out that these things don't change do people start to think about what it would actually mean to have that data fall into the wrong hands.

With traditional identity theft, banks and the Social Security Administration are able to work against criminals by changing details for us if our identities are stolen. However, health data is unchangeable this way. We can't change our blood type or our prescription lens. Worse still, we can't always change our mental health status or invisible injuries, such as anxiety, depression, schizophrenia, or bipolar depression nor diseases we've had or have. Data with any permanence makes it elite, and we, as the victims, can't always offset the consequences by reporting and disputing.

Taking it a step further, your genes play a massive role in who you are and what you are capable of. If you have taken a DNA test or something similar, your DNA has already been sequenced, at least in part. What if someone got ahold of this and sold it. But instead of the consequences being minor, they were published, and you had markers for a disease that made you seem very unattractive as an employee or for insurance (or both).

There's something else leaked elite data brings to the table: longevity of attacks. I can vish and phish you about that every day, forever. I can try as your insurance company, doctor, nurse, psychiatrist, therapist, psychologist, optometrist, or pharmacist; if you switch, I may be able to find out who you changed to and use the unchanging data against you again. That's the reality of the world we live in, so it's imperative that we all understand the risks and where they truly lie.

If you've read this book so far, you now know how an attacker thinks and targets. Apply this to your own life.

Behavioral Security

The concept of behavioral security needs one question put under the microscope if it is to succeed as a style of protection: why do we act in certain ways when we are being targeted? The response will inform how we go about mitigating the risks. To begin answering that, let's look at human psychology from the side of the target.

There are two fundamental components of our psychology and how they manifest as behavior. There's a cognitive component, which consists of your thoughts and beliefs about something. There's an affective component, which is how you feel about something. These form your behavioral outcome. AMs uses those two basic components against you as an individual, with the aim of shaping the outcome of your behavior to their advantage.

It's a hard game to win, mainly because you, as the target, don't know you are in a game. But by becoming aware of these biases that create human vulnerability and by lessening how much value you ascribe to interactions with strangers, and by following a process where there is no room for an exception to the rule, you will keep yourself safer, your employer safer, and the wider communities safer.

Defense starts in the brain. Because of this, I believe behavioral security deserves to be taken seriously as a branch of cyber- and information security. As I see it, and as some branches of science see it, too, we are all chock-full of weaknesses, irrationalities, and idiosyncrasies.

The best protection against a threat, physical or cyber-based, ultimately depends on the individual's own actions, knowledge, and attitude. It would be great if we were all emotional robots in a way; we could be programmed to act accordingly. But, as Richard Thaler pointed out in his book *Misbehaving* (W. W. Norton & Company, 2016), we are not rational beings, and from this, behavioral economics was born. Under the same lens, it's easy to see that we as humans do not act rationally when it comes to security. The effect of psychological, cognitive, emotional, cultural, social factors, and poverty of information on the decisions of individuals and institutions is often where security fails. Moreover, defense fails when people don't have the skills to think critically about what they're seeing and to examine claims of fact before accepting them as true. When we fully recognize this and put in place cognitive defenses, as well as physical and digital, our security posture as a whole will shift, helping you as a person, businesses, and communities as a whole get ahead of the attacker. The first step in building these cognitive defenses is to become familiar with how we are vulnerable to cognitive attacks.

We often act, or react, because we feel a certain way, and as you should know by now, the attacker mindset used in conjunction with social engineering is an effective tool for making a target feel the way the attacker needs them to feel to get their job done—whether it be fearful, joyful, or compelled. We can look at behavioral security in terms of irrational behavior and search for ways to counteract that behavior. Alas, we are all at risk of being a target, so target psychology is well worth our consideration, and combating weaknesses through behavioral security is the solution. The promise of behavioral security as applied to policy is to use people's weaknesses to help them achieve their business's goals. Make security seem simple and automatic. From things like the wording of policies to how they are disseminated, security must be shaped to make it easy to understand, remember, and act on. Behavioral security will allow us, as security professionals, to cease treating security only through ineffective technological defensive measures and start looking at the psychology of an attack and place defenses there, too.

We must take security and mold it for human behavior, not just for technological pursuits of crime.

When Thaler coined the concept of mental accounting, he stated that people think of value in relative terms and not in absolute terms; they gain pleasure from how good the deal is, not just from an object's value. According to this theory of mental accounting, people treat money differently, depending on things like the money's origin and intended use, rather than thinking of money as money. MIT's Drazen Prelec and Duncan Simester found that people are generally more willing to spend a larger sum of money when they pay with a credit card than cash ("Always Leave Home Without It: A Further Investigation of the Credit-Card Effect on Willingness to Pay," 2001, https://web.mit.edu/simester/Public/Papers/Alwaysleavehome.pdf). They are also more willing to spend $10 on a theater ticket if they have just lost a $10 bill than if they have to replace a lost ticket worth $10 (Kahneman and Tversky, 1984, referenced in "Choices, Values and Frames," https://web.missouri.edu/~segerti/capstone/choicesvalues.pdf). But it is all the same; losing the ticket worth $10 is the exact same event as losing the $10 bill. This brings into play *fungibility*—money is interchangeable and has no labels. Here's where I am going with this: most people see security through a similar mental filter. People think of security (and money) through a subjective lens that often intersects with their feelings rather than thinking of it in terms of the "bottom line."

Why should cybersecurity be treated any differently than physical security? Many people wouldn't try unknown doors on a dark night just to see what's behind them, but they will click unknown links from unknown sources, not looking too closely at the originating address. Many people wouldn't leave their cars or homes unlocked, but they will leave their computers unlocked. Many people will take the news seriously that thieves are operating in their area, going door to door, but not that hackers are always on the prowl and capable of getting on their network even though so much of our personal lives and details are held within the devices we connect to our networks. They won't stop filling in online forms with personal details that are collected and used maliciously. Most of us would not tell a stranger who happened to walk by us on the street where we had been and where we were going, but we will give people information on Facebook through check-ins or by labeling Instagram photos with location metadata. The parallels are endless, but the bottom line remains: people should think of security as, well, security. But to do so, they have to understand that there is crossover between what can be stolen from them online and what can be stolen on spied on in the physical world.

Reductively, security online is not so different from security in the real world: if you wouldn't tell a stranger, don't tell the Internet. Your privacy matters and is not the same as, but is linked to, your security. All data is sensitive data. If you can place yourself in the mind of an attacker, you will be able to assess more clearly and accurately what can be used against you and how. You might still choose to share information, but that will be your choice and at least it will be informed.

People should follow processes and treat security as an absolute, not as a relative and subjective thing, not based on how they feel about a person or email, and not based on where the requests and directives are coming from. Security should be fungible— interchangeable, not subjective. Creating simple policies that allow a person—any person, of any position or rank—to understand them easily and treat them as absolutes is a good start. And if you, as the individual supposed to implement the policies don't understand them, speak up. Ask people around you if they understand the policies, ask yourself how likely you are to uphold their directives. For the points that seem too far-fetched or unclear to you, raise them with your peers and management so that they can be carved into something more meaningful or clear—something you can follow. Following the right processes, no matter how they feel, is critical.

Recall the woman who really wanted to help me on my vishing call, which was meant to trick her. She followed every process the client had, was polite, seemed as though she really wanted to help, spent time trying to authorize herself to help, but ultimately ended the call when she couldn't verify me. She treated security as an absolute, not as a relative and subjective thing. She did not look at the circumstances and narratives I was presenting and find a way in her mind to let it work. She found no value in our unique interaction. It did not matter to her that I was trying to be sweet, charming. She beat me in a game of chess she didn't even know she was playing. But this is not common.

Finally, as a community, we can use every digital and physical tool at our disposal to protect people, communities, and businesses, and those efforts are a good start. But the real solution begins to take shape when people realize they're being subjected to cognitive attacks. Defense starts in the brain. Behavioral security should be taken seriously as a branch of cyber- and information security because, as humans, we do not always act rationally, so as security professionals, we must seek to understand individuals as they really are and how it matters to security. This has many contributing factors, such as cultures and subcultures within the workplace, the overall understanding of a company's optimal security posture and how far it is from achieving it, why it is important and how attacks might unfold.

Amygdala Hijacking

We know security—digital, physical, personal, and professional—can be a scary topic, especially if you've faced online harassment, identity theft, or other online attacks. As an individual intent on avoiding becoming a target, there are things you can do to mitigate your risk. But first, you have to know how it feels to be one.

The amygdala is actually the *amygdalae*. They are a bilateral structure, one on each side of our brains, behind the eyes and the optic nerves. Bessel van der Kolk, a prominent doctor, calls them the brain's "smoke detector." They detect fear and prepare your body for an emergency response. When you identify a threat, your amygdalae sound an alarm, releasing a torrent of chemicals, like adrenaline and cortisol. When this deeply instinctive function takes over, it is called an *amygdala hijack*, a term Daniel Goleman coined in *Emotional Intelligence* (Bantam, 2005). The common psychological phraseology states that you have been "triggered." And all of the responses you have to amygdala hijacking are designed to move you into action. Complex decision making departs, as does your ability to perform multiple evaluations.

The amygdalae work with the conscious and unconscious areas of the brain to determine how to react to situations. When a stress response occurs, the sympathetic nervous system is activated, which is part of the autonomic nervous system, which controls all of our automatic functions, like the immune response, hormones, digestion, heart rhythm, and breathing. This is what an attacker relies on.

If an attacker says they have an appointment and that if you don't let them in, something bad will happen—the elevators will have to be shut down, or your boss's request won't be honored, or that your action will impact the situation negatively—there's a likelihood the amygdalae will be provoked. The most effective way out of this state is to pause. It may sound hippy-dippy and like therapy parlance, but it's the best way to reset your defenses and reassume your composure. Follow the process set out for you. Simplify it in your brain to an objective. Now you are thinking like an attacker, and now you're on the path to beating one.

Just having awareness of this, knowing that it can be used against you with nothing more than a sentence, is scary. But it's the first step of defense. You can always pause. Regain your composure, take a few breaths, and wait until your mind can reassess the situation and reply as you see fit. Treat security as an absolute, not as a subjective thing. Place little value on unique interaction with someone trying to bypass normal processes. There's a chance they want you to *feel* and then *act* in a certain way.

Acting in a security-conscious way doesn't come down to how the situation makes you feel; it comes down to the process for the situation.

Another area where amygdala hijacking is rife is with a trendy phishing scam that relies on sextortion. A target will receive an email that claims their computer has been hacked and that intimate recordings of them, for example using a porn site or partaking in sexual activities, have been obtained. Some versions of this scam even include the person's password for an online account or may appear to have been sent from the person's own email address. It's hard, without the proper knowledge, to not fall for this. The email will then go on to blackmail the target, threatening to release the footage unless a payment is made. This is often an emotional event, and all the deep breaths in the world might not help because there's often no process to follow in our personal lives (unlike in our professional). This is where reasoning and education come into the mix. Still take the time to calm down and then perform research. Depending on how tech-savvy you are, your research might be reaching out to a friend or trusted source.

For closure's sake, for this sort of phish and any other, don't respond or send any payments. Immediately change your password(s). A good resource is the website Have I Been Pwned?. It allows you to check if your email address is listed as being affected by one of the large data breaches included on their database. If your email address is listed, go ahead and change the emails for all listed accounts, and if you reuse passwords over multiple accounts, change those, too. You should also mark the phish as spam and delete it.

If you ever end up sending money using your credit card, you must talk to the company, and the same goes if you happen to have paid from your bank account. If you pay with Bitcoin the transaction is likely untraceable.

Analyze Your Attack Surface

Think of yourself as one person with multiple attack points. Remember, as far as AMs is concerned, every piece of information that exists about you can be tied back to the objective of targeting you—the attacker will weigh up all the information they find about you and assess whether or not it is good or bad in terms of their objective. Learn and lean into the fact that privacy limits the amount of information an attacker can discover about you, and security prevents unauthorized access to your accounts/events. You need to implement both to have a cohesive strategy. There are *best practices* that apply to everyone, and there are practices that are specific to you and your footprint and needs only. See what an attacker could find on you, and think about how that would affect you.

You should eliminate all unnecessary pathways, including old posts on social media and emails no longer in use. Think like someone who wants to get your most valuable possession, your deepest secrets, or into your safest places. You might also attempt to OSINT yourself. See what you could put together, based on the information available online about yourself. You could include reverse searching and analyzing pictures you've posted to see if there is anything in the background that gives away information that could (a) locate you or (b) be sensitive.

You might also look at your location. Where does your house sit on the street? Who can see into your house and from where? These are important questions to ask if there's ever a chance you could be spied on. You might also consider the pictures you post of your house's interior online. If you post the cute picture of your cat on your keyboard, are you also posting the apps you have on your computer? What about the hardware you use? It can all be valuable to an attacker.

There's also the issue of when you decide to sell your home. Those images tend to live online for a long time. You might consider taking images of your family members down and also keeping other sensitive information, like mail and hardware, out of view.

Get educated on good techniques to protect yourself, like using VPNs, password protection, two-factor authentication, and privacy-centric email providers. "Extreme Privacy: What It Takes to Disappear," 2020, offers tips on how to hide, such as removing your information from databases, ways to circumvent providing your cell phone number, protecting your address, and registering your residence and vehicles in trusts or LLCs, etc. That might be too far for some readers and sound like the stuff privacy dreams are made of.

I recently gave an interactive speech to one of America's three-letter agencies, where I said that if you go to a hotel, check the position of the cameras relative to your room, have your room point onto the street, not somewhere obscure, so that, should someone try to break in, they will be seen. I also noted that you should ask for a room that is not on the ground floor to make access harder; when traveling, you should keep your devices under the seat in front of you where you can see them at all times; and that you should not check your accounts while traveling and that, if you can, avoid taking photos. To be honest, no one seemed very galvanized by the advice. It was taken with more of a "Well, yes, of course" reaction.

The advice applies to regular individuals as well. When I say it to "regular" people, however, they are always taken aback. They always want to delve into the topic and make me answer if that's something they should take seriously. . . I suppose it applies to some people more than others, but I don't know all of you. My suggestion is to take the advice if you think it's necessary for you to do so. Only you can decide that, but if you want to think like an attacker to beat one, you should consider it. After all, treating security as an absolute is the name of the game. Take the safer room; be cautious of your possessions as you travel. Be careful of the information you share at any time.

You should also be careful how you store confidential information. Use encrypted computer hard drives, USBs, and so on, to contain sensitive information. Never leave your systems unattended. Always protect them with strong passwords.

In all honesty, a sharp AMs pointed against you as an individual is a hard thing to dodge. It takes full awareness, knowing and accepting that an attack could target you without you knowing in the moment. Such attacks can be brazen, almost effortlessly convincing you to hand over items of access that are seemingly harmless.

There are a few steps you can take that I will list here, because they become more viable and valuable with the awareness of attackers and their mindsets now that you've read this book:

- Refuse to provide personal information or passwords over email or on the phone if you did not call the number yourself.
- Refuse to provide information about yourself over the phone or even in person unless you sought the person out—for example, if you go to your bank and they ask you to supply some verifying

information, you are most likely safe in giving it. If your bank calls you, you might want to reconsider. If they come to your house, you might want to call the police.

- Verify a request's authenticity by contacting the company directly.

With that said, there are other things, less often advised, you can do to protect yourself, such as redirecting and reflecting questions back at people who are inquisitive about your life. It's actually a good way to make friends, too, contrary to popular belief. People typically want to talk about themselves, not you. Let them.

At work, you should be wary of anyone asking what kind of software you use or the name of the person responsible for maintaining your computer network. We know attackers pose as coworkers, repair technicians, IT staff, and convenient outsiders with an apparent legitimate need to know such information.

Network security is also an area that requires attention. The traditional measures mean using antivirus, passwords, keeping your devices, browsers, and apps up-to-date, and similar steps. Measures introduced by behavioral security, where we treat security as an absolute, mean knowing and sticking to effective processes. Don't log on to public Wi-Fi without a virtual private network (VPN), *ever*. Delete sensitive information when it's no longer needed, and do it weekly. Do not fill out forms online, such as quizzes and informal questionnaires. Do not click on anything in an email without hovering over the link or checking it in a virtual machine. There's so much you can do to be safe. The bottom line is that you have to research best practices, decide which to use, and then carry them out religiously.

Finally, threat modeling looks within. An attacker's mindset is formed by also looking at you and your information. The less you give them, the better. For the information you do give out, threat-model it. Ask what is the worst that can happen with that information, and work backward from there to mitigate that risk or plan for the eventuality of it being used against you.

Treat your security as seriously as an attacker looking to harm you would.

Summary

- Security is not relative to any circumstance; you are not more secure online than you are in the physical world.
- Security is an absolute and should be treated without mental accounting of it. Your cybersecurity is not less important than your home security or any other type.
- There are ways to protect yourself, and there are steps you can take that will thwart attacks, stopping attackers in their tracks should they try targeting you.

Key Message

If you are security conscious, be security conscious everywhere. The real solution will begin to take shape when people start realizing they're being subjected to all attacks via cognitive attacks. Defense starts in the brain. The promise of behavioral security as applied to policy is to use people's weaknesses to help them achieve their business's goals.

Chapter 11

Staying Protected— The Business

Modern technology and globalization have made it possible for a single attacker to wage war against a company and even a country, and win! Technological advances make it possible for attackers to continuously develop and improve tactics. This results in everchanging threats which are made all the more pernicious by the interconnectivity we've grown into.

Moreover, technologies have led to extremely sophisticated and powerful criminal networks that are hard to identify and uncover even when operating under our noses. To thwart such attacks and threats, huge amounts of resources would have to be dedicated to security by the government, but those resources aren't there. The gap is therefore bridged more and more by the private sector.

Criminal organizations come in many forms and can take unlimited actions that aren't always accurately forecastable. This is where learning to think like them comes into play. Looking at your organization through their mental filter can show you not only how you are vulnerable, but where. Indicators of attack (IOA) focus on detecting the intent of what an attacker is trying to accomplish, regardless of the malware, tools or exploits they use. Indicator of

Compromise-based (IOC-based) detection approach does not identify the rising threats from malware-free intrusions or even zero-
day exploits. This is where an IOA-based approach, pioneered by
CrowdStrike, becomes useful (https://www.crowdstrike.com/
cybersecurity-101/indicators-of-compromise/ioa-vs-ioc/).

Indicators of Attack

Indicators of Attack are actions or a series of actions that an attacker
must execute in order to succeed. A spear phish is a good example
in order to illustrate the idea of an IOA.

A successful phishing email must persuade the target to follow
a link or open a document that will, in turn, infect their machine
and initial compromise takes place. They often aim to maintain
persistence and to make contact with a command and control site,
awaiting further instructions.

IOAs are concerned with the execution of these steps, the intent
of the adversary and the outcomes the attacker is pursuing. They are
not focused on the specific tools used to accomplish the objectives.

My position is not that IOA's should be used in place of IOC's.
I am of the opinion both are valuable. However, IOA's are especially valuable when trying to determine why your business will be
attacked instead of only how. No advance knowledge of the tools or
malware (aka: Indicators of Compromise) is required, and so many
points of view can be offered and listened to.

Nontechnical Measures

My understanding of the evolution of cyber security is that for a
long time, attackers went for data on networks and servers, so we
protected them as best we could; then data and attackers went to
the endpoints, so we protected them the best we could; then the
data, and so the attackers, too, went to Software as a Service (SaaS)
and we authenticated them, but protection was limited. Threaded
throughout is the social engineering aspect of attacks, too, which

has played a part steadily throughout the history of cyberattacks. And only relatively recently have we really tried to build out our defenses there. There are two categories of security: technical and psychological. Because of this dichotomy, cybersecurity's primary concern with technical features often leaves us all at risk. It's precisely why the community needs more discussion and thought around AMs for defensive and offensive measures.

As was egregiously apparent with the recent Bitcoin-Twitter scam, a win for an attacker doesn't have to be brilliantly technical to have adverse effects for hundreds of millions of people: ubiquitous and mainstream technology is easily weaponized through AMs. The attack itself saw prominent Twitter users, with the blue verification checkmark next to their names, tweet "double your Bitcoin" offers, promising their followers they'd double donations made to the included links and send them back. For example, former President Barack Obama's account tweeted: "I am giving back to my community due to Covid-19! All Bitcoin sent to my address below will be sent back doubled. If you send $1,000, I will send back $2,000!" The tweet has since been deleted. Elon Musk, Jeff Bezos, and Bill Gates were among many prominent US figures targeted by the scam.

In this case, Twitter employees were the targets and, as we know, if you aren't an attacker or thinking like one, it can be hard to stop the outcome.

The other thing that is needed if you are to protect yourself is teaching your employees what to look out for—what an attack feels like and how they can defend themselves even if they don't know they are in a position or situation where they need to. It's so simple, but it's also worrying due to repercussions if you fail: if your employees are unprepared to deal with current and growing threats, you do not have a shot at effective security. The threat landscape is always changing, advancing, and growing, and employees have to be prepared for this. It doesn't mean everyone has to be highly strung and forever on edge. But knowing what makes the company attractive, understanding how attackers operate, and giving your employees the power to treat security as something more than a concept is essential. Employees are typically the ones on the front lines when security incidents occur. However, many of them come into contact with their organization's cybersecurity policies through reminders and restrictions. Those who don't know about the policies, who haven't been able to commit them to memory, or who don't recognize attacks and remedies by reading what to do, are caught off-guard, ill-equipped, and vulnerable.

Eliminating this issue requires a commitment to the resources, personnel, and time to support an in-house or outside team to determine how vulnerable your organization is. This team will then be required to show you, without fancy frills, what your landscape looks like. This approach also requires corporate humility, which boils down to implementing changes based on results. This is part of a simple formula that will keep you safe as a company:

Employ tactical and combative methods internally through the attacker mindset to identify security gaps and be willing to change, employing corporate humility, to mitigate vulnerabilities and security gaps.

That's it. That explains how the most secure companies do the impossible and remain ahead of attackers. Innovative companies use this formula to change their position from defensive to offensive. Resilient companies use it to become stronger. But all companies require it. We are all at risk—the owners, employees, and service users—if this is not being done. Companies and government alike must always be able to identify dangerous shortcomings and react to any glaring limitations quickly. If you can't, you aren't being proactive. You aren't invested in security—yours, the customers', or the employees'. The best way for us, as a society, to achieve higher levels of security is to share information: share it with the authorities, with the security community, and with each other—business to business communication on what attack types and trends you are seeing is essential if we are to advance our position in terms of security.

Testing and Red Teams

If you're hiring a red team, pentester, social engineering team, or AMs expert, and if scope and the rules of engagement are significantly restricted, you will not receive effective testing.

If you are part of an in-house red team and you're restricted, you will struggle to effect real change, but you can aim to do so in baby steps. You might consider documenting your thoughts on where the company's security faults and vulnerabilities lie and getting them to an executive for potential future use and leverage (and in case there is a breach, and all eyes turn to you. . .).

If you are in charge of a red team in-house and cannot see the full spectrum of benefit when employing them at their fullest potential, you might consider looking further into this.

If you are in charge of a red team for hire but cannot see the benefit of looking at the world both offensively *and* defensively, you probably don't have an effective red team.

In any instance of a red team, looking at attack trends will not suffice. They are good to know about and to test, but your job is to think like an attacker, looking at environments in isolation and working out how to best exploit them. Then you must look at those same environments and determine how best to protect them. There is no one-size-fits-all in security, and every business, organization, and institution is vulnerable to attack, admittedly to varying degrees. Red teaming seeks to uncover these vulnerabilities through a sharp AMs.

Survivorship Bias

Survivorship bias is when you aren't working with all of the information needed to make a complete analysis. We tend to focus on the information we have and fail to consider the information we don't have. An example of this is illustrated in a story from World War II: During WWII a mathematician named Abraham Wald helped the US military determine where to add reinforcing armor on bomber planes. Reinforcing the whole plane would render it too heavy, so weight was added only where absolutely needed. Data and direction was collected and taken from returning planes based on where they had taken damage (from bullets, shrapnel, etc.), essentially mapping out where the damage tended to be. This is an example of full-blown survivorship and Wald realized this. The data collected could only account for the planes that made it back, and not for the planes that were shot down and never returned. The areas a plane could get shot, but still return, did not need additional armor to fly. This is essential to understand as a business and an ethical attacker.

As an ethical attacker employing AMs, you cannot lean into over-appreciating successes and underappreciate failures. Success stories are easy to find while failures are usually ignored or lost to time. You cannot look only at what made you successful as an attacker and fail to notice what aptly countered you. If you do, you will fail to grow, and you will fail to help your client see their whole organization. As a whole industry, we cannot endlessly turn our attention to the most successful ethical attackers. We must also be aware of why attacks fail so we can then analyze the situation and assess if it is truly secure or if the means of defeat lay elsewhere.

Businesses must also resist survivor bias. If you survive an attack, it is not your triumphant defenses that need bolstering, it is those that failed. Less obviously, as a business the culture cannot shift to believing it survived an attack because it is completely superior to those that didn't. Those that didn't may offer you more insight than the other way round. In the simplest simple terms, as a business that outperformed the rest, that concludes, based on their attributes, without looking more broadly at the whole dataset, including those with similar characteristics that failed to perform as well, mistakes and vulnerabilities will occur.

Finally, whilst successful businesses can give advice on what to do, businesses who failed in terms of security can give advice on what not to do (which is just as valuable). This is also where I return to the criticality of sharing information between businesses and organizations: understanding where one business was successful or unsuccessful can lead to helpful data and extrapolations that can help the whole of business.

The Complex Policy

Unfortunately, a cybersecurity policy does not equal cybersecurity. In May 2018, research firm Clutch found that almost half of employees don't pay much attention to their employers' cybersecurity policies (see `https://clutch.co/it-services/resources/how-employees-engage-company-cybersecurity-policies`). One of the biggest reasons internal cybersecurity practices are often ineffective is that they are overwhelming. If your policies are too complex, they will ensure people take shortcuts, thereby functionally circumventing them completely. This is where companies fail people. It is also where regulations fail businesses and people. A policy should be aimed toward giving anyone reading it a chance at understanding it.

Behavioral security tells us that defense begins in the brain. Let the policies reflect this. They should be comprehensible and reasonable, and they should not falter from their message: no matter what, adhere to the process.

Finally, if you are in charge of a red team, social engineering team, or pentest team, you cannot instill within your team members what they should think. That is not your job, nor should you want it to be. I don't even think you should tell them what to do directionally when in the planning phase—let the environment be open to all suggestions, and let the person who offered the idea talk it all the way through. If it falls dead in the room, great. Move on to the next, but do not make that individual feel bad. That suggestion might spark another idea or help narrow down attack vectors. Have your team learn how to form their own brand of attacker mindset. Only when each person has a strong AMs in place can they learn how to defend properly, because in doing so, they'll be able to assess a business and its defenses far more critically, describing blind spots previously unknowable or invisible upon first inspection.

Protection

If you are going to defend your company against an attack, you must first know who the enemy is by knowing what they want and what will make it easy for that (or difficult) within your environment.

Protection is no easy feat with external attacks and insider threats and two categories of employees aiding a security event (the neutral and the lucrative). A relentless and dangerous balance exists between offense and defense, deepened in its insidiousness when an attack is conducted in a stealthy manner. When the offense has the advantage, there will always be engagement. When it costs more to attack, or when the chances of an attack defeating the defenses is low, there will be less engagement and less success on the attacker's side. This is your ultimate aim. Show attackers that you are not "easy pickings"; use effective measures they can't plan for ahead of time. Be hard to defeat—use AMs to assess yourself. Defend your business one level higher than you think it needs.

Antifragile

Being *antifragile* is basically benefiting from volatility and shock. Being *robust* is not the same as being antifragile. Something that is robust will survive, but it will not benefit from harm. It will simply act as though there was no trauma at all. Being antifragile is being able to self-improve based on stressors and volatility.

In *Antifragile: Things That Gain from Disorder* (Random House Publishing Group, 2014) author Nassim Nicholas Taleb coins the word *antifragile*. He gives an example of its definition, stating that "logically, the exact opposite of a 'fragile' parcel would be a package on which one has written 'please mishandle' or 'please handle carelessly.' Its contents would not just be unbreakable but would benefit from shocks and a wide array of trauma" (p. 32).

The antifragility of something is determined by how fragile its parts are. Paradoxically, the more fragile the parts of a system are, the more antifragile that system can become; the parts that are fragile direct the antifragility of the future system. This is best thought of as trial and error. Taleb advocates for adding stress on purpose (in your life; in your organization)—not too much, as we've discussed before, because too much is detrimental. Exposure to a small dose of stress will, over time, make us and our companies immune to additional, larger quantities of stress.

An example of antifragility is the economy: its constituent parts, from a one-person business to the biggest bank on Earth (as of this writing Industrial & Commercial Bank of China), are all vulnerable to fragility. But when one fails, the others learn from those mistakes and are able to use those findings well into the future and become stronger. The economy is antifragile, whereas its constituent parts are all fragile.

In contrast, tranquility is not good for survival; shocks and the unforeseen come with valuable information. Making a system tranquil will not aid its survival, as it will lag behind and lose its potential for growth.

Bottom line: antifragility fuels progress and advances society. Failure of some things is okay so long as it is for the greater good and we learn from it, thus becoming antifragile.

This concept applies to your business as well; you do not want to mask, be blind to or ignore the gaps in your security. You should want to be antifragile; add stress to your organization in a semi-controlled way, thus allowing for growth and gaining from disorder. Keeping this process under your control—and out of the control of a malicious attacker—means being able to identify what's vulnerable and what's sensitive and then safeguarding it with everything at your company's disposal—technology solutions as well as people and process solutions. After all, this is exactly what an ethical attacker sees and acts upon: who and what is vulnerable and what is sensitive. It's, of course, what a malicious attacker sees and acts upon, too.

The Full Spectrum of Crises

The Internet is undoubtedly the largest public data network. It enables and facilitates both personal and business communications the world over. But although it can be used for good, it can be used for bad as well. The Internet provides many advantages but comes with many security threats. Having an Internet connection alters your security risk profile. For instance, an offshore platform doesn't *have* to be connected to its on-land counterparts. It's done to streamline some of the operations needed to run a platform. The platform's, as well as the company's, risk profile changes dramatically in light of this.

Your business can undergo the full spectrum of crises, from a data breach to an asset theft. On top of this, the threat landscape is evolving and new technologies are constantly being rolled out. Transformation is often disguised as evolution, like the "cloud." Even with this, you must have the ability to rapidly respond and decisively resolve crises, providing the most effective deterrents and setting the stage for future operations where possible. Should deterrence fail, it is imperative that you be able to defeat attacks of any kind. Especially important is the ability to deter or defeat simultaneous or nearly simultaneous attacks, even if they are happening at a distance but occurring in overlapping time frames—which means the whole organization must be on the same page, treating security as an absolute. Training and being able to recognize events for what they are is critical.

The ability to rapidly defeat initial attack advances means you must be prepared to conduct several smaller-scale contingency operations so that you can stabilize a situation. All of this proves that simply having a policy isn't enough. Communication and careful training, companywide, is called for, and in light of escalating security breaches, there is a need for decisive, mitigating action that is swift and effectual.

You will have to recalibrate your security approach from mainly technology-based defenses, including processes and education, to become proactive. It takes laser focus, commitment, and a sharp, modern leadership to do so in a way that sticks. This level of communication and ultimately foresight within your organization is the only way to change habits and culture.

Cybercrime is constantly evolving, and the growing increase in the number of threats that use social engineering techniques is a cause for concern in several businesses. All it takes is one user to click on a malicious link, and a firm's network can be brought to a grinding halt. Cyberthreats have increased in large numbers, and the transaction and compromise time has decreased.

It should be noted that, although sophisticated attackers might know much of the information contained in this book, most attackers only know it in essence, which is adequate, but not enough to effect real change in terms of security. Having an in-depth understanding of AMs will allow us, always, to be ahead of those less careful, less diligent attackers. This is a massive benefit to our clients, who depend on us to give them more than a step-by-step account of the actions we take to circumvent their defenses. To best protect them, we should be able to give our clients a comprehensive understanding of their whole landscape as we perceive it, not only how we bypassed some of their defenses arbitrarily. As a business, you should expect this. For businesses reading, employing AMs affords you exactly this.

Security as a whole needs to be broken down into the pieces recognizable to the cultural and technical backdrop you operate within. There is no one-size-fits-all for security. You must analyze each piece of your landscape and tooling, identify any faults, and perform regular maintenance. When it has all been sewn back together, the hope is that it equals more than the sum of its parts. You will experience unintended consequences of securing your business in this way. However, even if your changes do not seem good at first, it is critical to remember that antifragility comes through volatility: it's best *you* have put that into action rather than an adversary.

AMs on the Spectrum

America, possibly tied with the UK and Iran, is a sophisticated cyber superpower. America is good at offense, but we are also the most targeted. We have many systems of interest to profit from, to steal from and to spy on, so we are targeted frequently. We are one of the most vulnerable from this perspective, too, because we are one of the most connected—everything is connected, from our refrigerators to our water treatment facilities. Because of this, we face many challenges: one is to remain skeptical and honest in evaluating our utility as attackers—meaning we must also not become complacent and self-assured that we are ahead of the real bad guys or that because we can identify what tactics and strategies have been applied by them in the past we know what they will do in the future.

As companies engaging AMs experts, you face a similar problem. Business as a whole can struggle in identifying their own shortcomings and in realistically understanding how and why they will become targets. Corporate AMs is recognizing this and enlisting the help of experts. AMs specialist–proficient, unbiased red teams, pentesters and social engineers with the ability to look at the organization as a whole do make an irrefutable difference—specifically when they are correctly scoped, competently structured, and encouraged to carry out their objectives without improper influence or constraint. To reiterate: AMs is a way of thinking and acting that puts ethical attackers in the mind and shoes of the unethical. In doing so, we, as companies and industries, get to benefit from their work in the short term (in getting an honest assessment of our threat landscape, an alternative analysis of our vulnerabilities and security gaps and the chance to fix our shortcomings) and in the long term (through sharing information and being able to better recognize trends, similarities, and how threats evolve).

Your business is subject to the full spectrum of crises—a spectrum you as a business should understand but of which the complexities may allude you. AMs requires a distinct way of thinking and operating—employing a self-aware, curious, creative, confident, agile mentality and maintaining the ability to communicate and explain your organization through their eyes. Their methods cannot become predictable or culturally ingrained, nor will they become Complacent with your security and threat landscape. To help your business combat the full spectrum of threats, ethical attackers employing AMs will be disruptive, but this is the business's opportunity to become antifragile. Holistically, I believe this is our function aligned with each businesses. An additive would be sharing information within the community and subcommunities to identify trends and patterns more quickly and effectively, speaking for both the attacker in this case and the company. Assuredly, all data is sensitive data. Through employing the use of AMs, you will be able to assess more clearly and accurately what can be used against you and how.

Final Thoughts

Security is a tough task for many organizations. Most aren't in the business of security, which makes it hard to think through its lens. Organizations typically do not build security programs designed to be robust; they build them with defensive technology and test them offensively to the best of their ability. This approach can often fail to consider the users of that technology, their understanding of security and policy. Additionally, not all attacks use technology. Social engineering is the practice of using influence, deception and manipulation to breach security—it's human versus human. This is not solved if defenses amount to firewalls, intrusion detection systems, patch management, and compliance checks. Attackers, both ethical and malicious, count on this blind spot and use it to their advantage.

As an attacker, we are always acting as the adversary for the greater good of security. We think objectively about the environment we are aiming to secure, unencumbered by its cultural biases, internal assumptions, and the information that exists only in its literature, such as handbooks and mission statements, and not in its everyday workings. We know a skewed view of anything will gain us nothing.

Use AMs to your advantage as an organization. Use our curiosity and persistence to gain a new, informed perspective. Use our wily ways of processing information, even that which seems innocuous, to get smarter on how actual attackers size you up and plan their attacks. Employ our specific brand of mental agility to show you how we can adapt to your cultural norms to move around undetected. Finally, use our self-awareness: we know what we can leverage and through that, you can become a self-aware company that knows your current limits and your greatest strengths.

Finally, it has become increasingly clear to me that behavioral and cultural revolution in the realm of security and policy is imminent and, ultimately, business security will not be adequate unless the focus is centered on people.

Summary

- There is a simple formula to keep ahead of attackers and protect your business from a faceless, shapeless threat capable of striking at any time:
  Employ tactical and combative methods internally through the attacker mindset to identify security gaps + (b) be willing to change, employing corporate humility, to mitigate vulnerabilities and security gaps.
- Attackers will weaponize information for the good of their objective and every action they take will be in support of the objective; they will not break pretext and they will strategize and optimize an attack with only the end in mind. Be ahead of them. Think like them and mitigate accordingly.
- Start with the end in mind: security.

Key Message

If you aren't implementing AMs in some way to benefit your security posture, you aren't taking your own security, your employees' security, or your customers' security seriously.

You will not care about the money you should've spent on this type of security when you either cannot make money anymore or you have to pay a huge fine.

Index